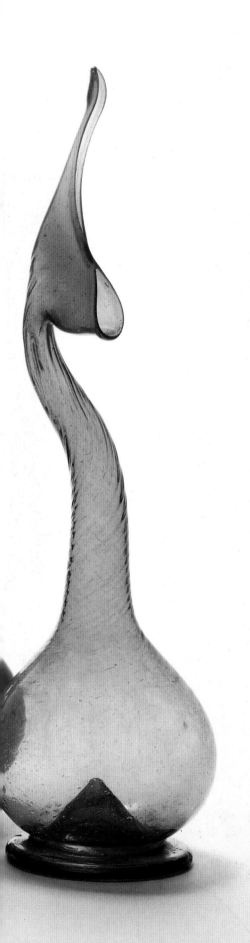

Contents

ACKNOWLEDGEMENTS *page 7*

Introduction *page 8*
HUGH TAIT

Faking *page 17*

CHAPTER ONE *page 21*

Before the Invention of Glassblowing
VERONICA TATTON-BROWN AND CAROL ANDREWS

The First Glassmakers 2500–1200 BC *page 21*
Egypt *c.* 1450–1100 BC *page 26*
Western Asia and the Mediterranean *c.* 900–300 BC *page 38*
Hellenistic and non-blown Roman glass *c.* 325 BC–AD 400 *page 47*

CHAPTER TWO *page 62*

The Roman Empire
VERONICA TATTON-BROWN

Early blown glass 1st century AD *page 62*
The Roman achievement AD 100–400 *page 79*

CHAPTER THREE *page 98*

Early Medieval Europe AD 400–1066
VERONICA TATTON-BROWN

CHAPTER FOUR *page 112*

The Islamic Lands and China

RALPH PINDER-WILSON

Early Islamic glass 8th–11th centuries *page 114*
Islamic glass 12th–15th centuries *page 126*
Later Islamic glass 16th–19th centuries *page 136*
Chinese glass *page 140*

CHAPTER FIVE *page 145*

Europe from the Middle Ages to the Industrial Revolution

HUGH TAIT

Byzantium and medieval Europe 10th–15th centuries *page 145*
Venice and Renaissance Europe 15th–17th centuries *page 156*
North of the Alps 17th–18th centuries *page 179*

CHAPTER SIX *page 188*

Europe and America 1800–1940

PAUL HOLLISTER

Cut and engraved glass *page 188*
Pressed glass *page 197*
Some special techniques and achievements *page 200*
Five formative artists *page 206*

Epilogue *page 211*

HUGH TAIT

Techniques of Glassmaking and Decoration *page 213*

WILLIAM GUDENRATH

GLOSSARY *page 242*

FURTHER READING *page 248*

ILLUSTRATION CREDITS AND MUSEUM ACCESSION NUMBERS *page 250*

THE CONTRIBUTORS *page 252*

INDEX *page 252*

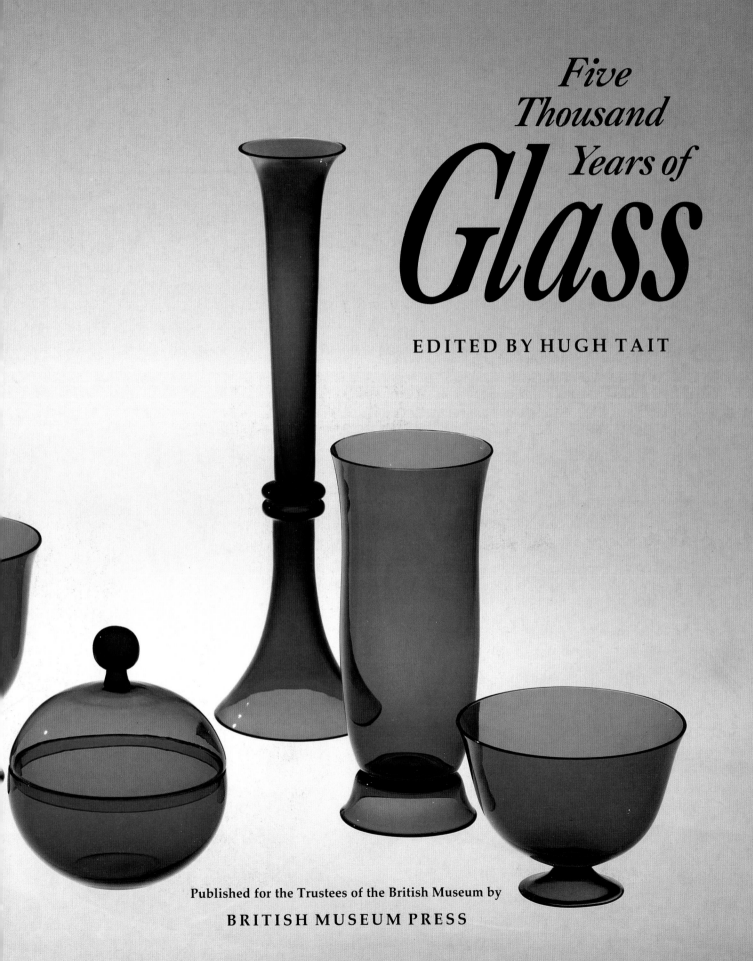

Five Thousand Years of Glass

EDITED BY HUGH TAIT

Published for the Trustees of the British Museum by

BRITISH MUSEUM PRESS

© 1991 The Trustees of the British Museum
Published by British Museum Press
A division of British Museum Publications Ltd
46 Bloomsbury Street, London WC1B 3QQ

First paperback edition 1995

A catalogue record for this book is available from the British Library

ISBN 0-7141-1756-0

Designed by Roger Davies

Set in Linotron Palatino by
Rowland Phototypesetting Ltd,
Bury St Edmunds, Suffolk
Colour origination by Colourscan, Singapore
Printed in Singapore by Imago

Acknowledgements

MANY and varied are the contributions that have gone into the making of this ambitious survey of the story of glass and, as editor, I would like to begin by acknowledging with profound gratitude the generous co-operation of the many institutions whose specialist photographers and scholarly staff have enabled key material in their care to be included in this book: Musée des Beaux-Arts, Besançon; City Museums and Art Gallery, Birmingham; Cambridge University Museum of Archaeology and Anthropology; Museo Archeologico, Cividale; Römisch-Germanisches Museum, Cologne; National Museum, Copenhagen; The Corning Museum of Glass, New York; The Rockwell Museum, Corning, New York; Topkapi Sarayi Müsezi Müdürlüğü, Istanbul; British Library, London; Sotheby & Co., London; Christie's, New York; Leo Kaplan Antiques Ltd., New York; The Metropolitan Museum of Art, New York; The Chrysler Museum, Norfolk, Virginia; Ashmolean Museum, Oxford; Musée des Arts Décoratifs, Paris; Municipal Museum, Prague; Vatican Library, Rome; Musée d'Art et d'Histoire de la Ville de Saint-Denis; Stuart Crystal, Red House Glassworks, Stourbridge; The Toledo Museum of Art, Toledo, Ohio; and the Treasury of San Marco, Venice. In addition, special thanks are owed to the following for helping with requests for photographs: Gary Baker, Chrysler Museum; Mario Carrieri, Milan; Karen De Ponceau Flint, Rockwell Museum; Charles Hajdamach, Dudley; Dwight Lanmon and Jill Thomas-Clark, Corning Museum; Jean-Luc Olivié, Paris; George Scott, Edinburgh; and Geneviève Sennequier, Rouen.

The extraordinarily challenging photography for Bill Gudenrath's demonstrations of glassmaking techniques was carried out at the glass furnace – often close to its hot and blinding light – over a lengthy period by the talented photographer Steven Barall, and Mr Gudenrath wishes to record his thanks both to him and to Tina Yelle, Director of the New York Experimental Glass Workshop, where all these sequences were conducted and photographed.

The British Museum's Photographic Service embarked on an extensive programme of new photography for this book, and I wish to thank in particular the following staff photographers: David Gowers (Oriental Antiquities), who also took the front cover photograph; Christi Graham, with David Agar and Peter Stringer (Medieval and Later Antiquities); Peter Hayman (Egyptian Antiquities); Sandra Marshall (Prehistoric and Romano-British Antiquities); Nick Nicholls (Greek and Roman Antiquities); and Barbara Winter, with Lisa Bliss (Western Asiatic Antiquities). The publishers and the authors are deeply grateful to their colleagues in the Departments for their constant support.

Indeed, colleagues in the Research Laboratory and the Antiquities Departments and outside the Museum have given unsparingly of their time and expertise. In particular, Veronica Tatton-Brown, who is especially indebted to the late Donald Harden, wishes to thank also the following for reading and commenting upon her text: Brian Cook, Vera Evison, Lesley Fitton, David Grose, Jennifer Price and Susan Woodford; and to express her gratitude for information communicated by Donald Bailey, David Buckton, Wendy Evans, Ian Freestone, Yael Israeli, Dafydd Kidd, Kenneth Painter, Nigel Ramsey, Paul Roberts, George Scott, Tim Tatton-Brown, Hafed Walda, Christopher Walker and Susan Walker. I am also grateful to David Whitehouse for bringing the Colinet MS to London (see Pl. 212) and to Anna-Elisabeth Theuerhauff-Liederwald for obtaining a precise identification of the coat of arms in Pls 207–8. The maps were drawn by Graham Reed.

Finally, my thanks go to Celia Clear of British Museum Press for suggesting that this material – much of it recently reinterpreted and reassessed – might be the springboard for a new survey, and to her colleague, Teresa Francis, for her truly devoted and invaluable work in putting this book together in 1991 and now for her patient help in incorporating revisions for this second edition.

HUGH TAIT, *August 1994*

Introduction

TODAY, glass is everywhere around us in our daily lives – and in such abundance and variety that its familiarity has blunted our sense of wonder at its fundamentally exceptional character. Glass may give the appearance of being hard and solid, like several other materials that man has been producing since prehistoric times, but (as we now know) it passes from a hot liquid state to a cold rigid one without undergoing the kind of internal structural change that occurs within most molten substances – such as iron – as they cool. In the latter, the component atoms rapidly become reorganised to form crystals, but glass, when it cools, has no crystalline structure. As it cools, glass becomes viscous, like toffee, and has the power to resist a change in the arrangement of the molecules; hence, it has been described as a 'super-cooled liquid'. For this reason, glass in its heated state can be blown to form a bubble or pulled out (and twisted) to form long thin canes. The inherent fluidity of the material has remained a fundamental property of glass since it was first made in the third millennium BC, and has always given glass objects their unique quality.

Since the time when the first glass was made by heating and fusing a mixture of sand, soda and lime (silica, sodium and calcium oxide), recipes for making glass have been written introducing countless variations. Essentially, however, the use of these three inorganic and very plentiful ingredients has continued throughout, although both potash and lead were introduced at different times to improve the quality. One of the very early glass recipes – and certainly the best preserved – was written in Mesopotamia on a clay tablet in a cuneiform script that is dated between the fourteenth and twelfth centuries BC. Surprisingly, it gives instructions on how to add lead, copper and antimony in differing proportions to two types of 'raw' glass, the making of which is not described. Other evidence from the Late Bronze Age also indicates that there was a well-established trade in raw glass ingots of different colours (see Chapter 1), and therefore that the manufacture of raw glass may already have become a highly specialised activity in a few centres, where glass furnaces were designed to reach high temperatures. Whereas the normal temperature maintained in a European glass furnace from the Renaissance onwards was about 1500°C, the earlier – and much smaller – glass furnaces were almost certainly incapable of such a high temperature; indeed, many may not have been able to reach 1100°. However, it is significant that from a very early date there may have been a clear-cut distinction between those makers who possessed the technical expertise to frit the ingredients (probably at about 900°) and then found the frit (at about 1100°) for some sixteen hours or more, and those who had

Unless otherwise stated, all objects illustrated are in the British Museum.
Abbreviations: D. diameter; H. height; L. length; W. width.

Numbers in the margin refer to text illustrations. *Fig. nos.* refer to the section on 'Techniques of Glassmaking and Decoration', pp. 213–41.

1 The sixteenth-century Medici glass furnace in Florence: a detail from one of the set of oil paintings on panel made between 1570 and 1575 by Giorgio Vasari and his school for the *Studiolo* of the Grand Duke Francesco de' Medici (reigned as Grand Duke of Tuscany 1574–87). The *Studiolo* was a room hidden in the heart of the Palazzo Vecchio in Florence; the paintings concealed cupboards in which the Grand Duke kept his mineral specimens, engraved rock-crystals, objects of 'curiosity', jewels, gold, silver, and so on. The Medici glasshouse, known to have been built in the Venetian manner, became operational by the end of the 1560s and is here depicted by Giovanni Maria Butteri with the annealing chamber at the top, into which a finished glass is being placed by a servitor (to the left of the furnace). Neither seated glassblower has a 'chair', but each is seated on the traditional three-legged stool near the glory-hole and is only partially protected from its heat and glare by the fire-clay screen.

2 Recipes for making two types of glass, written in a cuneiform script on a clay tablet. These instructions are the best-preserved and probably the earliest record concerning the manufacture of glass in the ancient world. Mesopotamia, 14th–12th centuries B C. H. 9.5 cm.

the skill to re-melt ingots of glass and make objects with it in small local furnaces. Even in modern times, the worst moment in a glasshouse's calendar was the 'setting of a new pot' – an operation of the most tremendous difficulty because of the ferocity of the naked heat that was unleashed when the wall of one of the arches of the furnace had to be taken down. If, in addition, the old pot had cracked, it would be firmly cemented to the floor by the glass that had escaped, and only repeated sorties (each lasting only a minute or two) by men clad in wet skins and wielding crowbars could loosen it and move it on to the waiting iron truck on wheels. The preparing of the clay floor for the new pot of molten glass (kept glowing bright in the annealing chamber, or lehr) was a blistering and slow process, but on its completion the new pot could be carefully wheeled to the furnace and held in position with crowbars while the low iron truck was swiftly withdrawn from under it. Without further delay, a party of men then quickly closed up the opening in the wall with fire-clay and bricks.

Through the centuries, glass furnaces had been fired by wood but in sixteenth-century England the overriding needs of the King's Navy and the dwindling size of the few remaining forests in the British Isles spurred the glassmakers to find an alternative. They set about devising a system for using coal, and by 1615 the burning of wood in the glass industry could be officially forbidden by a 'Proclamation touching Glass'. The use of coal as a fuel required a much greater draught to produce a sufficiently intense heat, and so the English glass cone was created. This was a unique contribution to glass technology, having no equivalent in Europe or America. Long before the end of the seventeenth century the tall brick cone – one reported in the *London Gazette* of 1702 was '94 Foot high and 60 Foot Broad' – became an impressively conspicuous feature of the landscape of such glassmaking centres as Bristol, Dublin and Nottingham. At Belfast, one of these cones rose to be as high as 150 feet (46 m). Often they enclosed two furnaces, and the Red House Cone at the Stuart Crystal factory at Wordsley (near Stourbridge), built in the late eighteenth century, continued to house a twelve-pot crystal melting furnace and some fifty glassmakers until it closed in 1939. It was here that in 1874 (and in the succeeding decades) the famous blue and white double-layered blanks were blown for John Northwood I to carve his 'cameo glass' replica of the Portland Vase, his famous Milton Vase and the three portrait tazzas of Flaxman, Newton and Shakespeare.

With the great cone acting as a chimney, a tremendous throughdraught could be created as the underground flues were opened and all other outlets from the cone at ground level were closed. The coals, however, had to be laid on a massive grill of iron bars, with a large pit below, into which the residue could fall as the coals were periodically raked. This grill system seems to have been copied on the Continent by the 1670s, if not before. Because the English lead crystal glass was quickly ruined by the sulphur compounds given off by the burning coals, glass manufacturers in Britain had to develop the covered glasspot and, though open pots continued to be used in bottle-glass factories where the fumes made little difference to the dark colour of the final product, the change to the covered glasspot became widespread – indeed, the merits of this innovation were soon recognised on the Continent. By the end of the eighteenth century, expert

3

opinion in France and other European centres was convinced that the English coal-fired glass furnace was by far the most efficient and productive, but today only four cones survive – at Alloa, Catcliffe (near Sheffield), Lemington (near Newcastle upon Tyne) and at Wordsley – to convey the powerful monumental scale of these once noisy and scorchingly hot places of creativity.

Unlike the potter, the glassmaker can only work his material when it is too hot to touch with the hands. It has to be withdrawn hot from the open furnace and either formed in a mould or shaped (and decorated) with tools – not with direct touch – while being held in the other hand at the end of a rod or, later, a blow-pipe. Speed was always important because the glass must not be allowed to cool and had therefore to be returned repeatedly to the heat of the furnace. Indeed, the need for speed and movement became paramount after the glassmaker discovered that glass, gathered at the end of a hollow pipe, could be shaped by inflation, because it is the glassblower's constant rhythmic swinging and spinning of the molten glass (between alternately blowing and reheating it at the furnace) that enables him to control the form and thickness of the blown vessel.

For that reason, this book is primarily concerned with the achievements of the craftsmen and artists who worked hot glass to fashion an infinite variety of objects from its molten mass. Because so many of the hot techniques and the complicated sequences of manufacture are unfamiliar and difficult to explain without illustration, the section on 'Techniques of Glassmaking and Decoration' provides a unique series of photographs taken over many weeks at a glass furnace during the re-enactment of many of the former methods of glassmaking in so far as the current state of knowledge permits. The accompanying texts contain some technical glassmaking terms – defined in the Glossary – and the photographs will not only serve to elucidate them but also to show the painstakingly complex methods by which, for example, many a fragile elegant glass object of the past was made and colourfully embellished at the blindingly hot 'glory-hole'.

The distinction between 'hot working' and 'cold working' is fundamental. Craftsmen who fashion or decorate the glass after it has become cold play a secondary – if not always a minor – role. From very early times, glass was frequently treated as if it were a stone, being ground and abraded to the required shape by lapidaries, who were experienced stonecutters or gem-engravers. Indeed, as early as the Roman period, glassmakers were led to experiment with the manufacture of a glass composed of two fused layers of contrasting colours – specifically made to imitate the layers found in natural stones such as onyx – so that glass versions of the technique of cameo carving could be produced: the Portland Vase is the most renowned example. [75] Wheel-cut decoration on rock-crystal and other hardstones was similarly a well-established tradition long before its exponents decided to use this 'cold' technique on the man-made (and probably much cheaper) material, glass. Cold working in antiquity achieved brilliant results, especially in Roman *diatreta* and the famous 'Lycurgus Cup', [116–17] but for these large pieces the glassblower would have been commissioned to make blanks of a very special thickness. More usually, the cold-working decorators were content to use routinely produced glass. With the advent of the pointed diamond, even the thinnest of

3 The Red House Glass Cone at the Stuart Crystal Factory, Wordsley, near Stourbridge, England, from an illustration in the *Gentleman's Journal* of 1902. Built in the late 18th century, it continued in use until 1939, housing some fifty glassmakers and a twelve-pot melting furnace. The English glass cone, a unique contribution to glass technology, enabled coal to be used as a fuel in place of wood by creating sufficient draught to produce a more intense heat.

soda-lime *cristallo* from Murano could receive cold engraved decoration and later, with the English discovery of a pure strong lead glass, Dutch glass engravers were able to invent another cold-working technique, the art of stippling (Dutch *stippelen*, pricking), in which the diamond point was no longer 'scratched' on the surface but tapped on the glass to produce innumerable dots in varying degrees of density. Just as the Dutch artists who stippled on English glasses were far removed from the place where the glasses had been made, so too it seems unlikely that many of the craftsmen who used cold-working methods to decorate the glasses of antiquity were part of the staff of the glasshouse. However, in the last few centuries many glasshouses had their own cutting and engraving workshops – usually located at some distance from the furnace where the glass itself was being made. The sense of contrast between these two working areas could scarcely be more marked.

222

242

Whilst the cold-working decorators of these glasses could follow – sometimes with great precision – designs produced by other artists, the glassblower working at great speed at the glory-hole of the furnace had to rely on his memory. He may, for example, have received from his Renaissance patron a batch of drawings produced by some court artist and, however impractical these fanciful designs for new glasses may have been, he would have been expected to memorise and, if necessary, modify them until he could create a comparable object. For this type of luxury glass, although success could be achieved only by the glassmaker with the most 'fantasy in him' – as the instructions of the Archduke Ferdinand of Tyrol expressed it in the late sixteenth century – the role of the patron and the designer has become, since the Renaissance, increasingly perceptible whereas, in antiquity (especially in Rome), their roles are still a matter for conjecture. At a more commercial level, there is written evidence by the seventeenth century to prove that the middlemen – the glass-sellers and merchants – would keep the suppliers informed of how the consumers were reacting and, very naturally, if sales were declining in any particular respect, they would make forthright recommendations for a change. One of the best-documented cases involved a London glass-seller, John Greene, who between 1667 and 1673 wrote numerous letters to his Venetian supplier, Allesio Morelli, about the growing demand in England for glasses of 'white sound mettal' and of more sober form: to make his requests unambiguously clear, he included numerous detailed drawings of the plainer forms he required for the English market. These drawings, sometimes in the margin of the letters and sometimes on separate sheets, have been preserved at the British Museum since 1753 among Sir Hans Sloane's collection of manuscripts (Sloane MS 857). However, the survival of such evidence is rare, and so our knowledge of the market forces that over the past 5,000 years have dictated the kind of glass produced at any given period in a particular centre is often very sketchy, even when the surviving glass itself may be sufficiently plentiful to enable reliable deductions to be made about other patterns of development.

186

4

The pieces chosen to illustrate the story of man's mastery of this difficult, but very versatile, material have in the main been selected from the British Museum's own wide-ranging collection – an impressive tribute to the wisdom and generosity of the many donors whose

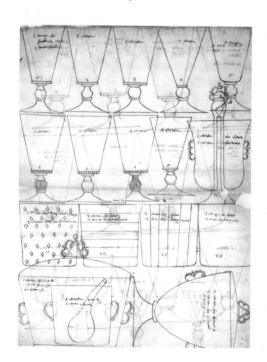

4 One of the many sheets of drawings with instructions for different designs and stronger glasses that accompanied the letters sent by the London glass-seller John Greene to Allesio Morelli in Venice between 1667 and 1672. London, British Library.

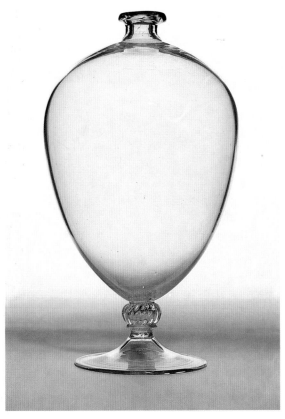

5 ABOVE, LEFT Tazza with wheel-engraved decoration, purchased for its excellence by Felix Slade (1790–1868) at the International Exhibition held in London in 1862, where it was exhibited by J. Maës, one of the founders in 1839 of the glassworks at Clichy-la-Garenne, near Paris. H. 16 cm.

6 ABOVE, RIGHT 'Vaso Veronese', one of a series of models designed by Vittorio Zecchin (1878–1947) for a new glasshouse founded by Paolo Venini (1895–1959) in Murano in 1921. Venice, about 1922–5. H. 55 cm.

gifts over the past 200 years have been regularly supplemented by shrewd purchases. Its universal character began in earnest at a surprisingly early date, largely because of the bequest of one man, Felix Slade (1790–1868). Born in London, Slade studied law before becoming a scholarly connoisseur and friend of Sir Augustus Wollaston Franks at the British Museum. He continued to live in his father's house at Lambeth, while energetically amassing a vast and varied collection, the chief glory of which was undoubtedly the glass. He began to collect glass soon after the Napoleonic Wars ended in 1815, while he was still in his twenties. Stimulated by a visit to Italy in 1817, his interests broadened so that he not only acquired incomparable specimens of Venetian Renaissance glass but also ancient glass from Egypt (as early as *c.* 1400 BC), Greece, the Roman Empire, India and the medieval Islamic Middle East. Although Slade showed little interest in English glass unless it had been finely engraved or stippled in Holland, his expert knowledge of Continental glass from the sixteenth to eighteenth centuries led him to form a substantial nucleus of masterpieces, those bearing signatures and dates being of lasting documentary significance. Even after a lifetime of collecting historic glass – and much of it had been purchased by 1850 (when he was 60) before the skilled fakers had muddied the waters (see below) – Felix Slade's approach remained open and receptive. For example, at the 1862 International Exhibition held in London, he bought a modern tazza of the purest quality. It was exhibited by J. Maës, who had helped to found in 1839 the glassworks at Clichy-la-Garenne, near

5

Paris, and Slade had his cataloguer, Alexander Nesbitt, record the reason: *'it was selected as one of the best examples of engraving on glass in the Exhibition, and this must be the excuse for introducing so modern a specimen into this catalogue'*.

From the time of the Slade Bequest in 1868 until 1978, no other examples of contemporary glass were collected by the Museum, even though there were a few exceptional gifts. However, with a change in policy, this omission is now being steadily rectified as the 'Modern Collections' are slowly built up every year. Most recently, the Museum purchased a glass vase, the model for which was designed in the early 1920s by the painter Vittorio Zecchin (1878–1947) for a new Murano glasshouse that had been founded in 1921 by Paolo Venini (1895–1959). This model, known as the 'Vaso Veronese', was in marked contrast to the previous fashion in Venetian glass, and in its reliance on form alone the vase seems to reflect Zecchin's artistic links with the Wiener Werkstätte and the works of Josef Hoffmann (1870–1956) as well as his awareness of Murano's own heritage and early traditions. The appointment of Zecchin to the post of artistic and technical director at Venini's was a turning-point in the modern history of Venetian glass.

No one collection can hope to be comprehensive and there are several other areas, especially in the Byzantine and medieval periods, where key pieces can be found only in ancient treasuries, like that of San Marco in Venice, or among the finds of some foreign excavation. On more than one occasion, archaeological evidence has shaken long-established theories and has led to healthy reappraisals with consequent modifications to the standard historical interpretation. The authors are therefore deeply grateful for the help they have received from colleagues abroad, and for the owners' permission to include these essential illustrations.

Very occasionally, a chapter in the history of glass has to be rewritten because some lost masterpiece is rediscovered. One such momentous event occurred in 1988 when a piece of glass furniture – the top of a unique table of exuberant Baroque design, worthy of a *Kunstkammer* – was recognised as having been listed during Louis XIV's reign among the items belonging to the French Crown before 1681 and as having the original inventory number, 276, still stamped on it (see T. Clarke and J. Bourne, 'Louis XIV's Glass Table', *Apollo*, November 1988). Furthermore, when it was again described in the royal inventory of 1729, a more precise entry established that the top had been supported on five glass columns (no longer preserved with the table-top): 'Une table couverte de divers morceaux de verre fondu et mele de plusieurs couleurs, liés par un compartiment de cuivre doré ciselé, fort leger, portée sur son pieds a cinq colomnes rondes, aussi couvertes de verre . . .' (a table covered with varied pieces of fired glass and mixed with several colours, placed within a chased gilt-copper compartment, very light, resting on five round columns, also covered with glass . . .). The survival of these five columns was first suggested by Paul Hollister, who in 1977 had discovered and recorded four matching glass columns in the Smithsonian Institution, Washington (where they are incorporated into a piece of American furniture) and a fifth – slightly stouter – column of similar length in the British Museum (acquired in 1873, by itself, slightly damaged and

6

title pa

187

191–4

7

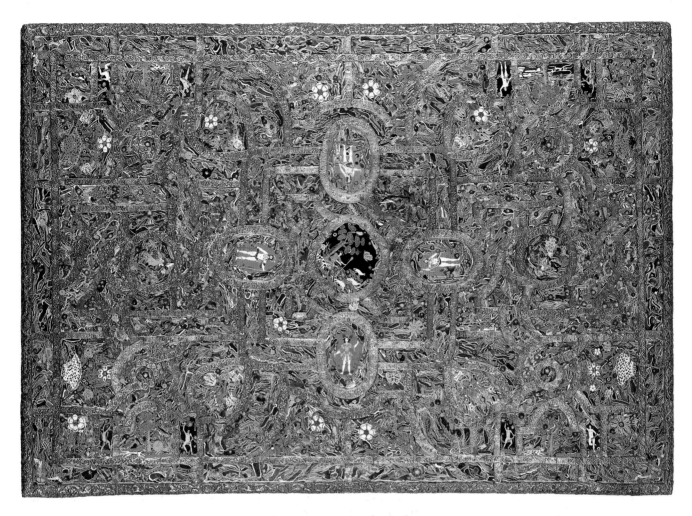

7 ABOVE The Louis XIV glass table: a view of the table-top showing its formal baroque design, emphasised by the decorated gilt-metal strips running between the shaped sections of *millefiori* and flame-worked glass on copper. North Italian, or perhaps made by Italians in France (Nevers or Orléans), third quarter of the 17th century (before 1681). 117 × 81 cm. Private collection, England.

8 RIGHT Detail of one of the four hunting scenes on the table in Pl. 7, each flanked by two nudes. Five *millefiori* glass columns now dispersed between the Smithsonian Institution, Washington, and the British Museum may originally have belonged to this table, which was sold in Paris in 1752 and remained unidentified until 1988.

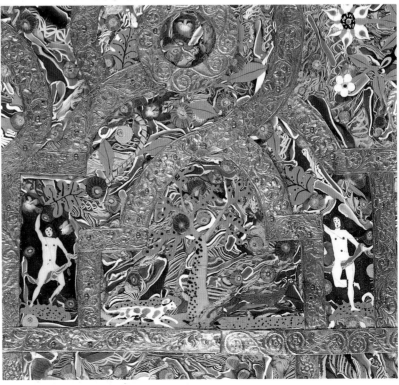

without any record of its earlier history). However, this important identification cannot be confirmed until the four columns can be detached from the modern cabinet and all five columns reunited for a comprehensive scientific study, preferably in London where the table-top has remained in a private collection: we are most grateful to the owner, who has very generously supplied the illustrations.

Apart from the unusual gilt-copper mounts with stamped ornament that conceal the joins of the numerous sections, this magnificent *tour de force* of glass fused on copper combines both Italian-looking (Venetian) *millefiori* glass of many different patterns and flameworked plaques with flowers, hunting scenes and other animals, and mythological figures that recall the French (Nevers) glass figures executed 'in the round' during the seventeenth century. Consequently, historians of French glassmaking are now seeking to incorporate this extraordinary achievement within the *oeuvre* of Bernard Perrot, who is generally regarded as the most eminent glassmaker in France during the second half of the seventeenth century (see J. Benard and B. Dragesco, *Bernard Perrot et les verreries royales du Duché d'Orléans*, Paris 1990). However, his Italian origin – and the correct date of his birth – have now been established: he was born on 26 June 1619 in Altare (near Genoa). Altare, at least since the formation of its Guild of Glassmakers in 1495, had been a very active competitor of the Venetian glass industry, but today not one of its products can be recognised. Like many other Altarists, Bernardo Perroto, who had learnt his trade from his father, Francesco, left for France, where in 1651 he is first recorded at the age of 31, working in a glasshouse in Nevers; thereafter, he had a distinguished career in France, mainly at Orléans. Consequently, if he did indeed create this exceptional table, his Altare background and training might have given it its very distinctive character – just as the earlier Altarists at Nevers had probably first introduced the three-dimensional glass figures that are now seen by historians as essentially French. This artistically ambitious masterpiece, made before 1681 and sold from the French Royal Collection on 4 August 1752, may yet prove to be the most significant tangible evidence of the Italian tradition which the Altarists introduced into France – and yet, dismembered and forgotten for more than 100 years, its vital connection with the court of Louis XIV might never have been rediscovered and, indeed, the table itself might so easily have been destroyed and lost for ever.

The story of this unparalleled glass table serves as a salutary reminder of the countless masterpieces of glass from all epochs that have *not* survived. Even some that had succeeded in reaching the relative safety of a twentieth-century museum have since perished in a wartime bombing raid or during a freak flood. The world's heritage of this most fragile of materials is dwindling; it adds a certain urgency to our study and enjoyment of those perfect specimens that, almost miraculously, have been neither broken nor buried but are as fine as on the day they were taken from the annealing chamber.

This book has throughout aimed to offer the reader a framework of the principal patterns of development from the earliest times to 1940 and if, within this general framework, the reader has found areas of particular interest, these can be pursued with the help of the list of 'Further Reading'.

9 Faked Late Roman vase of colourless glass with eight green hooks. When acquired in 1906, this vase was said to have been found near Olbia in the Ukraine. H. 11.9 cm.

10 The 'Bonus Eventus' plaque, imitating lapis lazuli. First published in 1818, it is no longer regarded as Roman glass of the 1st century A D. 18 × 18 cm.

10a Faked 'Persian 16th-century' decoration added to a plain Hellenistic glass bowl of the 1st century B C. Diam. 14.2 cm.

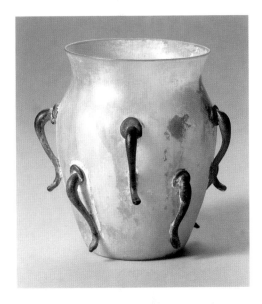

Faking

The catalogue of the British Museum's exhibition *Fake? The Art of Deception* (1990) contained only one glass object, but this was a piece that had been faked so skilfully and with such expert knowledge that it was to mislead several generations of scholars. Known as the 'Hope Goblet', because it was purchased by the Museum at Christie's sale of Adrian Hope's collection in 1894, it almost immediately became internationally famous. At first, it was quoted in books and articles in learned journals as one of the earliest and rarest of the enamelled glasses made in Venice. Its frieze of Western European religious figures is, indeed, painted in the Gothic style of about 1250–1300, but the form of the glass is Islamic. Later publications therefore proposed that it was made by a Syrian working in Venice, or in Crusader Palestine (before its total destruction in 1291), or even in Syria by a Venetian craftsman. Only in 1968 – in a British Museum exhibition catalogue – was it published, by the present editor, as a work of doubtful authenticity and now, as a result of the evidence gathered subsequently, almost every aspect of its decoration and its manufacturing techniques can be faulted. The Hope Goblet, probably made no more than twenty years before the 1894 sale by some exceptionally well-informed faker, perhaps working in London, is deceptively beautiful (as the colour illustration in the *Fake?* catalogue vividly confirms) and belongs, therefore, to the category that represents the greatest hazard for both the scholar and the collector.

Few glass fakes are thought to have been made before the middle of the nineteenth century, and so a collection like the famous Slade Bequest, which was principally formed between 1815 and 1850, has been thought to be free of fakes. However, between 1850 and his death in 1868, Slade made some spectacular purchases, a few of which can now be recognised as skilful Italian or German fakes, and because they predate his demise, these few fakes have acquired a new and special importance as early documented examples in the history of the art of deception within this field.

The constant reappraisal of the glasses within the British Museum's collections is a necessary exercise and each decade will witness doubts – often tentatively expressed at first – becoming more securely reinforced by the accumulation of evidence. With the scientific analysis of many excavated glasses from the ancient world, a corpus of reliable data has been built up, against which the dubious specimens can be measured. For example, a glass jar with green hooks, purchased by the British Museum from Messrs Rollin and Feuardent in 1906, was said to have been found in the neighbourhood of Olbia in the Ukraine, and was thought to date from the third to fourth centuries A D. During a recent reconsideration of this object, neither its shape nor its method of manufacture seemed consistent with this attribution and laboratory tests have now revealed that the composition of the glass is very significantly different from that found in glass of the Roman period. This fake, like many similar pieces, has a milky iridescence on the outside, but the incrustation in the area of the hooks is particularly deceptive. It now seems likely that this vase was produced towards the end of the nineteenth century.

Surprisingly, there has even been a reappraisal of the famous

9

10 'Bonus Eventus' plaque, which was acquired for the Townley Collection from the Museo Sabatini in Rome before 1817. Indeed, an engraving of it was published by Taylor Combe in 1818 and its subsequent history is fully recorded. From this it is clear that the plaque was acquired as a piece of carved lapis lazuli, a semi-precious gemstone highly prized at that time. It was not recognised as a glass relief until much later and, indeed, recent scientific analyses show that in virtually every aspect of its chemistry and technology, the glass is highly anomalous in the context – suggested by its style – of first-century AD Rome. The copying of gemstones in a glass paste was, however, a particular skill of the late eighteenth and nineteenth centuries, practised for example in Rome and Vienna by Luigi Pichler and in England by James Tassie and his nephew William. However, as the existence of the original 'Bonus Eventus' plaque is unrecorded, this glass plaque is best seen as a clever pastiche or fake.

Often the most difficult fakes to detect are those that incorporate authentic material but transform it into a much more unusual collector's item by the deceptive addition of certain elements (a signature, a date or some special decoration). An exceptional amber-coloured glass bowl, which has been in the British Museum since 1889, is gold-painted and enamelled with a winged angel in the style of Persian
10a miniature painting in the sixteenth century and has hitherto been attributed to glassmakers in Persia or Transoxiana at that period. However, recent scientific examination has confirmed Ralph Pinder-Wilson's opinion that its puzzling features seem to be the result of a faker acquiring a genuine, but plain, Hellenistic bowl (probably first century BC) and, after repolishing it, adding the gold paint and enamel colours. A Western centre, such as Paris in the late nineteenth century, seems the most likely origin for such a deception, especially after Persian antiquities became popular among European collectors.

Collectors of Renaissance glass, especially in Germany and England, soon became aware of the rarity of Venetian glasses enamelled with German coats-of-arms, apparently commissioned in the sixteenth century, usually by members of the patrician families of the great trading cities of Augsburg and Nuremberg, whose commercial enterprises often had close links with Venice. Whereas the rest of the enamelled decoration on these glasses was indistinguishable from the finest of Murano's work, the shapes were Germanic and not in the least like those of the Venetian repertoire. They became much sought after and, as the demand exceeded the supply of genuine pieces, fakes began to be made; for almost a century their authenticity was not questioned. An interesting example, known in German as a covered
11 *Scheuer*, is decorated in the typically Venetian manner of around 1500 except for the cover, which is enamelled with two coats-of-arms. These were identified and published in 1927 as the arms of Scharff and Hörlin, patrician families of Nuremberg and Augsburg respectively, although it now seems that the first shield may be copied from the arms of Seuthe of Augsburg. The date, '1518', enamelled above the two shields, was surprisingly early and consequently this perfectly preserved *Scheuer* was a tempting acquisition for any collector of Renaissance *objets d'art*. When it was bequeathed to the British Museum in 1898, neither its earlier history nor the existence of any similar pieces was known. By 1911 an identical specimen had appeared in the

11 ABOVE Faked covered cup in the form of a German *Scheuer*, enamelled with two German coats-of-arms and the date 1518; formerly thought to have been made in Venice as a special commission celebrating a union between two German patrician families. The location of this faker's workshop remains uncertain; probably German, third quarter of the 19th century. H. 15.5 cm.

12 BELOW Faked covered *Scheuer*, identical to that in Pl. 11, with the same pair of enamelled coats-of-arms and the date 1518. New York, The Metropolitan Museum of Art, Robert Lehman Collection.

13 ABOVE Faked covered *Scheuer*, almost identical to those in Pls 11 and 12, but the cover is enamelled with a different date (1512) and has a different design of ornament. Corning, New York, The Corning Museum of Glass.

14 BELOW Faked cover seen here on the Corning *Scheuer* (Pl. 13). This extra cover, decorated with the same distinctive ornament as that in Pl. 13, is enamelled with the surprisingly late date, 1615, and a single armorial shield. The cover no longer has the upturned foot of a typical cover belonging to a *Scheuer*. Corning, New York, The Corning Museum of Glass.

Prague auction sale of the Lanna Collection (lot 708), but expert opinion was generally agreed that the Prague specimen had been made in imitation of the genuine one now in the British Museum and this view was published in 1927. The London example continued to be published as genuine, especially in two important books in 1958 and 1965, until the Robert Lehman Collection Wing of the Metropolitan Museum of Art in New York opened in 1975. It contained an identical *Scheuer* and cover, also dated '1518'. Comparative studies revealed that they undoubtedly had a common origin, but neither the character of the glass nor the methods of decoration were consistent with an origin in the early sixteenth century.

These serious doubts were to be confirmed in 1980 when another similar *Scheuer* and cover appeared on the London art market: it was enamelled with the identical pair of coats-of-arms but the accompanying date was '1512'. Furthermore, although the lower half of the cup was gilded and enamelled in the same way with a shell pattern, the geometrical design used on the cover was entirely different – and, indeed, less convincing for a glass reputably made in Venice in 1512. Any lingering doubts of the spurious nature of this group of glasses was dispelled when, in the same year (1980), another similarly enamelled and gilded cover appeared in London. This cover, of slightly different form but almost identical size, is decorated with the same geometrical pattern that had been used on the '1512' specimen; however, in the centre, it is painted with only one heraldic shield (with a lion rampant) and the date '1615' (arranged on either side of the shield). The decoration of this cover offered irrefutable evidence of the activity of an over-confident faker and it soon became clear that none in this group is older than the late nineteenth century (a full account will be published in the forthcoming Volume IV of the *Catalogue of the Waddesdon Bequest*). The illustrations of the '1512' *Scheuer* and the '1615' cover have been kindly supplied by Christopher Sheppard; both pieces have a key reference value and were, most fortunately, acquired by the Corning Museum of Glass, New York, where they can be studied by future generations.

The policy of collecting fakes is both enlightened and necessary because every institution that is engaged in research into this subject needs direct access to a corpus of spurious specimens. Without the existence of such a valuable archive of fakes, errors can so easily be perpetuated and wrong attributions, with each succeeding repetition, become more difficult to expunge. Future generations will undoubtedly be better equipped to expose more deceptions, some of which may, today, be quite unsuspected. Nevertheless, the very process of questioning sharpens our awareness of the qualities that distinguish the genuine – and hence deepens our enjoyment of the best achievements of the past.

12

13

14

CHAPTER ONE

Before the Invention of Glassblowing

The first glassmakers
2500–1200 BC

There is a story that once a ship belonging to some traders in nitrum put in here [the coast of modern Lebanon] and that they scattered along the shore to prepare a meal. Since, however, no stones for supporting their cauldrons were forthcoming, they rested them on lumps of nitrum from their cargo. When these became heated and were completely mingled with the sand on the beach a strange liquid flowed in streams; and this, it is said, was the origin of glass. (Pliny, *Natural History*, XXXVI, 191–2.)

THIS IS how the Roman author the Elder Pliny explains the invention of glass in his *Natural History*, written in the second half of the first century AD. But we now know that this remarkable man-made substance was first manufactured further east, in the country called in antiquity Mesopotamia (meaning literally 'in the middle of the rivers', referring to the Tigris and Euphrates, the area now known as Iraq and northern Syria), and that this happened some 2,500 years before Pliny's time, in the middle of the third millennium BC.

Pliny's account nonetheless gives the three principal ingredients of glass in antiquity, namely soda, silica and lime. Nitrum (or natron, as it is usually called today) is a naturally occurring soda; sand was the silica, and this probably contained lime, the third necessary element. If nothing was added to the soda/lime/silica mixture, the resulting glass was usually bluish-green because of the presence of at least some iron in nearly all sand. Coloured glass was made by the addition of specific metallic oxides and by varying the furnace conditions (and so the temperature of firing). For example, in antiquity copper produced turquoise or pale blue, dark green, ruby red or opaque dark red, while the addition of cobalt resulted in a deep blue; manganese was required for yellowish or purplish glass, antimony for opaque yellow (or pale orange) and opaque white, and iron for pale blue, bottle green, amber or a dark colour appearing black. Almost colourless glass (akin to modern crystal glass) could be achieved by the careful selection of

15 Squat *alabastron* (perfume flask), now weathered but originally made of a clear green glass. It bears a faint but legible inscription in cuneiform, the wedge-shaped script of central Asia, on either side. On the front a lion precedes the lettering that reads 'Palace of Sargon'; on the back is 'King of Assyria'. This vase stands at the head of a series of perfume flasks (such as Pl. 41) whose original forms were made by lost-wax casting but whose final shape, including the central hole, was achieved by grinding and cutting when cold. Made before the death of Sargon II in 705 BC, and found in the North-West Palace at Nimrud, the capital of Assyria. H. 8.8 cm.

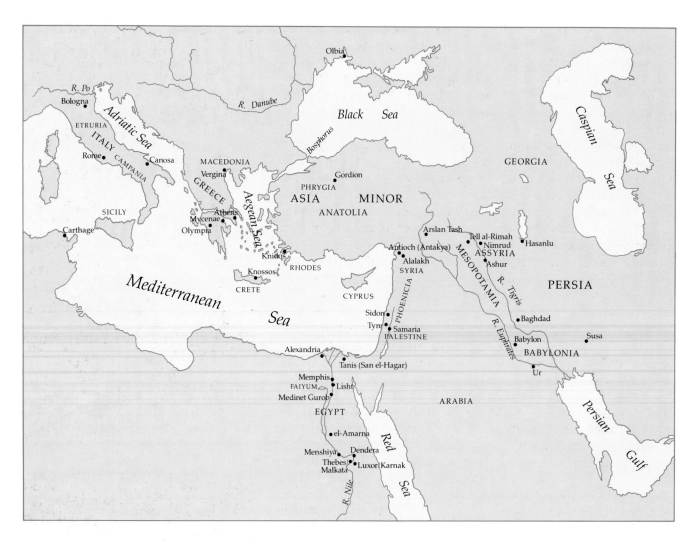

Map of part of Europe, North Africa and the Near East, showing the location of the principal glassmaking centres and other sites mentioned in this chapter.

fine silver sand free from iron, but manganese and, it seems, above all antimony, the most effective agent, were used as decolourants, at least in the Roman era.

Not surprisingly, the potentials of this new material were not immediately realised, and the initial stages produced only beads and other small objects, formed or cast using simple tools and finished by stoneworkers' techniques. Few glass items of any kind are known from anywhere until the first vessels were made in western Asia sometime before 1500 BC. Shortly thereafter, in the fifteenth century BC, the Egyptian industry was born. About this time, too, glass starts to be mentioned in Mesopotamian written sources (earlier references are perhaps to glazed objects, in one instance a bowl).

It was a technological breakthrough around the middle of the sixteenth century BC that had led to the creation of the first glass vessels and allowed the industry to become established in its own right. This was the core-forming technique, which was to remain the foremost method for the manufacture of vessels for the next 1,500 years or so. The first examples appear to have been produced in northern Mesopotamia. The shapes include long straight-sided beakers with button bases, similar to contemporary pottery vessels, and bottles of several varieties with pointed bottoms or disc bases. Round the rim there was often a 'network' cane of spirally twisted threads of different colours.

Figs 1–1

Figs 37–
50–53

Most were made between the late sixteenth and early fourteenth century BC, but an example from a thirteenth-century grave shows that such vessels continued to be in circulation, if not made, later on.

In the fifteenth century BC, not long after the invention of core-forming, polychrome vessels began to be made of mosaic glass, another technique apparently first discovered in northern Mesopotamia. These were made of pieces of monochrome opaque glass fused together and subsequently shaped around a core or possibly slumped over or into a form. Occasionally this same technique or an allied one produced marbled glass similar to veined stone. Beakers of this type of mosaic glass, which again resemble pottery vessels, date mainly from about 1350 to 1250 BC, while to the fourteenth century belong important mosaic glass fragments from a palace to the west of Baghdad and now in the Iraq Museum which are made of sections of multicoloured mosaic canes, so anticipating the practice of Hellenistic and Roman glassmakers. Red inlay plaques from the same site are decorated with patterns and birds in turquoise blue and white which were pressed into the red glass in its viscous state, another new technique. Exceptionally fine fragments of both plaques and vessels decorated with geometric or floral patterns and figured scenes, again formed of multicoloured mosaic canes, were found at Ashur in a thirteenth-century context.

Contemporary with the core-formed and mosaic glass vessels are a wide variety of objects including beads of many different types, jewellery insets, furniture inlays, pendants – both plain and decorated – and figurines of deities, demons and animals. A number of these are of one colour, cast in open or closed moulds; others are polychrome, made of mosaic or core-formed glass. In the ancient world there is a lack of evidence to show whether the glass was poured into open moulds and allowed to cool, so forming the large category of 'cast' flat-backed beads, amulets, inlays, statuettes and other objects. It is equally possible that many of these types were produced by pressing the mould onto the soft glass already poured onto the flat surface of a marver, i.e. 'mould-pressed'.

From the colours that survive and from textual references it is clear that the early glassmakers were imitating precious and semi-precious stones such as lapis-lazuli or turquoise (the blues) and gold (yellow). A distinction is made in the texts between lapis lazuli and its imitations, which were 'kiln-made' or 'produced by boiling'. It is clear, too, that glass was a luxury material in its own right, produced in major cities for an aristocratic market, generally royal or priestly, since most of the excavated pieces have been found in the ruins of temples or palaces or in tombs, rather than in private houses.

Thus, during the later sixteenth and the fifteenth centuries BC,

16 ABOVE, RIGHT Bottle of core-formed glass with dark brown body (now mostly weathered to grey) and turquoise blue decoration. This example was found in a 13th-century grave at Ur (Mesopotamia), but such bottles are among the earliest glass vessels, first made in northern Mesopotamia around 1525–1500 BC. H. 11.3 cm.

17 RIGHT Fragments of an almost cylindrical beaker of mosaic glass, made of sections of monochrome canes arranged in chevron patterns. This was the first type of mosaic glass to be made, another technique invented in northern Mesopotamia. Excavated at Tell al-Rimah, Mesopotamia; 1350–1250 BC. Largest fragment 7.7 × 6 cm.

glassmaking evolved rapidly in northern Mesopotamia. Mesopotamian glass vessels and objects have been found on many sites in the Middle and Near East, from Persia (modern Iran), Elam and Babylonia in the east to Syria and Palestine on the Mediterranean coast, and in other centres of Late Bronze Age civilisation in Cyprus and Mycenaean Greece. It is also possible that, encouraged by the military conquests of the Egyptian pharaoh Tuthmosis III in Syria and up to the Mesopotamian borders from about 1450 BC, the Asiatic industry had sent workers to Egypt to found the glass industry there (see below). It was in the mid-fourteenth century BC that the industry reached its peak in both western Asia and Egypt, but it continued to flourish until around 1200 BC and during these years it spread its influence further still.

The role of the Levant – the area from around Antakya (ancient Antioch) in modern Turkey down the coastal countries of Syria, Phoenicia (modern Lebanon) and Palestine/Israel, taking in the island of Cyprus – in the trade in raw glass and finished products at this time is illustrated both by diplomatic correspondence found in the royal archives of the new Egyptian capital at el-Amarna in Middle Egypt, which mentions consignments of raw glass to be sent by kings of Tyre and neighbouring cities, and by the discovery of cobalt blue glass ingots in the wreck of a merchant ship that sank off the coast near Kaş in south-west Turkey in the fourteenth century BC. Analysis of the glass has shown that more is in fact of Egyptian than Asiatic origin, but its destination is unknown. The find nonetheless illustrates how raw glass was circulated in the Late Bronze Age. Moreover, a group of core-formed vessels found on Levantine sites differ significantly from the Egyptian versions (which predominate) and so seem to be of local manufacture. These include jugs on high footstands and bottles in the form of pomegranates. The latter have been found mainly in Cyprus, where they were probably made. With their short necks and pointed leaves, they are truer likenesses of the fruit than their Egyptian counterparts.

Very few glass vessels have been found on Late Bronze Age (Mycenaean) sites in Greece, but exclusive to that area are ornaments of translucent glass, mainly bright blue, normally with flat backs and suspension holes. Most date from 1400 to 1200 BC. They occur in many different shapes, the most common being rosettes and spirals, the latter perhaps representing curls of hair. Moulds for such ornaments have been found on several sites. They are made of stone, notably steatite, and it is clear that there were a number of centres of manufacture. The same moulds could have been used for ornaments of gold foil which are often found with the glass examples, and indeed sometimes the gold and glass fit together. The ornaments were for

18 Plaque depicting a nude female figure, often identified as the Phoenician goddess Astarte. The visible rim suggests that the mould was pressed onto the soft glass already poured on the flat surface of a marver. The original colour of the glass was probably translucent dark blue, but it now appears light bluish-grey. Excavated at Alalakh, north Syria; 1400–1200 BC. L. 8.5 cm.

19 Sixteen ornaments in the form of stylised curls of hair, now threaded together and perhaps originally part of a diadem. Of translucent blue glass, now rather discoloured, they were made in moulds in Mycenaean Greece in the 14th or 13th century BC. Excavated at Ialysos on the island of Rhodes. L. of each 2.9 cm.

personal use, often strung together to form necklaces or diadems, or sewn on garments as appliqués. Documents in Mycenaean Greek give us the name for glass, *kyanos*, and from these, and also from the later Homeric poems, we learn that glass was used along with gold and ivory as inlays for weapons and palace furnishings, another indication that it was a luxury at this time.

Other cast objects from Mycenaean Greek sites and probably of local origin include gaming pieces, and a tiny bull figurine and a hilt from a distinctly Mycenaean type of sword (both Athens, National Museum). The last two items are made of blue glass similar to the majority of the ornaments, but were found in later sixteenth- and fifteenth-century BC contexts and so predate them. Other notable pieces, also usually made of blue glass and found on Mycenaean Greek sites in earlier contexts than most of the ornaments, are disc-pendants decorated with eight- or ten-pointed stars in relief and ribbed spacer beads of unquestionably Mesopotamian origin. By contrast, only a few fragments of Egyptian core-formed vessels have been found here.

While the Mycenaean Greeks certainly manufactured glass objects, the limited range of colours – or rather the almost exclusive use of bright, translucent blue – suggests that the raw material was imported, probably in the form of ingots like those on the Kaş wreck. Recent chemical analysis has shown that the composition of the blue glass ornaments is the same as that of the blue glass used in Egypt at this time, and so, in spite of their connections with the Mesopotamian glasshouses, it must have been from there, either directly or by way of the Levant, that the Mycenaeans imported their glass.

Towards the close of the thirteenth century BC this first flowering of

20 Core-formed bottle in the form of a pomegranate. Probably made in Cyprus, where it was found in a tomb at Enkomi; about 1400–1200 BC. H. 7.4 cm.

For the making of a core-formed vessel, see pp. 214–15, Figs 1–15.

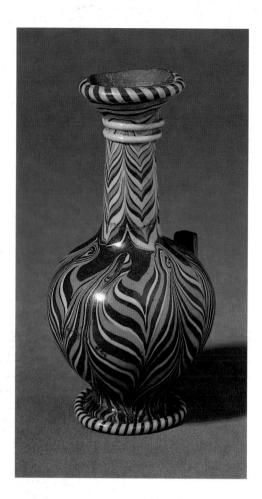

the glass industry came to an end. The destructions and disasters that brought the Bronze Age civilisations into a period of near anarchy no doubt closed the market for glass vessels, which had depended on the palace cultures. Very little vessel glass has been found for the period between about 1200 and 900 BC, although small objects such as beads, seals and trinkets were probably still being made, especially in Syria.

Egypt

*c.*1450–1100 BC

The Egyptians were foremost among ancient peoples in their mastery of manufacturing techniques, yet they did not begin to produce glass in any quantity until the New Kingdom and in particular from the reign of Amenophis III onwards (*c.*1390 BC), far later than any of their neighbours. Although individual beads of glass occur as early as the Old Kingdom a thousand years before (probably manufacturing aberrations of glazed composition) and there are some isolated glass scarabs of Middle Kingdom date (*c.*1900 BC), it looks as though the production of objects in this luxury material was the result of some new influence, in all probability the introduction of Syrian craftsmen to the Egyptian workshops. At any rate, it cannot be purely coincidental that the earliest glass vessels date from the reign of Tuthmosis III (*c.*1479–1425 BC), who conducted a number of successful campaigns in Syria as far as the Mesopotamian borders. It is only reasonable to suppose that local craftsmen with more than a century of experience in manufacturing objects from this difficult medium should now have introduced their expertise into Egypt, whether they were brought forcibly as prisoners of war or entered freely as travelling workers within the newly created Egyptian empire.

What makes the late production of glass in Egypt even more surprising is that the basic material – an alkaline calcium silicate – is the same as that of the glaze used as early as the predynastic Badarian period (*c.*4000 BC) to coat stone beads and also a little later in the manufacture of glazed composition. The only real difference lies in the method of employment: if the raw product was to form glass it was used independently, while if it was to form glaze it was provided with a permanent core of a different material. Appropriately enough, the Egyptian name for glass was *iner en wedeh* or *aat wedhet*, both meaning literally 'stone of the kind that flows'.

One of the earliest datable Egyptian glass vessels, now in the British Museum, almost certainly came from the burial of Tuthmosis III in the Valley of the Kings at Thebes. It takes the form of a turquoise blue jug with an elaborate yellow and white patterning of stylised tamarisk trees, threads, dots and scales incorporating a hieroglyphic text with the king's prenomen, Menkheperre. This decoration was created by enamelling, and the vessel is the earliest so far known employing the technique. The decoration of the outer surface of the handle, however, which was added separately, is more conventional, with parallel threads of white, yellow and dark blue. Like most dynastic glass vessels, the Tuthmosis III jug was core-formed. It is the remains of the core, which was never totally removed, which renders most Egyptian glass vessels opaque: fragments which can be completely cleaned reveal that the medium was nearly always translucent.

21 ABOVE A rare Egyptian glass version of a well-known type of Cypriot pottery ring-based jug; even the two bands at the top of the neck have been faithfully copied by raised yellow threads. Although it has been suggested that such vessels were used to transport opium – indeed, an opium-based residue was reputedly found in some of them – there is no evidence that Egyptian glass vessels were intended as containers for anything other than cosmetic and toilet materials; presumably this jug once held scented oil. The handle is lost. 18th Dynasty, about 1352–1336 BC. H. 9.3 cm.

22 OPPOSITE One of the earliest datable Egyptian glass vessels, its colouring no doubt imitating turquoise stone. The hieroglyphs naming 'the good god Menkheperre [Tuthmosis III] given life' and the decoration of stylised tamarisk trees, threads, dots and scales are enamelled, the earliest example of the technique so far known from Egypt. The yellow and white is probably intended to imitate gold and silver. This core-formed jug probably came from Tuthmosis III's tomb at Thebes, one of a set of seven for the sacred oils used during the burial ritual. 18th Dynasty, about 1425 BC. H. 8.7 cm.

 22

As in Mesopotamia and Syria, so in Egypt most vessel shapes in glass were copies of those which already existed in other materials. A jug with globular body, ringed base and cylindrical neck joined by a single handle to the shoulder, is a perfect copy of a pottery form well known throughout the Levant which, because of its resemblance when inverted to the opium poppy, has been suggested as the means of transporting that drug. Glass vessels in Egypt, however, were intended for the most part to hold cosmetics and toilet materials: kohl to paint the eyes, unguent shaped into a conical lump to be worn on top of the head, or scented oil to anoint the body. The remaining larger pieces probably served as luxury tableware in palaces or graced the houses of favoured courtiers. The jug from the tomb of Tuthmosis III probably contained a sacred oil used during the burial ritual.

A superb example of a uniquely Egyptian fancy-shaped vessel which, because of the narrowness of its mouth, also presumably once held oil, takes the form of a *bulti*-fish in polychrome glass. Although there are a few other examples in this shape and material, they are usually monochrome; this piece is therefore by far the most spectacular, with its pinched-out tail, high-relief fins, gaping mouth and pop eyes, decorated in light and dark blue, yellow, white and turquoise blue, all on a bright blue ground. Curiously enough, all such fish-shaped vessels require a support of some kind, for they cannot stand alone. This example, worthy to have graced the toilet box of Queen Nefertiti herself, was actually excavated at el-Amarna, the site of the new capital city founded by her husband Akhenaten (*c.*1352–1336 BC). However, it came not from any of the palace areas but from beneath the floor of a rather poor house, where it was found with a number of other objects, suggesting that it may well have been looted from a more appropriate original location.

As we have seen, it is unlikely that any new shape was invented exclusively for the new medium, and toilet vessels in glass imitated their counterparts in other materials. One of the most popular shapes for an unguent container, whether in stone or glass, was a footed squat vessel with or without handles but, *de rigueur*, with a very wide

21

23

24

23 A uniquely Egyptian fancy-shaped core-formed vessel in the form of a *bulti*-fish, the narrowness of the mouth suggesting that it was intended to hold scented oil. Although fish-form vessels exist in other materials and there are even other examples in glass – though they are usually monochrome – this piece is by far the most spectacular and may once have graced a palace at el-Amarna, where it was found. 18th Dynasty, about 1352–1336 BC. L. 14.5 cm.

24 A squat handleless unguent jar originally in lavender-purple glass which has deteriorated. The monochrome colour is unusual, as is the fact that the flared foot is solid. This shape in alabaster is one of the most characteristic for cosmetic containers of the 18th Dynasty, but is far less common in glass. 18th–19th Dynasties, about 1330–1200 BC. H. 8.6 cm.

25 A particularly fine and characteristic example of an unguent jar, with an especially broad neck to allow the greasy contents to be removed easily. The hemispherical core-formed body stands on a high trumpet-shaped foot, the neck is short and there are two strap handles. Said to be from Memphis. 18th Dynasty, about 1390–1352 BC. H. 8.7 cm.

cylindrical neck. The broad aperture made it equally easy for an ointment spoon or fingers to remove the contents and also allowed the complete removal of the core after manufacture. The decoration of glass toilet vessels usually consists of patterns of chevrons or festoons, but a wide diversity of effects is achieved in a number of ways. The variety possible within a single form of vessel can be seen in two ovoid jars of the Eighteenth Dynasty, dating from about 1390–1336 BC, both with handles and hollow flaring foot and presumably intended to hold scented oil. Although the more complete example has four rather than two handles and its body colour is dark blue rather than turquoise, a real difference in appearance has been achieved by other means. In the second example the handle still remaining is larger and set lower on the body, the foot is less high, more flared and encircled at top and bottom by a raised relief thread. In the four-handled jar the decoration consists of polychrome festoons on the body and similarly coloured chevrons on the neck, transmuted in the two-handled example to monochrome blue chevrons on the body and neck framed by a single thread of yellow and enclosing a single white thread at their centre. The effect is startlingly different.

In the case of glass lentoid flasks, so called because they are lens-shaped in section and which, in their 'classical' form, have a vertical handle at each side of a tall thin neck, joining it to the shoulders, the relationship with vessels in other materials is more complex. They

26 Two core-formed unguent vessels which demonstrate the variations in both shape and decoration that are possible within a single basic form. The blue-grey fabric of the left-hand jar is quite unusual, and the use of simple festoons in pale turquoise blue as the sole decoration on the body and neck produces a very different effect from that of the right-hand jar. This latter piece was excavated in the Faiyum in a modest reed burial dating to a period when such a fine vessel might be expected to be almost exclusive to the court. Both 18th Dynasty, the left-hand jar about 1390–1352 BC and the right-hand jar about 1390–1336 BC. H. of left-hand jar 8.8 cm.

27 Two ovoid jars, presumably intended to hold scented oil. Both core-formed and said to be from Memphis, 18th Dynasty, the left-hand jar about 1390–1352 BC and the right-hand jar about 1390–1336 BC. H. of left-hand jar 10.3 cm.

appear in Egypt as early as the reign of Amenophis II (*c.*1427–1400 BC) but at first lack handles. It was at the end of the Eighteenth Dynasty, however, and especially during the Nineteenth (*c.*1295–1186 BC), that they enjoyed their greatest popularity, when they were even reproduced in miniature. Indeed, this may be one shape in glass which influenced other media rather than the other way around, for it presages the glazed composition New Year flasks of the Late Period eight centuries later. Yet some examples in monochrome creamy white give an exact imitation of Egyptian alabaster or calcite, even though stone vessels seem rarely to have been made in this shape. Only the cane of spirally twisted threads of two colours which usually encircles the rim of such flasks would have no parallel in stone. Other glass lentoid flasks, however, make no attempt to ape stone, being manufactured in highly coloured body material and decorated with chevrons and flame patterns in standard colours.

From the earliest times the Egyptians, both men and women, outlined their eyes with eye-paint made from mineral colours, partly as decoration but mainly to give protection and to ward off infection. The eye-paint containers manufactured from glass during the New Kingdom in general take the characteristic shape of the palm column, retaining such elements from the architectural prototype as the bindings immediately below the fronds of the capital. A good deal of variety was still possible within this single shape, which was core-formed. The body material might be lavender, sapphire or dark blue, or even green; the bindings monochrome or two-coloured; sometimes the lower part of the shaft is extended into a ring base. The fronds of the capital may be so flattened as to be almost horizontal, and the opening at their centre prominently raised above them. In some rare instances the original rod-like applicator has also survived.

Very rare examples of glass vessels unique to Egypt include a glass version of one type encountered, but still rarely, in pottery. This is a dark blue glass vase with a tall cylindrical neck and a long ovoid body tapering towards a rounded base. The conventionally coloured decoration of the neck and body comprises chevrons and clustered festoons, some of them inverted; this may point to the place of production as Medinet Gurob in the Faiyum, a possible source of glassware for the northern court at Memphis from at least the time of Amenophis III (*c.*1370 BC) until the reign of Ramesses II well over a century later. However, what makes this piece even more interesting is that impressed into its surface above the upper row of festoons on the body are two bosses, each with a blue and yellow centre encircled by a cane of spirally twisted black and white threads. These are clearly intended to represent breasts – indeed in one of only two other known examples (Bonn, Akademisches Kunstmuseum) they are totally three-dimensional and provided with nipples – and above them, at the top of the neck, is the remains of an applied yellow detail now largely lost but presumably once indicating a face. Clearly this vessel is anthropomorphic, aping its better-known pottery counterparts which date to the Eighteenth Dynasty. That they were connected in some way with female fertility is undisputed, but their exact function is unclear unless they were intended to contain milk or a supposedly aphrodisiac substance.

Almost as limited a survival in glass is the Egyptian version of the

28

29

30

31

28 OPPOSITE, ABOVE LEFT The metal of this core-formed lentoid flask perfectly imitates Egyptian alabaster, although stone vessels appear only rarely to have been made in this shape. The twisted cane encircling the rim certainly had no stone precedent. Glass containers in this form were undoubtedly intended to hold scented oil, but because in Christian times souvenir pottery versions were produced for visitors to holy places they are still often known as pilgrim flasks. 18th–19th Dynasties, about 1330–1250 BC. H. 12.8 cm.

29 OPPOSITE, ABOVE RIGHT Lentoid flask for scented oil, core-formed in translucent amethyst glass. The practice of overlaying handles with different coloured vertical threads and framing the body decoration with horizontal ones may be indicative of an origin in or near Medinet Gurob, where this flask was found. Although no evidence of glass-working, as opposed to finished pieces, has been found at the site, the chronological gap between the 18th Dynasty workshops at Malkata and el-Amarna and those of the Ramesside period at Lisht and Menshiya would thus be filled. This piece is dated relatively firmly by inscribed objects of the reign of Ramesses II which were found with it. 19th Dynasty, about 1250 BC. H. 10 cm.

30 OPPOSITE, BELOW LEFT Two core-formed kohl tubes in the shape of palm columns, the most popular form for eye-paint containers in glass; one still has its original glass applicator. *Left*: 18th–19th Dynasty, about 1375–1275 BC; *right*: 18th Dynasty, about 1390–1336 BC. H. of left-hand tube 8.7 cm.

31 OPPOSITE, BELOW RIGHT Rare glass anthropomorphic vase, with two bosses representing breasts. The remains of a yellow detail on the neck, between the two raised bands, may once have indicated a face. Core-formed, 18th Dynasty, about 1400–1300 BC. H. 15.3 cm.

32 RIGHT Egyptian glass vessel fragments, 18th Dynasty. In the centre is a shallow dish of mosaic glass, presumably made in imitation of a stone such as diorite-gneiss. So many fragments in this technique have been found at Malkata that this fine example is probably to be dated to the reign of Amenophis III (c.1390–1352 BC), who had a palace there. The other fragments include two almost certainly from the burial of King Amenophis II in the Valley of the Kings, about 1400 BC (*top right*, with rosettes and swirling patterns); the remainder include several from el-Amarna, about 1352–1336 BC. D. of central fragment 7.1 cm.

vessel in the shape of a pomegranate, with convex base and roughly cylindrical body, horizontal shoulders and a nipped-in denticulated mouth. The feathered decoration of the body is always confined between horizontal bands. The fact that one of the three known examples was excavated near Menshiya in Middle Egypt suggests that the glass workshops there might have produced this local version of the better known and more naturalistic Cypriot form.

It is hardly surprising that far more fragments of glass vessels have survived than complete or even partially complete examples. Yet these remnants, often little more than slivers, serve not only to give a glimpse of spectacular pieces which would otherwise be totally lost but by their numbers can help to pinpoint the location of ancient glass-producing workshops of which no trace has otherwise survived. Thus it would appear that there were no glass workshops in Egypt before the reign of Amenophis III, but then, to judge from the number of fragments found at Malkata on the Theban West Bank, the palace there played host to an important production site. Glass was certainly manufactured at el-Amarna during the reign of his son Akhenaten and, by the Nineteenth Dynasty, workshops at Lisht catered for the northern capital at Memphis while others at Menshiya had probably taken over from Malkata in supplying the religious capital at Thebes.

On the other hand, enough vessel fragments of New Kingdom date have been found at Serabit el-Khadim in Sinai to raise the suspicion that 'he local extractors of turquoise lived an abnormally luxurious lifestyle so far away from civilisation. Yet there is no evidence of any glassworks. In all probability, the vessels were taken there specially to be dedicated at the local shrine of Hathor, 'mistress of turquoise'.

In addition to producing core-formed vessels, the Egyptians also cast glass in moulds. A fine early piece whose exact method of production is disputed but which must at some point have involved the use of a mould, is an eye-paint container in pale turquoise blue. The likeliest explanation is that it was cast in a mould and only its

central tubular opening was made by the technique known as cold cutting. It has also been suggested, however, that the whole vessel was made by this process, whereby a block of glass was worked into shape by grinding and drilling just as though it were a stone vessel being extracted from a stone block. This container, with sheet gold edging on the rims of the cover, mouth and base, has the ringed base and swelling body with sharply delineated shoulders and pinched neck below a flat projecting rim which are characteristic of toilet vessels made popular during the Middle Kingdom four centuries earlier but still in fashion during the early Eighteenth Dynasty, the date of this example. They were usually made of a pale blue stone variously described as blue marble or anhydrite, and the medium here is clearly in imitation of its stone prototype. Unusually, it still retains its lid, a flat disc with a small boss at the centre of the underside to hold it in place inside the narrow opening of the neck.

Undoubtedly cast is a dish in translucent turquoise blue glass in the shape of a clam shell: the walls are so thin as to be almost transparent, and the edges sharp. Although this particular shape was popular in other media, probably serving as a scoop for unguent, and actual clam shells were used to hold coloured inks, it is extremely rare in glass and certainly a product of the palace workshops at Malkata or el-Amarna.

A magnificent mosaic shallow dish, of which there is only one other known comparable example (Brooklyn Museum, New York), was made from small irregular segments of white, red, dark blue, black and turquoise blue glass. A single thick yellow thread encircles the rim. Although the type is known as early as the reign of Amenophis II

33 An eye-paint container, with lid, in pale turquoise blue glass; the base, mouth and rim of the lid are edged with sheet gold. The shape is an exact copy of a type of stone cosmetic container popular since the Middle Kingdom, around 1900 BC; the colour may even imitate the blue marble or anhydrite from which these were often made. A boss on the underside of the lid would have held it in place inside the narrow mouth. Probably cast in a mould; 18th Dynasty, about 1457–1425 BC. H., with lid, 6.3 cm.

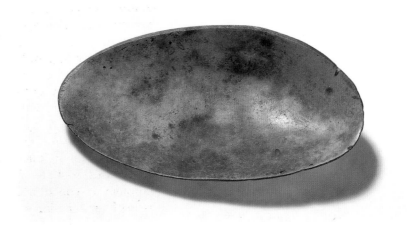

34 A glass clam shell in wafer-thin translucent turquoise blue glass, perhaps intended to be used (with great care) as an unguent scoop. It was undoubtedly made in a palace workshop, but whether at Malkata or el-Amarna cannot be certain. Only one other example, in Brooklyn Museum, New York, is known. 18th Dynasty, about 1390–1336 BC. L. 12.7 cm.

35 The damaged head and much of the right shoulder of a pharaoh as sphinx, in turquoise blue glass: he wears the *nemes* wig cover with two lappets, the uraeus (cobra) on the forehead, and the false beard. The stylised markings on and behind the right shoulder make it clear that the piece originally took the form of the hybrid sphinx (a lion's body with a royal human head). In spite of the damage, enough of this miniature masterpiece survives to suggest the chubby features of the youthful Amenophis II. Lost-wax cast; 18th Dynasty, about 1427–1400 BC. H. 3 cm.

and continued in use until the time of Akhenaten, so many fragments of the ware are known from the remains of the palace at Malkata that this all but complete example – a chip is missing from one side – probably dates to the reign of Amenophis III.

Lost-wax casting (*cire perdue*) in a closed mould was the method used to produce small-scale sculpture, which is often very fine but never as common in glass as in glazed composition. From what must have been a miniature masterpiece there survives only the head and part of the shoulder of a pharaoh as sphinx; the medium is opaque turquoise blue glass with a glossy surface. The features are tiny, yet sufficiently clearly delineated to suggest an idealised portrait of Amenophis II.

Closed moulds might also be used to produce glass amulets, pendants and ornaments in the round. Ear-studs of dumb-bell shape, however, often with a trailed thread encircling the rims, were not made in this way, nor was a particularly barbaric form which entailed a great distension of the hole in the earlobe. The shape of the latter type is two large circular convex domes separated by a groove, and so great is the size of some examples that they have in the past been incorrectly but understandably identified as glass knobs for furniture. Other glass earrings were made by drawing a cane, often rimmed by a thick thread, into an open circle and pulling out the ends into two loops to accommodate the wire or rod which would have passed through the pierced lobe. Leech-shaped earrings were usually formed around a wire which remained in place. Other penannular examples, however, are mere open circles made from a cane of a single colour or intertwining threads. All were worn pushed through the lobe and twisted into place.

Wrapping molten material around a rod or wire with a separating agent and shaping it could produce the simplest of beads or the more complex but characteristic pomegranate pendant, to which a suspension loop was usually attached. This was also the method of production for palm- and papyrus-column ear ornaments which have a narrow piercing from end to end and are typically Eighteenth or Nineteenth Dynasty in date. These were intended to be worn on a wire, often with other elements, which passed through the pierced ear, unlike the similar elongated mushroom-shaped unpierced ear-plugs made from glazed composition or even stone, with plain shafts but elaborately decorated domed tops, intended to be worn pushed

through pierced earlobes with the polychrome patterned dome showing at the front.

Far more often, however, pendants and amulets were produced like inlays, by casting molten glass in an open mould or mould-pressing so that the resultant piece has a flat back. Indeed, the ability of glass to imitate semi-precious stones, which were far harder to model and carve, meant that during the New Kingdom and later it was often substituted for inlays which in earlier periods would have been manufactured from lapis lazuli, turquoise, feldspar and jasper. Much of Tutankhamun's jewellery is little more than magnificent costume jewellery, consisting of precious metal settings for what are predominantly glass inlays. As early as the later Eighteenth Dynasty, however, larger-scale glass inlays with highly modelled details were manufactured to form figured scenes when inset into other materials. A male face of red glass, in profile looking right, if correctly dated to the Amarna period, is one of the earliest known in the colour. The long arched neck marked with folds of flesh, the thick lips and blunt nose, the heavy-lidded eye and pierced earlobe, certainly suggest the well-known physical characteristics of Akhenaten himself. Another of turquoise blue glass with slanting oriental eye and eyebrow once inlaid with glass of a different colour, while undoubtedly of the same reign, has a distinctly feminine look and presumably represents Nefertiti or one of the Amarna princesses. This piece well illustrates the inability of the early glassmakers to produce flesh colours in accordance with the normal Egyptian conventions of reddish-brown for men and yellow or pale brown for women. Both pieces irresistibly call to mind the inlaid throne-back from the tomb of Tutankhamun. Other parts of the body produced in relief for use as inlays in figured scenes include hands, feet, legs, arms and torsos; there are also headdresses, clothing and jewellery, and hieroglyphs from the accompanying texts.

Flat-backed amulets are surprisingly rare during the formative years of glassmaking in Egypt. Their forms, too, are in general restricted to

prescribed funerary shapes such as papyrus sceptres and Girdles of Isis, which were manufactured only in green and red respectively as required by the relevant chapters of the Book of the Dead. However, a characteristically colourful amulet of late Eighteenth Dynasty date (c.1300 BC) is the heart amulet pulled into shape at the end of a pontil and resembling a pot with knobbed top and two lug handles. Whether the body material is black, dark blue, turquoise or sapphire blue, it is always decorated further with trailed threads of white, yellow, green or, more unusually, red. Manufactured in the same way at the end of a pontil are equally colourful amulets with suspension loop which depict Taweret, hippopotamus goddess of childbirth. She stands on stumpy legs so rudimentary as to be almost non-existent. Her black body is decorated with embedded blobs of red and white glass which give a spattered effect very reminiscent in appearance, if not in technique, of composite mosaic dishes of the mid- to late Eighteenth Dynasty which are probably contemporary.

Fig. 89

Thus, by the mid-Ramesside period (c.1200 BC), the Egyptians had perfected virtually all the glassmaking techniques which were to be employed during the remainder of the dynastic period, yet a hiatus followed the end of the New Kingdom (c.1070 BC) when scarcely any glass seems to have been manufactured. Instead glazed composition became ever more prevalent, and even in jewellery there was a return to inlays made of semi-precious stones.

Western Asia and the Mediterranean
c.900–300 BC

The renaissance of the glass industry in the ninth century BC took place against a background of cultural revival that affected the whole of western Asia, the Levant and the Mediterranean world. The earliest use of glass on a large scale in the Iron Age was as inlays, often in ivory plaques and panels used to adorn furniture. The inlays themselves were either of monochrome glass, usually different shades of blue as well as red, green or yellow, sometimes with painted or possibly enamelled designs, or of polychrome mosaic glass forming rosettes, circles and square patterns. The inlays in ivory plaques were all of monochrome glass, and most plaques have been assigned on stylistic grounds to craftsmen from Phoenicia (modern Lebanon). Large numbers of these plaques have been found in the Assyrian palace at

39
41

39 Phoenician-style ivory plaque showing two enthroned goddesses or queens holding royal sceptres and saluting a cartouche. They sit on thrones decorated with a scale pattern of blue glass inlays; the hieroglyphs of the cartouche are also inlaid in glass. Inlays represent the earliest use of glass by the revived industry in western Asia in the 9th century BC. This plaque was found in the North-West Palace of Nimrud, the capital of the kingdom of Assyria; 8th century BC. H. 7.6 cm.

40 Hemispherical bowl of greenish-colourless glass, now largely covered by a layer of brownish weathering. One of a series of drinking vessels probably made by Phoenician glassmakers. Found in the North-West Palace at Nimrud; about 725–600 BC. H. 6.2–7.5 cm (it stands askew because the thickness of the glass varies).

For the making of such bowls by the slumping process, see p. 221, Figs 54–8.

41 Glass inlay plaque, probably originally colourless with a greenish tinge but now opaque. It is decorated with a Phoenician winged male sphinx, painted or more probably enamelled, as the design has survived, at least in part. Found in Fort Shalmaneser at Nimrud and probably made as one of a set to decorate furniture during the reign of the Assyrian king Tiglath-Pileser III (744–727 BC). W. 4.2 cm.

Nimrud (modern Iraq), at Arslan Tash (Syria) and Samaria (modern Israel). Most are said to date from the eighth century BC, but the earliest (which certainly include a group – now in the Iran Bastan Museum, Tehran – from Hasanlu in northern Iran in the Syrian style, which would have had glass inlays) are of the ninth century BC. The source of the glass used by the ivory-carvers is a problem: western Asia is the most likely candidate, as chemical analysis has shown that the composition of the inlays differs from that of the glass of New Kingdom Egypt. However, while the ivory-carvers themselves would have been capable of casting monochrome inlays from ingots (and finishing them to fit after cooling by grinding and polishing to make bevelled edges), considerably more skill would have been required to produce inlays of mosaic glass, which suggests that these are the work of specialists. Were the Phoenicians responsible for both types of inlays, or were they imported from a different source? Glass technology also reached Italy at about this time. Beads were being made near the Po delta in the tenth or perhaps the eleventh century BC.

It was around the middle of the eighth century BC that glass vessels began to be produced by the reborn industry. These were of monochrome glass, cast by the lost-wax method or slumped, or polychrome and formed around a core: although, as we have seen, inlays of mosaic glass were made, mosaic glass vessels were very rare until the later third century BC. Perhaps also the work of Phoenician glassworkers was a class of luxurious vessels of clear monochrome glass, usually in natural greens or yellowish or greenish colourless glass. More rarely they are of deliberately coloured glass, namely blue, purple or aquamarine. To the eighth and seventh centuries BC belong drinking vessels, mostly in the form of hemispherical bowls that were no doubt made by the slumping process, undecorated or with simple decoration of horizontal cut grooves or ridges or, exceptionally, with more elaborate geometric patterns or inlays of coloured glass (like those of the ivories). These have been found in large numbers in the Assyrian homeland and only rarely outside, like one from Fortetsa in Crete and another from Palestrina in central Italy; none so far in Phoenicia.

Rather more widespread is a group of tall perfume flasks (*alabastra*)

40

42

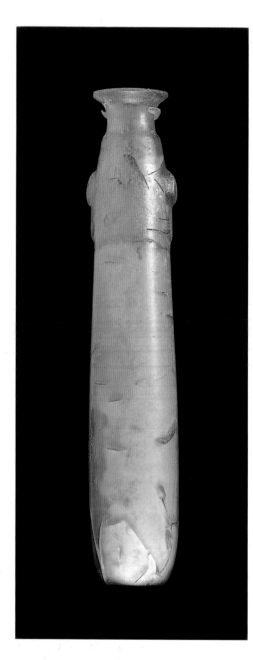

42 Tall *alabastron* of sea-green glass. Said to be from Pozzuoli (ancient Puteoli) in Italy, but probably made in western Asia in a Phoenician glasshouse in the 7th or 6th century B C. H. 21.1 cm.

known from Cyprus, Italy and Palestine (but not, it seems, Mesopotamia). Made of fabrics similar to those of many of the bowls, their original form was most probably produced by lost-wax casting but their final shape, including the central opening, was achieved by grinding and cutting when cold. A squat example bearing the name of the Assyrian king Sargon II (721–705 BC) and found in his palace at Nimrud stands at the head of the series, which as a whole belongs to the seventh, sixth and perhaps fifth centuries BC. Other vessels which belong to this general group are a jug of the seventh century BC from Aliseda in central western Spain (Madrid, Museo Arqueológico Nacional), an *amphoriskos* (flask) of the sixth century BC from Bologna in Italy (Bologna, Museo Civico), and a remarkable *phiale-mesomphalos* (bowl with a central boss on the inside) from a tomb at Gordion, Phrygia (Ankara, Archaeological Museum). Of virtually colourless glass, the bowl is decorated on the inside with radiating petals. It was found in a late eighth-century BC context and is therefore one of the first examples of virtually colourless glass with elaborate cut decoration. It must be emphasised that no example of these vessels has been found in Phoenicia itself, but they are generally discovered in areas with which the Phoenicians were in contact and often in conjunction with other Phoenician products, such as ivories or metalwork. The jug from Spain is more of a puzzle, since it was not found in an area known to have had contact with Phoenician traders, nor was it associated with other Phoenician objects. Its shape, however, is typically Phoenician, known also in pottery and metal, and it bears a muddled Egyptian hieroglyphic inscription such as could have been copied by an ignorant Phoenician.

While there is, therefore, reason to believe that the luxurious monochrome cast or slumped glass vessels were made by Phoenicians, it was in Mesopotamian workshops that core-forming was revived, at about the same time, the mid-eighth century BC. Compared with the products of the Bronze Age, however, the vessels are rather dull. Bottles and jars have dark translucent bodies and simple thread decoration limited to opaque white or yellow, or occasionally both together. The loop handles with tails (known as duck-head handles) on the shoulders of many of the vessels are an innovation, but a feature also of some of the tall cast *alabastra*. Prominent among the types of this core-formed group are rather ugly *alabastra* with short necks and broad cylindrical bodies. A few examples, mostly fragmentary, have been found in Mesopotamia itself, but of particular significance is the discovery of at least five complete, or virtually complete, examples of the seventh century BC on the island of Rhodes. It has been suggested that the Rhodian pieces were made there by migrant Mesopotamian glassworkers who were to inspire the setting up of a local industry, the prolific output of which will be considered below.

In the seventh century BC Mesopotamian core-formed vessels also reached Persia (modern Iran) and seem to have led to the establishment there of a local industry responsible for numerous pointed bottles found at Susa. It is possible too that a more minor industry established in central Italy (Etruria) in the seventh and sixth centuries BC had its beginnings in direct contact with Mesopotamia. Its products included core-formed *oinochoai* and *lagynoi* (jugs), and *alabastra* of blue, brown or yellow glass decorated with spikes drawn out from their

43 Core-formed *oinochoe* (jug) decorated with spikes drawn out from its walls. Made in Etruria, central Italy, where the core-formed industry was evidently inspired by Mesopotamia, but indirectly, via Rhodes. 7th century BC. H. 6.5 cm.

44 BELOW Mesopotamian core-formed *alabastron*. Imported from a glasshouse in western Asia or perhaps made by an immigrant craftsman on the island of Rhodes, where it was found during excavations at Camirus, this *alabastron* belongs to the group that led to the local production in Rhodes of core-formed glass vessels. About 700–600 BC. H. 16 cm.

walls; also core-formed beads, brooch-runners and bracelets decorated with the more usual coloured trails. Migrant Italian glassmakers, moving on when Rhodian glassware (see below) flooded their markets, were probably responsible for objects found further north in the area of the Alps and at sites on the Adriatic coastline. These date from the later sixth and fifth centuries and include brooch-runners of blue, green and brown glass with spiked decoration, and cups – some without handles, made of monochrome ribbed glass, and others with handles and decorated with trails. The brooch-runners were probably core-formed, and the cups were evidently made by slumping.

Core-formed glass was produced in other centres in western Asia and the eastern Mediterranean. To the latter area belongs a series of tall tubular bottles which may have contained kohl. They have dark bodies, and are decorated with zigzag yellow trails. Somewhat similar bottles which were made in much the same way but which are often confusingly and erroneously described as 'rod-formed', are sometimes provided with stoppers. Another series of core-formed kohl tubes with cylindrical bodies, found exclusively on sites in modern Iraq, is probably of Mesopotamian origin. All these groups were made in the sixth century BC. Somewhat later, probably of the fifth to fourth

centuries BC, and made in an area of western Asia that was part of the Achaemenid Persian empire, are three more classes of core-formed kohl tubes found principally on sites in what is now north-west Iran and the neighbouring areas of north-west Turkey and Georgia. The most distinctive of these have square bodies with four flat sides and shoulder knobs. The ground and the decoration are of many different colours, including translucent dark green, yellowish-green and a variety of blues, as well as opaque orange, white, brown and a dark colour appearing black. The trails form a variety of patterns such as festoons, chevrons and zigzags.

By far the most numerous and widespread of the core-formed vessels are the products of Mediterranean workshops which were in operation from about 550 to 50 BC. Designed to contain perfumes, scented oils and cosmetics, they form a homogeneous group sharing the same technique and taking their shapes from the repertory of Greek vases in pottery and metal. The most common types are flasks in the form of *alabastra, amphoriskoi* and *aryballoi* and jugs (*oinochoai*). These forms are varied to follow contemporary fashions in Greek pottery and there are other rarer shapes such as *hydriskai* (three-handled flasks) and unguent bottles. The most common body colour is translucent dark or cobalt blue, but perhaps more attractive are those of opaque white glass; others may be opaque brown, red or olive-green. Decoration usually consists of opaque orange, yellow, white or turquoise trails, but dark red also occurs, especially on opaque white. On the body the trails are normally combed into zigzag, festoon or feather patterns. Traded far and wide, perhaps initially in the hands of the Phoenicians, these core-formed vessels reached every major site in the Mediterranean and also travelled as far as the Black Sea, the

45 A group of early Mediterranean core-formed vessels which served as containers for scented oils or perfumes. All made on the island of Rhodes, where the jug (*oinochoe*) was found in a tomb in the Fikellura cemetery at Camirus (the find-spots of the others are not known). About 550–400 BC. H. of jug 10.5 cm.

Balkans and Gaul (modern France). Recent studies of the group as a whole have identified three main divisions, assigned to about 550–400 BC, 340–200 BC and 150–50 BC, although examples are occasionally found in first-century AD contexts. No firm evidence for the location of any of the factories has yet been found, but possible candidates for the three groups are, first, Rhodes, second southern Italy and Macedonia, and finally countries of the Levant (Syria, Palestine and Cyprus).

Rhodes is suggested as the location of the first workshops by the large numbers of vessels of this early group found in cemeteries on the island, and indeed the concentration of such glass vessels in other areas of the Mediterranean and the Black Sea that were then in the milieu of Greek commercial activity. Added to this is the overwhelmingly Hellenic character of the early shapes as well as evidence for the production in Rhodes at this time of scented oils and perfumes, which could have led to a demand for glass containers.

If, as seems likely, this Rhodian production was inspired by the arrival or local manufacture of the Mesopotamian core-formed *alabastra*, there is an uncomfortable gap of at least fifty years between the Mesopotamian group of the seventh century BC and the first of the Mediterranean series, none of which can convincingly be dated earlier than about 550 BC. This time interval may, however, be filled by the production of core-formed pendants and beads made in the same way as the vessels and employing the same range of colours. The earliest of these, in the form of heads of demons and male figures, date from the late seventh and early sixth centuries BC. Although those from Rhodes are far outnumbered by others from areas in close connection with the Phoenicians through trade or colonisation (and some have also been found in the Phoenician homeland), the lack of any other evidence that the Phoenicians made core-formed vessels or objects at this time adds fuel to the theory that the earlier group of pendants were made in Rhodes, like the core-formed vessels which they resemble and predate. It is nonetheless possible that the Phoenicians made this single foray into core-forming at this time, just as the Mesopotamians appear to have done with casting in the eighth and seventh centuries BC, when they made parts of statues in cast blue glass as a substitute for

46 BELOW, LEFT A selection of core-formed head pendants from necklaces, mainly of the 4th-3rd century BC and probably made in the Levant (Syria, Palestine or Cyprus), though the male head with plain hair is an early type first made on Rhodes around 600 BC and the large ram's head was perhaps made in North Africa, at Carthage (Tunisia). The negro head was found in a tomb at Mostagedda in Egypt, and the satyr and small female head are also said to come from Egypt, the former from Karnak. L. of ram's head 4.7 cm.

For the making of head pendants, see p.216, Figs 16–21.

47 BELOW, RIGHT Core-formed pendant in the form of a large male head, with hair and beard composed of spiral ringlets of clear monochrome glass applied separately. Many pendants of this type come from the western Mediterranean and have been assigned to a Carthaginian workshop, but the discovery of a number from further east, like this example said to come from 'south Russia', probably the Black Sea region, suggests that there was at least one production centre in the eastern Mediterranean as well. 4th–3rd century BC. H. 6.2 cm.

47 lapis lazuli. Some particularly attractive pendants, dating from the fourth and third centuries BC, may have been made in Carthaginian workshops. They often represent men's or rams' heads, the former having hair and beards composed of spiral ringlets applied separately and made of translucent monochrome glass.

The Rhodian factories ceased production at the end of the fifth century BC. More than two generations passed before core-forming was revived in new glasshouses some time after the middle of the fourth century BC, coinciding with the conquest of the Persian Empire by Alexander the Great, king of Macedon and leader of the Greeks, and the start of an era of Macedonian supremacy. Many fewer vessels were produced by this new industry, and they are concentrated in Italy, especially the south (the area known as Magna Graecia because of the large number of Greek colonies founded in this area). Distinctive of the Italian finds are white speckles on the surface (the result of scum in the mixture). These facts suggest that factories were established in southern Italy, but recent discoveries in northern Greece and neighbouring areas indicate that other workshops were located in Macedonia. Many of the forms of this group are more massive than those of their predecessors, and new types were added to the repertory, notably jars, three-handled flasks and bottles (*stamnoi*, *hydriskai*
48 and *unguentaria*). Miniature vessels were also made.

The final flowering of the Mediterranean core-forming industry took place in the later Hellenistic period, between the second half of the second century and the mid-first century BC. Vessels were generally rather smaller, with long necks, and only *alabastra* and *amphoriskoi*
49 were made. The former have simple lugs and the latter have strap handles, sometimes formed into an s-shape, of clear translucent glass

49 OPPOSITE Three core-formed perfume flasks, one with handles and a base knob of clear amber glass similar to that used for contemporary bowls probably made in the same or neighbouring workshops in the region of Syria or Palestine. That example and the one with small ring handles come from tombs at Amathus in Cyprus. About 150–50 BC. H. of flask with clear glass handles 16.5 cm.

48 BELOW Three miniature core-formed perfume vessels with simple decoration. Probably made in southern Italy (Magna Graecia), where the jug and globular flask are said to have been found at Ruvo di Puglia (ancient Rubi). About 340–200 BC. H. of jug 4.7 cm.

like contemporary monochrome slumped vessels (see below). The majority of examples in this group have been found on Levantine sites in Syria, Palestine and Cyprus, and the factories must have been located in that area.

Mediterranean core-formed vessels were even imported into Egypt, where the renaissance in all branches of the arts which took place during the Saite Twenty-Sixth Dynasty (*c*.664–525 BC) had led to a revival of the glass industry. From this time dates a superb example of sculpture in the round, depicting a walking ram in turquoise blue with a heavy mane and a socket on the head for an *atef* crown, almost certainly symbolic of the god of Mendes in the Delta. Curiously, it is depicted with six legs so as to be viewable from either side – only the leg at the front and that at the back being common to both. This multiplicity of legs is so reminiscent of Assyrian sculpture that the Egyptian craftsman who made the piece may well have been conversant with the art of Egypt's recent conquerors. It is also now known that the technique of inlaying glass into another material to form figured scenes, once thought to have disappeared in Egypt by the end of the New Kingdom, not to reappear until the time of the Thirtieth Dynasty (*c*.380–343 BC), actually re-emerged there during the reign of Amasis (*c*.570–526 BC).

The Greeks had two names for glass, one of which means 'poured or melted stone', an apt description of core-formed vessels, assuming that they were considered to be imitations of stone vessels. The second signifies 'transparency' or 'clarity', and would apply to mono-

50

62

50 This magnificent glass sculpture, cast in a closed mould, demonstrates the revived skills of the Egyptian glassmaker during the Saite artistic renaissance. The curly-horned, heavy-maned ram is depicted walking on a base. The material below the body and between the legs has not been removed; indeed, six legs have been carved into it – each side having two legs and the front and rear legs in common, so that four legs are visible from each side. A socket in the head must once have held a headdress, presumably the *atef*-crown, suggesting that this ram represents the god of Mendes, in the Delta. 26th Dynasty, about 600 BC. L. of base 9 cm.

51 Shallow bowl cast in almost colourless glass with a cut design of sixteen petals alternating in relief and in intaglio, so forming two superimposed rosettes. Bowls of this type seem to have been made in the Persian Empire and used as drinking vessels in the later 5th and 4th centuries B C. This example is reputed to come from Cumae in southern Italy, which, if correct, would make it one of the few examples found outside the Persian Empire. H. 4.1 cm.

chrome vessels of translucent glass, such as the products of the Phoenicians that we have already considered, and more particularly to elegant highly polished bowls and a few other types of clear greenish or colourless glass with cut decoration that were made in the Persian Empire in the fifth and fourth centuries BC. The shapes and decoration mirror Persian vessels of silver and bronze. The glass versions were highly prized and were distributed throughout western Asia and the Mediterranean. Some may have been produced in factories in western provinces of the empire in Asia Minor (modern Turkey), but their use in Persia itself is attested by the Greek playwright Aristophanes, who in the *Acharnians* of about 425 BC tells of Athenian ambassadors at the court of the Great King of Persia drinking from vessels of clear glass. Several of the excavated examples of this group come from mid- to late fourth-century BC contexts, that is the years just before the fall of the Persian Empire in 330 BC. Indeed, it is likely that some were made later than this, in the same way that certain Persian styles of silver (and bronze) outlived the destruction of the empire by Alexander the Great.

It seems clear that the Greeks themselves were also making yellowish and greenish clear glass in the fifth and fourth centuries BC. Excavations at Olympia in the workshop of Phidias, the Greek sculptor best known for overseeing the work on the Parthenon in Athens, have shown that he was himself casting such glass in clay moulds, no doubt in connection with his great gold and ivory statue of the god Zeus. The shapes include three-pointed stars and parts of palmettes and flowers (Olympia Museum).

Hellenistic and non-blown Roman glass
c.325 BC–AD 400

The core-forming industry has already brought us into the Hellenistic period, the name given to the years between the death of Alexander the Great in 323 BC and the firm establishment of the Roman Empire in 31 BC. Alexander's vast empire had included the whole of western

Asia and Egypt as well as Macedonia and Greece. On his death this was divided up among his generals (all Macedonian Greeks), who founded separate kingdoms in their newly acquired territories. For glass the story continues into the early years of the Roman Empire, until around AD 100, when the recently discovered technique of blowing (see Chapter 2) finally led to the almost total disappearance of other methods of manufacture, at least for vessels. The Hellenistic period was to see the glass industry flourishing as never before, in an era marked by the diffusion of a basically Greek culture (hence its name, which comes from 'Hellenes', an old term for the Greeks). The growth of manufacturing industries was coupled with the opening of new markets for luxury wares brought about by an increase in long-distance trade.

It was in the second half of the third century BC that a purely Hellenistic style of glassware emerged. This first group of Hellenistic vessels, made between the third and the mid-second century BC, is perhaps best represented by finds from tombs at Canosa in southern Italy. To it belong some magnificent vessels of mosaic glass, heralding the start of a tradition that was to become one of the hallmarks of Hellenistic and early Roman production. Large plates were made of multicoloured canes, usually forming spiral or star patterns and often interspersed with segments of plain-coloured or occasionally sandwich gold glass (gold leaf sandwiched between two colourless layers). A new type of mosaic glass described as 'lacework' or 'network' is represented by hemispherical bowls made

52 Bowl of 'network' mosaic glass, composed of canes of spirally twisted threads of different colours laid side by side; a single network cane forms the rim. Made in the eastern Mediterranean, about 2nd century BC, and said to be from Crete. H. 6 cm.

For the making of a network rim, see p. 219, Figs 37–9, and pp. 220–21, Figs 50–53.

53 Large plate of mosaic glass formed from sections of multicoloured canes interspersed with segments of yellow, opaque white or occasionally gold foil sandwiched between two colourless layers. From a tomb at Canosa in southern Italy, where it was found with nine other glass vessels, including those illustrated in Pl. 54. About 225–200 BC. D. 30.8 cm.

For the making of a mosaic bowl, see pp. 219–21, Figs 36–58.

of canes of spirally twisted threads of different colours laid side by side, later known as *vetro a retorti*. Complete dinner services, comprising vessels for both serving and drinking, were made of monochrome glass, often intentionally decolorised so that it has a pale greenish or yellowish-greenish tinge. After cooling they were carefully ground and polished, and decorated with fine linear cutting in the form of flutes, grooves, rosettes and other patterns. Some are of deliberately coloured glass, deep blue, purple or aquamarine. The most common shapes are fairly large plates, dishes, hemispherical bowls, large footed bowls (*kraters*, for mixing wine and water), bowls with projecting bosses on the outside and linear-cut splayed lotus petals spreading from a rosette on the bottom, and cups with winged ring-handles (*skyphoi*). Like their Persian predecessors, these were luxury items imitating vessels of other materials such as silver and bronze. The occasional example carries gilded decoration on the outside and in addition there are bowls of sandwich gold glass, some of which probably date from the early third century BC. Those with known find-spots come from southern Italy (four), Rhodes, Gordion, and Olbia on the Black Sea. The illustration of a very Egyptian landscape on one fragmentary example (Moscow, Pushkin Museum) suggests that it may have been made in Egypt, though such Nilotic landscapes were a popular theme in many parts of the ancient world.

By this time it seems that sandwich gold glass, or at least gold leaf applied to the underside of a layer of colourless glass which would protect it, was being made and used in a number of different places. Not only are sandwich gold glass vessels quite widely distributed in the earlier Hellenistic period, but motifs in gold leaf (and silver) covered by colourless glass had also been used in the fourth century BC in the decoration of luxury items, such as a wooden couch encased in ivory and a ceremonial shield (Thessaloniki, Archaeological Museum), both found in the tomb at Vergina in northern Greece of Philip II, king of Macedon from 359 to 336 BC and father of Alexander the Great.

Perhaps the best known of Hellenistic mosaic glass vessels are fused and slumped hemispherical bowls made of polychrome canes with spiral or star patterns, often interspersed with monochrome seg-

54 TOP Three elaborate vessels of virtually colourless glass: a bossed bowl with a fine linear-cut rosette pattern on the bottom, a wing-handled cup on a tall foot-stand, and a bowl of sandwich gold glass. Found in a tomb at Canosa, southern Italy, with the mosaic dish in Pl. 53 and six other glass vessels. About 275–200 BC. H. of cup 11.1 cm.

55 Detail of the gold-glass bowl in Pl. 54, showing its fine decoration of a floral design in gold leaf sandwiched between two layers of colourless glass. In this early period, the layers were not fused together, as in Late Roman and Renaissance sandwich gold glass.

56 A bowl and dish of mosaic glass, each with the typical 'striped' rim made from a single 'network' cane. Both were probably made in the eastern Mediterranean, the bowl (said to come from Vulci in central Italy) in the 2nd century BC and the dish in the later 2nd or 1st century BC. D. of bowl 12.7 cm.

ments, as in the large plates described above. With only a few exceptions all these polychrome glass bowls, as well as other shapes such as the dishes and jars to be discussed below, have rims formed of a 'network' cane of spirally twisted threads of different colours which gives a 'striped' effect. This feature was to survive into the Roman period as well, and had of course already been used by early Mesopotamian and Egyptian glassmakers. The earliest of these hemispherical bowls may belong to the second half of the third century BC, but most were made in the second century BC. Almost as common (though slightly later, of the second to first century BC) and made in the same way, are shallow dishes with upright sides or outsplayed rims. An example of a less common type, made of the typical star- or spiral-patterned canes and roughly contemporary with the dishes, is a jar on a base ring from Italy. Other examples of this shape are known, but these are made of a distinctive and beautiful type of mosaic glass of the second to early first century BC that imitates onyx, a semi-precious stone. When finished, these vessels – mostly jars or *alabastra* – show meander or spiral decoration on a golden brown or purple ground.

The location of the glasshouses responsible for these magnificent vessels remains uncertain. The colourless and monochrome tableware has been found mainly in Greek settlements in southern Italy and Sicily, with other examples from sites in Greece, Asia Minor, around the Black Sea and possibly Cyrenaica (North Africa). Of the mosaic glass vessels, the large plates and the dishes with known find-spots come exclusively from Italy, mostly from Magna Graecia and Etruria. The bowls, both the more usual polychrome glass and the lacework mosaic examples, are more widespread: examples are known from sites in Greece, the Aegean islands, Anatolia, Syria, Mesopotamia and Egypt, as well as southern Italy. But all these areas were ready markets for other luxury goods of the time, and so do not really shed any light on the source of the glassware.

Alexandria, the new capital of Egypt founded by Alexander the Great in 332 BC, has long been thought to have been a major centre for the manufacture of Hellenistic glassware as well as many other luxury products. Cicero, the Roman orator and politician (106–43 BC), is the

56

57

58

57 ABOVE This mosaic glass bowl is a typical product of an eastern Mediterranean glass workshop of about the 2nd century BC. H. 8.3 cm.

58 RIGHT Jar of mosaic glass which closely imitates the semi-precious stone onyx. The pattern seems to have been achieved by using enlarged ends of canes (called 'cowhorns' by modern glassmakers) of golden brown with white spirals at the centre. Made in the eastern Mediterranean, probably in the 2nd or early 1st century BC. H. 13.7 cm. New York, The Metropolitan Museum of Art, Bequest of Edward C. Moore, 1891.

first to mention glass imported from Alexandria, and the glassmakers who gave the Greek geographer Strabo (64/3 BC–AD 21) his information about the excellent Egyptian sand were Alexandrians, but the principal written sources responsible for the city's reputation are of the Roman Imperial period. The archaeological record for glass production in Egypt at this time has been dismissed as poor, but, as shown below, it is quite clear that mosaic glass was being produced there. This, together with other evidence now coming to light, may yet vindicate Alexandria. The number of examples of this type found in southern Italy shows at least that the inhabitants had a taste for fine glass tableware, while increasing quantities are also being found in the Greek world and the eastern Mediterranean, together with some evidence for glass factories. It is therefore impossible at the moment to identify with any certainty the manufacturing centre or centres of these splendid and innovative glass vessels, and the origin of the remarkable sandwich gold glass bowls remains, if anything, even more of a mystery.

Indeed, it is quite certain that mosaic glass was again being produced in Egypt at least as early as the reign of Nectanebo II of the Thirtieth Dynasty (c. 360–343 BC). Moreover, the Egyptians developed the technique to a point of complexity far beyond anything comparable at so early a date. Small coloured canes and variously shaped elements were bundled together to form the desired pattern or figure (visible at each end of the bundle), heated until they fused, then miniaturised by being drawn out. The resultant cane was then sliced exactly like bread. Particularly characteristic is the form in which the slice depicted only half a face, human or otherwise, and two slices from the same cane were joined down the centre to produce a full face on a square ground. Quite instructive are those instances in which, although the subject of each half of the slice is the same, the dimensions are not quite identical, showing that they probably came from different canes.

Most slices, however, depict a complete pattern or figure. Many were used as inlays inset into other materials, such as wood; indeed, wood was probably the material of a discarded shrine once decorated by a large number of glass elements found in a jar in the animal catacombs at Dendera. Although the jar has been dated to the time of Constantine (AD 306–37), the shrine was certainly a good deal earlier. Many of the inlays are polychrome: a set of mosaic wings would have framed the top of a scene, and a fine falcon head may have been the terminal to a collar worn by one of the figures. There were also a number of highly coloured moulded glass squares of bright red or turquoise blue, yellow, white or dark blue, inlaid with a central polychrome design. The favourite motif is a flower head with each petal set in a bronze cloison against a different coloured ground. But splendidly colourful *udjat* eyes and *ankh*-signs occur too. The date is somewhere in the third to first centuries BC.

Because hieroglyphs always remained a pictorial script, a wooden furniture element faced with gesso and inlaid with part of the titulary of Ptolemy V (205–180 BC) in both monochrome and polychrome glass is representative of contemporary inlaid figured work. Hundreds of similar hieroglyphs and parts of figures, all cast in open moulds, were found at San el-Hagar in the Delta, which must have been the site of a factory operating in the Ptolemaic period (third to first centuries BC). In iconography the relief heads of the period are so similar to those of the New Kingdom that mistakes of dating have often been made.

After about 400 BC the number and range of flat-backed glass amulets produced by the Egyptian industry increased enormously, but they are in general small, made in worn moulds and not subsequently retouched. Virtually the only innovation lies in the use of two or three contrasting colours, each added separately in a small quantity to fill just part of the mould and allowed to set before the next colour was added. In a slightly different technique, variously coloured strips might be impressed at irregular intervals into the body material.

By the mid-second century BC the Hellenistic glass industry was firmly established, and production increased quite dramatically. Hemispherical bowls, dishes and some other types of mosaic glass vessels were being made, as we have seen, and it was at this time too that the manufacture of the last group of Mediterranean core-formed bottles began in the Levant. A new type of slumped tableware was made in considerable quantities, probably at sites on the coast of Syria and Palestine, illustrating the commercial exploitation of this particular process. Only bowls of various shapes were produced, most often hemispherical or conical with pointed bottoms, at first of clear greenish, brownish or almost colourless glass and later sometimes of green, amber, blue or wine-coloured glass as well. They were polished all

59 A group of Egyptian mosaic glass slices, all dating from the Ptolemaic period, about 1st century BC. *From top left:* the right half of a chubby female face, the colours suggesting a mask rather than a human head; two slices joined together to form the face of Bes, dwarflike helper of women in childbirth and one of the few Egyptian deities ever to be depicted full-face; two slices joined to form a pale green square with an animal head, possibly that of a lion; two slices joined to form a female head; and two slices joined on an original wood backing and forming a grotesque male face, suggesting a Greek mask; 2.9 cm square.

60 ABOVE Egyptian mosaic glass slices. *Top*: a row of palmettes, probably from a border, of particularly fine workmanship. Ptolemaic period, 1st century BC. *Bottom, left*: a standing falcon. Ptolemaic period, 1st century BC. *Bottom, centre*: a standing *ba*-bird: as is usual, this hybrid creature which represents the characteristics, personal traits or the 'self' of the deceased, has a human head. Although the scale is tiny, the workmanship is again exceptionally fine. The frame is modern. Ptolemaic to Roman period, 1st century BC to 1st century AD. *Bottom, right*: a falcon wearing a double crown. Ptolemaic period, 1st century BC. L. of palmette border 4.7 cm.

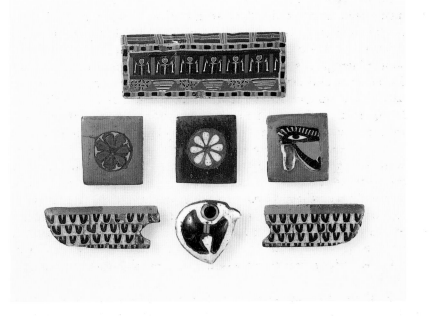

61 Glass elements from a wooden shrine, found in a jar in the sacred animal catacombs at Dendera, Egypt. *Top*: a mosaic border composed of *ankh* signs flanked by animal-headed *was* sceptres, with below, six *neb* baskets. Each grouping spells out the message 'all life and dominion'. *Centre, from left*: two cast glass squares each filled with a flower head in a contrasting colour, and a square inset with an *udjat* eye facing left. *Bottom*: a pair of mosaic glass wings, possibly from the top of a figured scene, and a falcon head facing right, possibly one of the terminals to a broad collar or else the actual head of one of the deities depicted in a figured scene. All Ptolemaic period, about 1st century BC. L. of mosaic border 8.4 cm.

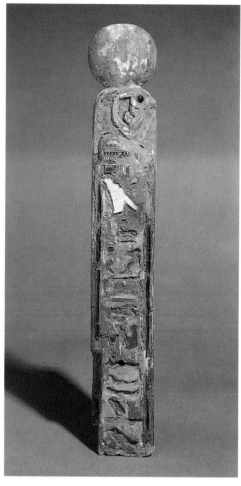

over, although the need for this to be carried out as an additional process was reduced by the slumping technique which meant that only the interior of the vase was in contact with the mould (in this case a form), so that the exterior remained glossy. They were also usually decorated with linear-cut concentric circles on the bottom or horizontally cut grooves near the rim on the inside or outside. These bowls were made with very little variation for nearly 100 years and were widely exported, reaching many sites in the eastern Mediterranean and occasionally further west.

Of similar glass to the bowls (and so approximately contemporary), mostly in various shades of yellow and green, is a group of little boxes, found principally at sites in Crete, suggesting that they were made somewhere on that island.

The first century BC witnessed the introduction of new types of mosaic and monochrome glass vessels. Core-formed bottles and slumped grooved conical and hemispherical bowls continued to be produced in the Levant, at least in the earlier part of the century (the bottles possibly for slightly longer), and it seems likely that the workshops producing the grooved bowls were also responsible for a new class with ribs on the outside that were mould-pressed and slumped. These ribbed bowls were the forerunners of a very widespread and well-known class of bowls of the Roman period, from which they can be distinguished by their asymmetrical and uneven

62 ABOVE, LEFT This firmly dated figured scene on a panel from a wooden shrine proves that the glass inlay technique re-emerged earlier than the 30th Dynasty, as once supposed. The Persian ruler Darius the Great makes an offering to Anubis and Isis, all once inlaid with polychrome glass. This panel illustrates the inlaying technique of the Saite-Persian period (c.570–486 BC), termed 'cellular' because each piece is set within a hollow, or cell. In the later Sebennytic-Ptolemaic style of the 30th Dynasty and Ptolemaic period (c.380–100 BC), the inlays are inset so as to abut one another. 27th Dynasty, about 522–486 BC. H. 28.3 cm.

63 ABOVE, RIGHT A wooden furniture element surmounted by a falcon head with a black glass eye. It wears a sun disc and a broad collar inlaid with elaborately patterned mosaic glass. Below it is a hieroglyphic inscription containing the beginning of the titulary of Ptolemy V. Gesso, a base for gilding, covers the rest of the surface, so that the glass inlays would have appeared to be set in gold. Ptolemaic period, 205–180 BC. H. 33.2 cm.

ribs and exclusive use of translucent monochrome, rather dull, colours (like the grooved bowls).

Mosaic glass of this last phase of the Hellenistic period is best known from a group of vessels found in a ship wrecked near Antikythera, off the south-west coast of Greece, in about 80 BC (now mostly in Athens, National Museum). It included five small bowls, either hemispherical or with outward-curving sides, on applied ring bases, new shapes in the repertory, though the bases are shared by other glass vessels such as the jars discussed above, which may be contemporary. The mosaic patterns include spirals and lacework with 'striped' rims of spirally twisted coloured threads such as we have seen before, but new is a true striped effect achieved by fusing together canes of different colours laid side by side (coloured-band glass).

Another innovation of this time was gold-band glass. This was used to make *alabastra* for scented oils and perfumes, and takes its name from bands of gold sandwiched between two layers of colourless glass which are interspersed among bands of translucent coloured glass, usually green, blue, purple or golden yellow. Some are provided with monochrome stoppers, pierced to act also as sprinklers. Since these exceptional pieces are found at sites in the eastern Mediterranean and Italy which received other luxurious glass vessels in the Hellenistic period, it is probably to that era that they belong, as precursors of the Roman production. For their place of manufacture we can only suppose the eastern Mediterranean, most probably on the Syro-Palestinian coast. This is the area of manufacture of our last group of Mediterranean core-formed bottles, whose basic process of manufacture is shared by these gold-band *alabastra*, though some scholars would rather divorce the production of these handsome mosaic glass vessels from the workshops or areas associated with the monochrome grooved and ribbed bowls.

As we enter the age of Augustus, the first Roman emperor (27 BC– AD 14), the glass industry is in the process of being revolutionised by the invention of blowing. Nonetheless, non-blown glassware con-

65

66

64 Conical bowl of amber-coloured glass, evidently made by the slumping process in a Syro-Palestinian workshop between about 150 and 50 BC. H. 8 cm.

65 Mosaic glass footed bowl composed of single-coloured canes laid side by side to give a striped effect, together with sections of multicoloured canes showing white spirals in a brownish-yellow ground. Made in the eastern Mediterranean in the 1st century BC, and said to be from one of the Greek islands. H. 4.4 cm.

tinued to be made in a wide range of colours and types until about the middle of the first century AD, and ribbed bowls and a few other types of monochrome glass for a further fifty years or so. The most significant step at this time was the establishment of factories producing these non-blown vessels in Roman Italy, where many examples have been found on sites previously altogether void of glass. The precise locations of the first Italian factories are unknown except for one in Rome, whose workers, according to the geographer Strabo writing in the early first century AD, were responsible for certain innovations in colour and production. Sixty years later a passage in the Elder Pliny's *Natural History* suggests the presence of another glasshouse further south, in Campania. Manufacture continued in the eastern Mediterranean, and it seems likely that migrant glassworkers from the east had arrived in Italy to establish the industry, since it demanded skill and expertise.

Many types of non-blown glassware of the early Roman factories have their origins in the preceding Hellenistic era, but innovations include a much wider variety of patterns and more brilliant colours for mosaic glass vessels found almost exclusively on Italian and other sites in the western Mediterranean. Ribbed bowls were produced in large numbers. Many were of single colours, and those forming a particular group with evenly spaced ribs are usually described as 'pillar-moulded'. These seem to have been made in both eastern and western factories and perhaps provide a point of contact between the two. A speciality of Italian factories was colourful mosaic glass: striking examples of gold- and coloured-band and lacework glass can be seen in bowls of different shapes, little box-like receptacles and perfume bottles. A notable series of cups, plates, dishes and bowls, made mainly of single colours – either translucent greens or blues or opaque red, light blue or pale green – but also occasionally of mosaic glass, resemble Roman fine pottery vessels and in many cases the glass versions predate the pottery. Some of the shapes were also made in silver. More unusual types of monochrome glass are represented by model boats and a magnificent very large box.

69, 70

By about AD 50 blown glass had become the norm and by the end of the century most production of non-blown vessels had ceased, the later ribbed bowls being made mainly in monochrome (blue-green) glass only. There is also a later series (about AD 70–300) of mosaic vessels, some of which were blown: unknown in the east, most examples come from the western provinces. In the third quarter of the first century AD tableware of cast (probably by the lost-wax process) colourless glass made its first appearance in the Roman world. It was no doubt to these, rather than the blown versions, that Pliny was referring when he wrote in his *Natural History*, 'the most highly valued glass is colourless and transparent, resembling rock crystal as closely as possible'. The series, made over a period of about fifty years, included simple plates, and dishes with overhanging rims and facet-cut decoration, like a contemporary group of blown glassware de- 97 scribed in Chapter 2. A number of similarly cast and colourless wing-handled cups (*skyphoi*) with relief-cut decoration have been found in tombs of the third century AD in the Rhineland. These may indicate a

66 Three perfume flasks, two of gold-band glass evidently formed around a core and the third perhaps made in the same way but composed of two bands of dark blue separated by one of colourless glass. The stoppers are pierced to act as sprinklers. All made in the eastern Mediterranean, probably in the 1st century BC; the gold-band example with a stopper is said to come from Sidon. H. of gold-band flask from Sidon 11.2 cm, H. of stopper 3.5 cm.

For the making of a gold-band flask, see pp. 217–18, Figs 22–35.

67 OPPOSITE, TOP Two ribbed bowls of the 'pillar-moulded' variety, made in the western Roman Empire. The mosaic marbled example, from a cremation burial at Radnage, Buckinghamshire, England, was probably made in Italy about AD 1–50; the green bowl, from a burial at Vaison, Vaucluse, France, was probably made in Gaul about the mid-1st century A D. H. of green bowl 19.5 cm.

For the making of a 'pillar-moulded' bowl, see p.222, Figs 59–64.

68 OPPOSITE, CENTRE Three cast glass boxes, all with separate lids. That of translucent yellowish-green glass was probably made in Crete in the 2nd–1st century B C; that of 'lacework' mosaic glass, composed of canes of spirally twisted threads of colourless and opaque white glass (said to come from Crete), and that of gold-band glass were both probably made in Italy in the first half of the 1st century A D. H. of Cretan box, with lid, 4.5 cm.

69 OPPOSITE, BOTTOM Two cast glass model boats, faithful imitations of Roman cargo vessels. Both were made in Italy in the first half of the 1st century A D; the blue example is said to be from Aquileia and the green one from Pompeii. L. of blue boat 17.7 cm.

70 ABOVE A very large cylindrical box of deep greenish-blue glass, with a separate lid. Evidently cast, perhaps by the lost-wax process, and decorated with cut grooves. No other box of this size is known, although the Corning Museum of Glass, New York, has an equally large shallow dish of the same date and similar glass. The box is said to have contained ashes and so may have served as a cinerary urn, though whether this was its original purpose is not known. Said to be from near Rome, where both it and the dish were probably made in the first half of the 1st century A D. H., including lid, 18 cm.

revival by certain glassmakers of the casting technique for vessels, or perhaps these fine examples were buried as heirlooms. The *skyphos* shape occurs in pottery and silver as well, but is generally an early type that seems for the most part not to have continued after the first century AD. Of the same shape is a silver and glass cup from another third-century AD tomb but in Denmark, beyond the frontiers of the Roman Empire.

Throughout the Roman Imperial period, glass formed by non-blown techniques also continued to be used for a wide variety of items other than vessels. It was popular in jewellery making: bangles and beads were made completely of glass and there were many decorated glass gems and also plain glass settings for finger-rings and glass insets for pendants. Stirring rods of different varieties, some with a twisted stem surmounted by a bird, were made of translucent glass, while gaming pieces, probably for a board game, were of opaque white and 'black' fabrics, or occasionally of more varied colours decorated with eyes, like a remarkable set from a grave of the late first century BC at Welwyn Garden City, Hertfordshire. There are also a few glass mirrors from the Roman era.

'The lowest storey of the stage was of marble, and the middle one of glass, an extravagance unparalleled even in later times', is how the Elder Pliny describes a theatre built in 58 BC. Other literary references

confirm that throughout the Roman era the use of glass in both public and private dwellings remained a luxurious form of internal decoration, available only to the wealthy. Glass *tesserae* (cubes) were quite often incorporated in both floor and wall mosaics. Another type of wall (and ceiling) decoration known as *opus sectile* made use of coloured marbles and on occasions also glass cut in geometric patterns. In the late Roman period figures were sometimes included in the designs, and some fourth-century AD panels of probable Egyptian manufacture were made completely of coloured glass. Windows could have panes of glass from the first century AD.

Plaques made in open moulds showing both figured and foliage designs may have decorated walls or perhaps furniture or containers in the same way as those in cameo glass described in Chapter 2. Perhaps as late as the second century AD, Egypt was still the main

74 producer of rectangular tiles with a characteristic grey-blue field crowded with groups of stylised flowers and plants, not always easy to identify. At the centre of variously coloured and shaped small flowers and what look like inverted bunches of grapes, there appear as a standard feature three large Indian lotuses, a plant unknown in Egypt before the third century BC. The only slight variation is the presence or absence of what appear to be red tulips, but must represent thistles. Presumably these tiles were intended for inlaying into boxes or other furniture. The final flourish of glass inlaying in Egypt is probably to be seen in a set of heraldically opposed funerary

73 deities and emblems, whose garish combinations of colours and debased iconography suggest a date in the first to second centuries AD.

Of particular interest are circular medallions of blue glass backed by

72 a thin white layer and mounted on bronze which show members of the Imperial family. They belong with a group of related objects which were used to promote various members of the ruling family after the death of Augustus. Probably issued in sets of nine, they would have been given as parade decorations to soldiers and worn as *phalerae* (medals) on their breastplates. The glass *phalerae*, being of less intrinsic value than examples of silver or silver-plated bronze, were probably

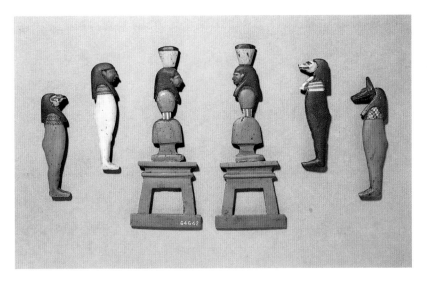

mass-produced for the lower ranks of the legionaries and auxiliary troops. Most with known find-spots come from the north-western provinces or Italy, but a single example from east of the Bosphorus is now in Ankara Museum. Related to these, in that some are portrait heads or busts of Roman emperors, is a small group of exquisitely formed glass statuettes cast by the lost wax method in the same way as bronze figurines. Two (Corning Museum of Glass and Boston Museum of Fine Arts) are miniature versions of the Aphrodite of Knidos (a Greek city on the south-west coast of modern Turkey), a life-size marble statue of the goddess dating from the fourth century BC and famous on account of its nudity (this was the first representation in Greek art of a completely naked woman) and frequently copied in stone and bronze in the first and second centuries AD.

The older techniques were therefore neither forgotten nor completely abandoned in the face of the revolution brought about by the discovery that glass could be blown. While there were to be some blown glass vessels in antiquity of high technical and artistic merit, none ever quite reached the colourful and luxurious nature of the earlier production, and a certain diversity was lost.

73 ABOVE, LEFT A set of flat-backed relief inlays of heraldically opposed funerary deities and two funerary emblems, obviously intended to be inset together into a piece of funerary equipment. The four Sons of Horus, who protected the embalmed internal organs, are shown in mummy form, with their characteristic heads: a falcon's for Qebhsenuef, human for Imsety, a baboon's for Hapy, and a jackal's for Duamutef. Each wears an elaborate broad collar in mosaic glass, no two alike, and a long wig in dark blue. Between the gods are two symmetrical emblems, probably intended to represent the Hellenistic funerary deity Canopus. The garish colours and debased iconography suggest a very late date, probably Roman period, about 1st–2nd centuries AD. H. of deities 5–6 cm.

74 ABOVE, RIGHT A rectangular tile with a translucent grey-blue ground into which have been set conventional floral motifs in mosaic and monochrome glass. In the centre are three Indian lotus stems, surrounded by fruit and flowers. Egypt, Ptolemaic to Roman periods, 1st century BC–1st century AD. H. 9.5 cm.

71 OPPOSITE, LEFT Four gaming pieces from a set of twenty-four, made up of four groups of six in opaque white, opaque blue, opaque yellow and translucent light green glass respectively, all decorated with 'eyes'. From a very rich grave at Welwyn Garden City, Hertfordshire, England; late 1st century AD. H. 2.0–2.2 cm.

72 OPPOSITE, RIGHT *Above*: a glass stirring rod with twisted stem, the top bent round to form a ring handle. 1st or 2nd century AD. *Below*: a bangle and two medallions. The bangle, said to be from the Faiyum, was probably made in Egypt in the 2nd or 3rd century AD. The medallions, of the 1st century AD, show portraits of members of the imperial family, one with his children, and were evidently issued in sets of nine to soldiers as parade decorations, to be worn as *phalerae* on their breastplates. L. of stirring rod 15.1 cm.

CHAPTER TWO

The Roman Empire

Early blown glass
1st century AD

THE MOST far-reaching innovation in the manufacture of glass in antiquity was the invention of blowing. This happened in the first century BC, probably in the Syro-Palestinian area long associated with glassmaking. In the middle of the first century BC a collection of waste from a glass factory was dumped in a stone stepped bath in the Jewish quarter of the old city of Jerusalem, but the small number of tiny blown bottles and inflated glass bulbs in this deposit (Jerusalem, Israel Museum) were made by using the glass tubes found with them. One end of a glass tube was pinched shut and then inflated by blowing through the open end while still hot to form a small bottle. Bottles may well have continued to be produced simply in a manner requiring no elaborate furnace or technology, although only by using a metal pipe could a glassmaker in antiquity produce tableware and storage containers in many shapes and sizes in a much wider variety and more easily and quickly than by any other technique known to him.

Blowing therefore heralded a complete change in the industry that was never to be matched or, rather, surpassed until the development of a power-driven machine for glassmaking in the 1820s to 1840s. Nonetheless, blowing has remained to this day the foremost method for making glass by hand. While the available evidence suggests that credit is due to the east for the invention of this new technique, it is not so apparent whether it reached its full potential first in the east or the west. At present the earliest known examples of true blown glass are for the most part small perfume bottles of coloured glass found chiefly on sites in Sicily, Italy and southern Switzerland and evidently produced in newly founded factories in central and northern Italy. They were found in contexts of the last quarter of the first century BC and the first decade of the first century AD. To the same period belong deposits from sites in Rome which contained fragments of blown glass, some identifiable as dishes of a typical western variety, together with non-blown glass vessels of the period.

The eastern evidence consists of a quantity of early Roman blown glass, mainly everyday natural greenish- or bluish-colourless vessels, found on sites in Syria, Palestine and Cyprus, although few groups can be dated more precisely than 'first century AD'. However, early blown glass, again principally small bottles for perfume or oil, is

Figs 65

75 Cameo-glass amphora known as the Portland Vase after its former owners, the Dowager Duchess (d. 1785) and the Dukes of Portland. The bottom was broken in antiquity, but evidently ended in a point like that of another cameo-glass amphora found in a tomb at Pompeii and now in Naples Museum. The identification of the figures, and therefore the meaning of the scene, is much disputed, but the scenario appears to be one of love and marriage with a mythological theme and in a marine setting. Perhaps from Rome, where it was probably made in the early 1st century AD. H. 24 cm.

For the making of a cameo-glass vessel, by flashing ('dip-overlay method') see pp.227–8, Figs 98–108.

known from elsewhere in the eastern Mediterranean, as at Priene on the west coast of Asia Minor (modern Turkey), on the Greek island of Samothrace and at Corinth in mainland Greece, these last examples being found together with non-blown glass vessels. These groups come from contexts of the first half of the first century, if not the first two decades, suggesting that already in the age of the emperor Augustus the technique was rapidly being adopted in many parts of the Roman Empire.

The familiarity of the Romans in Italy with blown glass towards the end of the first century BC is also shown by representations of obviously blown vessels in paintings on the walls of villas in Rome and at sites such as Pompeii and Herculaneum around the Bay of Naples. Most of the glass vessels are large bowls, no doubt chosen for illustration because their transparency allows the fruit with which they are filled to be seen clearly. The paintings are usually dated to the first century BC, but no blown glass vessels of comparable shape or size have been found in excavations of that date in Italy or elsewhere. Painters in antiquity made use of 'pattern books' and so need not necessarily have had 'hands on' experience of such blown glassware, but one may assume that the Romans who commissioned or painted these pictures were acquainted with blown glass vessels in representations, if not in reality.

It was probably in this experimental age, when the blowing technique was still in its infancy (the years around the turn of the first century BC/AD), that cameo-cut glass vessels were first made. The majority being certainly blown (and therefore not earlier than the time when the technique was properly practised) and demanding particular care and attention, they may well be seen as products – or rather masterpieces – from one or possibly more workshops exploring the potential of a new technique. As such, they were probably all made within a comparatively short period, not more than about two generations. Amphorae like the Portland Vase, jugs, cups (*skyphoi*) and bottles of cobalt blue, purple or occasionally green glass were flashed in white and the designs formed – perhaps by a gem-cutter – by

77 Cameo-glass disc cut down from a larger composition. It shows a pensive young man, possibly Paris, the son of King Priam of Troy, called upon to judge between the charms of the goddesses Hera, Athena and Aphrodite, who were perhaps portrayed in the missing portion. The disc was added as a new base to the truncated Portland Vase (Pl. 75), perhaps even in antiquity, but it clearly does not belong to it, differing in colour, composition and style. Perhaps from Rome, where it was probably made in the early 1st century A D. D. 12.2 cm.

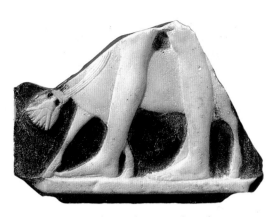

78 A fragment from what must have been a magnificent cameo-glass plaque. In white glass against a deep blue ground are the legs of a male figure, attended by a bull of tiny proportions, of which only the body, legs and lotus garland around its neck survive. The iconography and style appear to be completely Egyptian. Presumably early Roman period, about 1st century B C–1st century A D. W. 9 cm.

cutting away part of the outer white layer. The scenes show Egyptian or Egyptianising motifs, love scenes, elaborate vine scrolls and cupids and various paraphernalia associated with the myths and rites of the Greek god Dionysos. Cameo-glass plaques similar to the vessels in *77, 78* their range of colours and designs, but evidently made in open moulds with one colour overlaid on the other, were used as wall decorations or perhaps sometimes for furniture. These cameo-cut glass vessels and plaques have long been thought to be the products of Alexandria, which had an established tradition for the stone vessels on which they were thought to have been modelled. However, the fact that known find-spots are predominantly in Italy, notably Pompeii, and the similarity in the designs of vine scrolls with those of certain first-century AD Roman monuments, together with other evidence for a flourishing early Roman blown glass industry, make Italy the most likely source. Bowls of flashed glass used as drinking vessels, undecorated except for abraded or deeper-cut horizontal lines on the outer surface, were made in the middle years of the first century AD, probably in the same or neighbouring factories. These are white on the inside and coloured on the outside. Monochrome glass examples of this particular shape and decoration are common, and are known as 'Hofheim' cups after a site in the Rhineland where many have been found. They were probably made in several western centres and traded locally.

By the close of the second quarter of the first century AD blown glass vessels had become the norm, and within the next fifty years other techniques had all but disappeared, at least as far as vessel manufacture was concerned. A new development of about AD 25 was that of mould-blowing. Factories already established in the Syro-Palestinian area and in Italy increased their output and new glasshouses were set up, so that blown glass tableware came to be produced throughout the *79* Roman Empire and became as ubiquitous as fine pottery. It is indeed one of the means of identifying Roman contact with areas at the confines of the Empire. The fictitious *nouveau riche* Trimalchio, in the *Satyricon* written in the early AD 60s by the Roman author Petronius, laments that he would have preferred vessels of glass to gold and silver, had glass not recently become so common.

Glass factories at Rome and in Campania are mentioned in literature

79 Glass lamp, the body blown and the handle and nozzle attached afterwards. Lamps of this shape are much more common in pottery and bronze, but quite a few similar Roman glass necklace pendants have been found. Perhaps made in Italy, 2nd century A D. L. 10.3 cm.

of the first century AD, as we have seen. The existence also of factories in northern Italy, in the Po Valley and at Aquileia, is suggested by the numerous finds from sites in this area as well as from Switzerland, notably from Locarno and Vindonissa. This is confirmed by the signature of one glassmaker, Sentia Secunda, who records her origin as Aquileia on the bases of two late first-century rectangular bottles found at Linz in Austria (Linz, Oberösterreichisches Landesmuseum). This is also a rare example of a female glassmaker. Other signatures are male, and documentary evidence suggests that glassmaking was generally a male preserve.

Still favouring coloured glass, these Roman-Italian factories produced a series of attractive blown vessels which to some extent imitate the colours and decoration of their non-blown counterparts. These include bottles for perfume or oil, and bowls usually of purple, amber or blue glass. The bowls have ribs decorated with marvered white trails; the bottles, too, may be decorated with marvered white trails or unmarvered threads of various colours, or be made of bands of different coloured glass. Other vessels, often jugs, jars or flasks, are decorated with white or coloured blobs embedded in the surface. Less often the specks or blobs are in relief. These early Italian glassmakers were therefore blowing polychrome glass vessels, and for the banded variety must first have fused together monochrome canes of different colours. Very occasionally a gather of slices of monochrome or mosaic canes was blown to form a complete vessel or to decorate one. Curiously, Roman glassmakers never exploited the technique: this was to be left to their Venetian successors more than a thousand years later.

Particularly attractive is a group of jugs and jars of coloured glass with masks attached under the handles. Bird-shaped flasks for perfume or cosmetics were often of natural bluish or greenish glass, but bright colours were also used. The tails were sealed by heat after filling and so needed to be broken before the contents could be used. Another series of bowls are decorated by enamelling, principally with animal and floral scenes. They usually have a rosette on the bottom, indicating perhaps a single factory, probably located in the northern part of Italy. It was from these western (Roman-Italian) glasshouses that vessels travelled further westwards and northwards to military sites in Germany, Gaul and Britain, as well as to Austria (as we have seen), Switzerland and Spain. A few characteristically Italian types have also been found elsewhere, such as a jug with blobbed decoration from a site on an island in the Aegean Sea (British Museum) and enamelled bowls from Algeria.

It is not always apparent when glass was first made at, as well as imported to, these northern and western sites, but excavations at Cologne in the Rhineland have pointed to the existence of a glasshouse there from quite early in the first century AD. It was perhaps founded in AD 50, when the emperor Claudius made the town a colony at the request of his wife, Agrippina the Younger. Among the earlier products of the Rhineland workshops (made in the second half of the first and the second centuries) are flagons and jars decorated with ribbing. They are often of coloured glass, usually amber, blue or yellowish-green, but some are of natural greenish or bluish glass. The flagons have long necks, angular handles – usually attached like a claw on the shoulder – and globular or conical bodies. The handles of

80

81
82

83, 84
85

86

80 OPPOSITE, LEFT Squat bowl of blown glass with pinched ribs decorated with marvered white trails, now mostly weathered away. Probably made in Italy or another western province, where such bowls are particularly common; AD 50–100. H. 3.9 cm.

81 OPPOSITE, RIGHT Blown glass oil flask with embedded white blobs. Made in northern Italy about AD 1–50 and probably found with an imported pottery cup of about AD 80–90 near Richborough in south-east England. H. 9 cm.
For the technique of blobbing, see p.266, Figs 88–92.

82 OPPOSITE A small speckled blown glass jar and a jug with embedded opaque white and blue blobs. The speckles on the jar are proud and so must have been picked up on the gather towards the end of the manufacturing process. The jar is said to come from Pozzuoli near Naples, in Campania (Italy) where both were probably made in the first half of the 1st century AD. H. of jug 13.4 cm.

83 LEFT Blown jar of wine-coloured glass with opaque white theatrical masks and white stripes embedded in the handles. The effect of the contrasting colours resembles that of cameo glass, but the manufacture of this piece would have required none of the skill of the cameo glassmaker or cutter. Said to be from Santelpido near the ancient Atella, in Campania (Italy) where it was probably made in the 1st century AD. H. 24.8 cm.

84 ABOVE Close-up of the jar in Pl. 83, showing the masks under one of the handles. Blobs of white glass were applied and mould-pressed *in situ* before the handles were attached.

85 LEFT Bird-shaped flask for perfume or cosmetics. The vase was blown and filled, after which the tail was sealed by fusing; it therefore had to be broken before the contents could be used. Probably made in northern Italy, since such flasks are particularly common there and in the Alpine region; about AD 50–100. L. 17.1 cm.

86 Two flagons with handles and ribbed conical bodies, typical products of the early Roman glass industry in the Rhineland, centred at Cologne. The angular handles have a central rib extending in a long tail down the body; in the two-handled piece this rib is pincered. Both were found in eastern England, the blue example in the cemetery at Barnwell in Cambridgeshire and the green one in a grave at Bayford in Kent, and date from about A D 75–125. H. of blue flagon 29.3 cm.

the conical-bodied flagons have a single rib which extends in a long tail down the body. The globular-bodied flagons usually have a three- or four-ribbed handle, sometimes with a medallion showing a head of the mythical Medusa added underneath the handle attachment. The jars are globular, with folded collar-like rims. The letters CCAA or CCA which occur on a few glass vessels of similar date – including square bottles or flagons of a type to be considered below, one from Bonn in Germany and two from Silchester in Britain, and a perfume bottle from Cologne itself – probably stand for *Colonia Claudia Agrippiniensis*, the Roman name for the city, a further indication that this was a glassmaking centre. In addition, a terracotta mould probably for such a square bottle was found in the city and is now in the Römisch-Germanisches Museum there. It has a negative impression of four concentric circles with right-angled lines in the corners.

Enamelled vessels including flasks (*amphoriskoi*) of a type not known in the west have been found at Kerch (ancient Panticapaeum) on the Black Sea (St Petersburg, State Hermitage Museum) and in Cyprus (Corning Museum of Glass), and a bowl with a pointed star rather than a rosette on the bottom comes from Greece. Was there therefore a factory in the east as well? A group of tall beakers with polychrome enamelled decoration are similar in shape to colourless glass beakers with facet-cut designs (discussed below), with which they also share a

87

87 Blown glass bowl with enamelled decoration of a duck and a basket of flowers. On the underside is a star, which distinguishes this example from a group of enamelled bowls from a north Italian factory which have rosettes on the bottom. The fact that this bowl was found in Greece is another reason for suggesting that it is the product of an eastern workshop. About A D 50–75. H. 7 cm.

particular feature, a ledge below the ornamented field. They must therefore be contemporary, as must some undecorated examples (*c.*AD 70–117). Several of the enamelled beakers come from Begram in Afghanistan, beyond the political frontiers of the Roman Empire but on an important trade route leading to India and the Far East. Similar enamelled glasses are known from Egypt, North Africa and also the west, and some have facet-cut panels underscoring the enamelled decoration.

It is not always easy to determine the relationships between the eastern workshops, located principally – at least in the first century AD – in the region of Syria, Palestine and Phoenicia, and those in Italy and the west. In both areas vessels were decorated with trails wound around the outside of the body. These may be of the same colour as the body of the vessel, but a fine jug of opaque white glass from an Italian workshop has a trail of opaque light blue glass. Found in Italy, its date in the late first century AD is confirmed by the handle, which splays out at the rim in the same way as those of the contemporary metal jugs that it obviously imitates. Another link is illustrated by the work of a group of glassmakers, including those named Artas, Philippos and Neikon, who were probably active in the second and third quarters of the first century AD and so virtually contemporary with the early group of named makers of mould-blown glass which we shall be considering shortly. Together, these are the first named glassmakers. Artas and his fellows made free-blown two-handled cups, often signed on the thumb-pieces in Greek and sometimes in Latin as well. Their names were impressed together with that of their home town, 'Seidon' (Sidon), a city in Phoenicia. The use of Latin suggests that they were working in Italy where, as in the western provinces, it was the *lingua franca*, while Greek was generally used in the eastern parts of the Empire. In addition, the handles of one of Artas' signed cups are of blue glass streaked and speckled with opaque white, a decorative technique exploited in Italian workshops, as we have seen.

Mould-blown glassware, too, seems to have developed along similar lines in both regions. A fine earlier group, made for one or two generations after about AD 25 when the technique was introduced, consists of jugs, beakers, cups and two-handled bottles of clear yellowish-brown, blue or greenish-colourless glass blown into decorated moulds. They may carry Greek inscriptions, often drinking slogans such as 'your good health' and 'success to you' (literally 'seize the victory'). More significant is the presence of the names of the makers, Ennion, Jason, Meges and Aristeas. These usually occur in a formula with 'made me' and sometimes 'let the buyer be remembered' on the other side of the vessel, but in one case Aristeas is described as 'Cypriot'. The discovery of so many of Ennion's cups in northern Italy has given rise to the suggestion that, having started work in the Levant, he moved there, perhaps with other glassmakers from Syria and Phoenicia, to found factories making mould-blown glass vessels of similar varieties before the middle of the first century AD. A further connection between these eastern and western glasshouses is provided by two mould-blown jugs found at Kerch on the Black Sea which so closely resemble Ennion's signed pieces that they were probably made by him, or at least in his workshop. They have embedded blob decoration like that favoured by the Italian work-

88 Blown opaque white glass jug with a blue trail wound all around it. Similar in shape to contemporary metal jugs, it was made in northern Italy in the late 1st century A D, and found in a tomb at Ventimiglia (Roman Albintimilium) on the modern border between Italy and France. H. 15.2 cm.

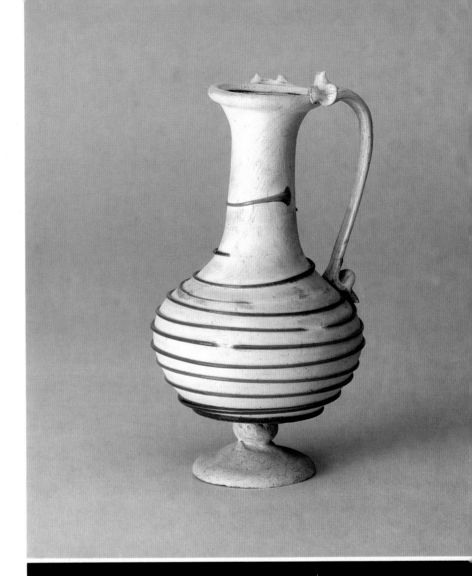

89 Box of opaque white glass with a separate lid, round at the top and bottom but with eight sides in the middle. Mould-blown, probably in a four-part mould, and decorated with palmettes, leaves and geometric motifs. Said to be from Sidon, in Phoenicia where it was probably made about A D 25–50. H., including lid, 8.5 cm.

90 ABOVE, LEFT Mould-blown glass cup signed by Ennion, one of the known glassmakers of the early Roman period. The Greek inscription, in two parts of four lines each enclosed in rectangles, reads on the illustrated side 'Ennion made [me]' and on the other 'Let the buyer be remembered'. Found in a tomb at Tremithousa, Cyprus, and probably made in Syria or Phoenicia about AD 25–50. H. 9.7 cm.

91 ABOVE, RIGHT Mould-blown beaker with three zones of decoration showing a Roman circus (arena for chariot-racing). In the top zone the names of the charioteers are inscribed in Latin, each ending in an abbreviated greeting. The middle zone shows the central barrier of the circus, adorned with monuments. The turning-posts continue down into the lower zone, which shows four four-horse racing chariots. Made in a western workshop, probably in Gaul or Switzerland in the mid-1st century AD and found at Colchester, England. H. 7.9 cm.

shops. On the other hand, the discovery in recent years of more examples of mould-blown cups and other vessels in the eastern provinces means that the precise location of the workshops must for the moment remain uncertain. All mould-blown glass vessels of this group could have been produced in one centre in the Mediterranean, reaching their different destinations in the hands of traders.

Almost all examples of another fine series of decorated mould-blown vessels, consisting of cups and bowls of blue-green or greenish-colourless glass, have been found on military sites in Switzerland, France and Britain. These normally show chariot races in the Roman arena or gladiators in combat, or sometimes the two scenes combined. The contestants are nearly always named in Latin. The find-spots, as well as the language of the inscriptions, suggest that these are products of a western workshop, probably in Gaul or Switzerland, and fragments of a mould which may have been used to make cylindrical cups showing chariot races have been found at Borgo in Corsica. However, about ten years ago a fragment of a chariot race scene was found with an inscription in Greek (Paris, James Barrelet collection). This appears to have an Egyptian source, and it therefore seems possible that such cups and bowls were also made in the east. The same western workshops were probably responsible for a small group of mould-blown beakers whose bodies are in the form of Negro heads. Two found in Britain (Cardiff, National Museum of Wales, and British Museum) have the same Latin inscription on the back of the neck and appear to have been made in the same mould.

An interesting series of small bottles, jugs and boxes (*pyxides*) made in three- or four-part moulds have several sides, normally six, decorated with fruit, flowers or other symbols whose meanings are now obscure. They are made either of translucent glass in deep shades of amber, green, blue or violet, or of opaque white or blue glass. Some of the motifs compare with those decorating the mould-blown vessels of Ennion and his fellows, suggesting that they were made in the same workshops together with some rarer decorated types such as small cylindrical boxes. Confirmation of this is provided by a unique two-handled hexagonal scent bottle with floral designs in the panels (British Museum), which is a smaller version of a signed Ennion bottle from Cyprus in the Metropolitan Museum, New York. The distribution of the examples of opaque glass, at least, suggests that such workshops were located in the east, perhaps in Phoenicia. Of western manufacture are four-sided flasks of deep coloured translucent glass decorated with masks. Other mould-blown pieces of the first century AD, such as a flask of cobalt blue glass whose body is in the form of a shell, could have come from either end of the Roman Empire.

New mould-blown wares were made in the later part of the first century and are well represented among the finds from the cities of Pompeii and Herculaneum, which were destroyed by the eruption of Vesuvius in AD 79. These include flasks for perfume or oil, shaped like dates and usually of yellowish-brown or purple glass, made at least initially in Syrian or Phoenician workshops and found in contexts of about the mid-first to mid-second century AD. Less numerous but contemporary with these are flasks shaped like bunches of grapes. Both types no doubt came to be made in the west as well. Another type of flask, also represented at Pompeii, has a long neck and body in the form of a human head, often with two faces looking in opposite directions, Janus-fashion. These, too, came to be made in western as well as eastern workshops and were popular until the end of the Roman period. Many of these small flasks are of coloured glass.

Yellowish-green or brown are the shades favoured for some tall mould-blown beakers which were also made of more natural

92 BELOW, LEFT Mould-blown glass flask, the body in the form of a shell. Made about AD 25–50 in either an eastern or western Roman province. H. 8.5 cm.

93 BELOW, RIGHT Mould-blown flasks in the form of a date and a bunch of grapes. These varieties of mould-blown glass were made initially in Syria or Phoenicia, but later probably in the west as well, between about AD 50 and 150. H. of grape flask 8 cm.

greenish-colourless glass. These were also found in profusion at Pompeii and Herculaneum, but are known from all parts of the Mediterranean world. Some are decorated with almond-shaped bosses, sometimes described as lotus buds, while others show figures from Greek mythology or representations of the seasons (an early appearance of a theme that was to become very popular in Roman art) between leafy garlands or in niches. Beakers decorated with almond-shaped bosses come in several sizes, one particularly large example in the British Museum being of translucent amber-coloured glass. The same motif decorates a drinking horn, which must be contemporary.

A special technique, described by the Elder Pliny and probably fashionable in his day, was the cutting of openwork designs in thin metal (silver), perhaps as casings for glass or some other materal. One example, which may belong to the early Imperial period, was apparently found in Italy, where it could have been made. There is no real evidence for its date except that the deep blue glass beaker with bosses that protrude through the openings in the silver case is not unlike the tall mould-blown versions. The silver case of another example (Copenhagen, National Museum) is in the form of a cup with winged handles (*skyphos*) of a type usually dated no later than the first century AD. It has a blue glass lining, again blown into the case, and round the rim is an inscription in Greek suggesting that it was made in an eastern workshop or for an eastern (or Greek) client. It was, however, found in a tomb in Denmark with coins of the third century AD and so must either be an heirloom or belong with other openwork metal vessels with glass linings made in the later Roman Empire. Perhaps significant is the series of relief-decorated lost-wax cast glass *skyphoi* from tombs in the Rhineland of the same date, discussed in Chapter 1.

By AD 40 the first mould-blown square bottles, each with a single handle, of blue-green or light green glass were being made. The early examples were small. More common and widespread are taller polygonal versions that were first made in large numbers about AD 70. Most of these are square in section, but some have as many as thirteen sides or as few as three. Among the square group most are mould-blown, but some are free-blown with the sides simply flattened. Examples of another version, also usually mould-blown, have cylindrical bodies. All these were utilitarian vessels used to transport liquids: being easier to inspect and clean, they were rather more practical than their pottery counterparts. There was no standard size or capacity, the smallest being no more than about 5 cm (2 in) tall and the largest over 50 cm (20 in), although examples over 40 cm (16 in) or under 10 cm (4 in) are not very common. They were sometimes re-used as cinerary urns. More are known from Italy and the western provinces than from further east. The western square bottles often have designs on their bases, ranging from concentric circles to scenes and inscriptions naming the proprietor or the location of the glasshouse, or the maker. A particular group found in Britain and the Rhineland are inscribed with the letters AF, or AF enclosed in a Q. Many of those from the east are undecorated, though some have inscriptions with Greek letters or geometric designs. These vessels went out of circulation in the late second or early third century AD (the large cylindrical type seems to have ceased somewhat earlier, around AD

94 OPPOSITE, LEFT Mould-blown drinking horn with a metal cap on the nozzle. The decoration of bosses resembles that on one of the beakers in Pl. 96. Made about AD 50–100. L. 12.5 cm.

95 OPPOSITE, RIGHT Beaker of cobalt blue glass blown into a silver case with oval openings, through which the glass protrudes. Perhaps made in Italy, where it is said to have been found, possibly at Brindisi on the south-east Adriatic coast; about AD 50–100. H. 9.3 cm.

96 OPPOSITE Two mould-blown beakers. That on the left shows apparently mythological figures in niches, including the god Hermes (Roman Mercury) with his staff (*caduceus*) in his right hand and purse in his left. The other beaker is decorated with almond-shaped bosses. Both are said to come from the vicinity of Cyzicus on the south bank of the Bosphorus, and were probably made in an eastern workshop (or even in Asia Minor) about AD 50–100. H. of bossed beaker 13.3 cm.

110–20) and were joined and eventually replaced in some areas by another type, as we shall see.

The first century AD also saw the introduction of other forms which were to be made with variations for the next two to three hundred years. These include small bottles for perfume, often called 'tear bottles', and larger versions, probably for oil or wine, which were made in numerous different varieties and occur frequently in our early groups of blown glass vessels. Free-blown cups, plates, bowls, jugs and other vessels for eating and drinking, plain or with simple decoration of cut lines, were also made of natural bluish-green and light green glass from about AD 25 to the end of the Roman era. A complete set of coloured glass tableware was found in the ruins of a shop at Cosa (modern Ansedonia) in central Italy which was destroyed about AD 40. There are often subtle differences in the forms of these common blown vessels that make it possible to distinguish eastern from western products and even to assign certain groups to particular areas, though many of the types particularly popular in the west are not completely unknown in the east.

From about AD 70 much of the finest glassware was made of intentionally decolorised glass. This colourless glass came to replace not the natural shades with a greenish or bluish tinge, but those deliberately coloured such as blue, purple and amber. Among the earliest, if not the first, completely transparent blown glass vessels of the Roman era are pieces decorated with facet-cut designs, made between about AD 70 and 117 at about the same time as the colourless lost-wax cast series, some of which carry similar facet-cut decoration. Most are cups or tall beakers, but a few other shapes are known, such as jugs of a type made also in pottery. These were particularly popular in Italy and the western provinces, but not unknown in the east. Cut and engraved figured decoration was rare at this time, but fragments of a cup (Cardiff, National Museum of Wales) similar in shape to many of the faceted pieces show a cut scene of a chariot race in the zone usually filled with facets. In the upper zone are traces of an inscription in Greek, indicating an eastern origin, but perhaps of the client rather than the cutter and so not providing indisputable evidence for an eastern origin for the technique of facet-cutting, although it was certainly practised by glass-cutters in that area. A small number of glass vessels, of shapes similar to those of the facet-cut group but with a few additions such as amphorae, have decoration cut in high relief. Almond-shaped knobs, ivy leaves and berries, shells, masks and other stylised motifs are depicted, most of which are known from contemporary vessels of mould-blown glass or precious metal.

Diatreta, literally meaning 'cut vessels', are mentioned as a new type of glass by the Roman poet Martial, whose works were published between AD 84 and 102. Vessels to which he might have been referring are represented by two beakers with openwork decoration, one found in the cemetery of the Roman town of Ulpa Noviomagus (modern Nijmegen in the Netherlands) and the other at the trading post of Begram in Afghanistan. In shape they compare with the tall enamelled and faceted beakers already discussed, and the cutting technique has something in common with that used in the relief-decorated series. The burial date of AD 80–100 for the Nijmegen example (Nijmegen Museum) shows that they must be roughly contemporary,

97

97 Jug of colourless blown glass decorated with hexagonal facets cut with a wheel. It was probably made in the Rhineland between about AD 70 and 117, alongside a larger class of beakers of similar glass with facet-cut decoration, although pottery jugs of this particular shape are usually dated AD 200–250. H. 12 cm.

dating from the later first or early second century AD. On the Nijmegen beaker twigs of an oak tree with leaves and acorns are carved in high relief and the decoration is shaped by grinding away the glass around and underneath the leaves, branches and acorns to form an openwork pattern. The surviving decoration on the beaker from Begram (Kabul Museum) shows three boats and a building consisting of a tower surmounted by statues, all partly cut away underneath. This scene has been identified as the famous lighthouse at Alexandria, one of the Seven Wonders of the World, and the neighbouring harbour filled with ships. However, as some recent excavations have shown, all Roman lighthouses were somewhat alike, and the distance of both Nijmegen and Begram from Alexandria (and from each other) make that city an unlikely source of these remarkable vessels, whose origin, even if the same, must remain a mystery for the moment.

Not a technique specific to glass working, cutting was nonetheless one of the most common decorative processes of the Roman era, as in earlier times. Glass-cutters must have been aware of the practices of other craftsmen, notably hardstone workers, and employed similar tools, no doubt including the bow-drill, known in Egypt from the middle of the third millennium BC. Wheels seem to have been used for certain linear and also facet-cut designs, as well as for some relief cutting, but these were no doubt always small and easily made, even of a hollowed stone supported on a stick and inserted into a hand-worked turning device. They would have been fed by damp grit such as sand, wood ash or other easily available abrasives. Some engraving was achieved freehand with a flint or similar tool. Simple files, narrow flattened implements of metal or even wood, sometimes bent at the end to reach, for example, under the bridges of cage cups, together with abrasives were used both for polishing and for some linear cutting. The easiest way to cut the decorative grooves around the circumference (often below the rim) of many glass vessels would have been with a file and abrasive, while the vessel itself was rotating slowly on a turning device like a potter's wheel.

Thus during the first century AD the Roman glass industry became fully established and prolific. This led to the rapid spread of glass-houses throughout the Empire, so that they were soon operating in all the major centres. Two pottery lamps of the second half of the first century AD, one from Dalmatia and the other from Italy, show glassblowers before their furnaces. The Roman Empire at this time extended from Britain in the west to parts of Iraq in the east. On the eastern side it embraced Asia Minor as far north as the northern shores of the Black Sea and inland to the frontiers of Armenia, running southwards to include most of modern Iraq, Syria, the Lebanon, Palestine, Israel and Arabia. In the north it was bordered by the Rhine and the Danube rivers, and in the south it encompassed the whole of the Mediterranean, North Africa and Egypt. Its influence, however, extended beyond its political boundaries. It is again the Elder Pliny who tells us that Spain and Gaul were making glass by the end of the first century AD, and this is borne out by the finds. The Latin name Aramantus (or Aramanthus) appears in the second half of the first century AD on glass vessels of different shapes, notably jugs with masks at the handle attachments, whose distribution suggests that they were made in south-eastern France, whence they were exported

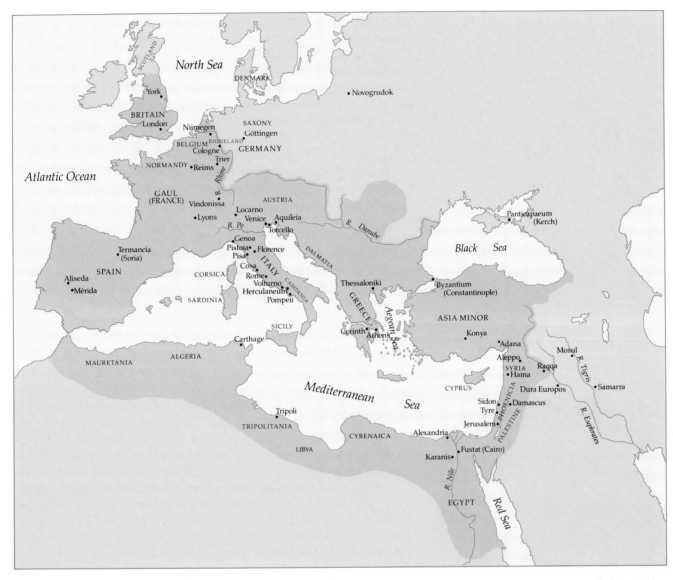

Map of Europe and North Africa, showing the extent of the Roman Empire in the 2nd century AD (in brown) and the main glassmaking centres and other sites mentioned in Chapters 2–4.

to Normandy and the Rhineland. The stamp AVG apparently identifies products of southern Spain and Portugal, since it occurs on unguent bottles of the later first and second centuries found principally in that region. Cologne is not mentioned by Pliny or other ancient authors, in spite of its obvious prolific production from soon after the mid-first century AD, Neither is Britain, but we now know that there were glasshouses in London from the AD 70s, and elsewhere in the second and third centuries AD.

The Roman achievement

AD 100–400

The story of glass continued without any real interruption up to the end of the third and into the early years of the fourth century AD. The fairly frequent literary references show that, while becoming more common, it retained its fascination; but after the first century AD no information is given about where glass was actually being made. Although makers sometimes signed their glass vessels, none mentions his home town. Nor is any help as to the location of glasshouses

98 Large urn with a lid, but plain rather than the more usual M-shaped handles. Like the jar in Pl. 99, it still contains cremated bones, but this was probably its secondary purpose. Made of natural bluish glass, often used for utilitarian ware, it must have been produced in one of the western provinces of the Roman Empire between about A D 50 and 200. H. of urn 31.7 cm, lid 5.7 cm.

provided by any other written evidence, except the records of disputes in the early third century between the glassmakers and glass-cutters of Aquileia in northern Italy. From these we learn how the glass industry was organised, since they draw a distinction between the *vitrearii* (glassmakers) and *diatretarii* (glass-cutters). Although this was about 100 years later than the mention of *diatreta* by the poet Martial, the distinction between the trades was obviously well established. It received confirmation about a century later still, in a decree of AD 337 issued by the emperor Constantine.

Glassmaking sites can be identified from finds of furnaces, tools and unworked glass lumps and stocks of vessel fragments that might be re-used by the glassmaker, but only a very few are known compared with the great number that must have existed to produce the vast quantity of Roman glass vessels and other objects. The only obvious Roman glassmaking tools found so far are hollow iron rods from Mérida in Spain (Mérida, Museo Nacional de Arte Romano). These were found with blown vessel fragments and glass waste of the fourth century AD, confirming that they were used as blowing irons. Some have a slightly thickened end like that of modern blowing irons used to gather molten glass from the crucible. The pair of shears found with them was also probably used in glassmaking. Funerary inscriptions mentioning glassmakers occur in Lyons, Athens, Mauretania (Morocco) and Dalmatia, but give no indication of the kinds of glass they were making. Our supposition of where particular series of vessels were made therefore relies on methods such as grouping together examples inscribed with the same name or of a particular shape or style of decoration, and relating such information to the distribution of the type. As we shall see, there remained strong connections between the eastern and western parts of the Roman Empire, illustrated in particular by the passing on of new decorative fashions. Abundant finds of glass used for vessels and other purposes in Rome, the capital of this great empire, show that it continued to be a major centre for both the production and consumption of this versatile and attractive material.

Until the fourth century, intentionally coloured glass became very rare for vessels. However, it continued to be used for some of the decorated mould-blown types, such as head-flasks of the variety introduced in the later first century and made in perhaps greater numbers in the second and third, and it seems to have become something of a speciality of the glassmakers at Cologne. They produced a number of mould-blown and other decorated glass vessels in quite deep shades of blue and green. Nonetheless, the finest or most luxurious pieces were now for the most part made of colourless material, while natural greenish and bluish-greenish glass was employed for some decorated vessels but in particular for utilitarian ware, which was produced in profusion. After the first century AD the proportion of decorated wares seems to have declined sharply in relation to glass tableware and storage vessels. Owning glass was no longer a novelty or a preserve of the rich.

A number of the distinctive forms introduced in the second half of the first century AD continued to be made in the second century. Among these were everyday wares like the tall mould-blown square bottles sometimes re-used as cinerary urns, as already discussed.

99 Large jar, or urn, still containing cremated bones, although this was doubtless its secondary use: it must originally have served as a storage jar. The deep green colour is unusual. Found at Box Lane burial ground, Hemel Hempstead, Hertfordshire, southern England, and made in one of the western Roman provinces, A D 50–200. H. 23.1 cm.

Large jars, too, served in the second place as containers for cremated bones at this time. Although those from excavated contexts regularly contain cremations, the version without handles, if not the handled types as well, must, like its pottery counterparts, originally have had a domestic purpose. Distinctive are examples with M-shaped handles and lids. Glass cinerary urns of this type were in common use throughout Italy, North Africa and the western provinces but were unknown in the east, Tripoli in modern Libya being the easternmost find-spot to date. Variations in detail suggest that they were made in many different western workshops.

The new types of mould-blown ware introduced in the second century were functional rather than decorative. Tall, square mould-blown bottles were still in circulation, but they were now joined by a smaller version. This type is again square in section and is known as a 'Mercury' flask because a figure of that Roman god appears, together with Latin initials or names such as Hylas or Hilarus, on the decorated base of many examples. They were made in western workshops in Gaul and the Rhineland, no doubt including Cologne, in the second and third centuries. Also of western, or perhaps specifically Rhineland production, of the third or fourth century, were flasks with three connected globular bodies and a single handle, not unlike some modern oil and vinegar bottles. These were free-blown and the vertical partitions made by drawing a wooden tool up and down the body. While it is quite easy to make a bipartite flask, a three-part vessel is no mean feat.

By the third century the production of tall square bottles had ceased. New types of containers in the north-western parts of the Empire

included mould-blown barrel-shaped bottles with one or two handles, often called 'Frotinus bottles' because of the abbreviated name found on the base of many of them. Large numbers have been found in north-western France, where they were probably mostly made in the second, third and fourth centuries, the one-handled version having originated in the late first century AD. They are widespread in the Rhineland as well, and some have been found in Britain, including one with one handle inscribed on the base FELIX FECIT, meaning 'Felix made [me]'. A series of bottles popularly described as 'eau-de-Cologne bottles' was produced in Cologne from early in the third century into the fourth. They were blown into cylindrical moulds and sometimes decorated with cut lines. Their distinguishing feature is that the handles are shaped like dolphins. Similar handles are provided for a rarer type of flask shaped like a barrel and decorated with trails wound around the extremities. Among their eastern counterparts is a third-century group of cylindrical free-blown flasks with similar dolphin handles made in Egypt and decorated with cut lines and facets.

It was in decorated wares that the glassmaker and his associates really excelled in the second and third centuries (and also the fourth, but more on that below). None of the decorative techniques was entirely new. Rather they illustrate the exploitation by the artists of tried and tested methods. The glassmaker himself might blow glass into decorated moulds which could determine the form of the actual vessel and also impart designs. He was also responsible for various types of applied decoration, including trails, blobs and mould-pressed medallions in the form of masks. Cut decoration, however, was

100 TOP *From left*: a mould-blown square bottle of a type commonly used to transport liquids, later 1st or 2nd century AD; a blown triple-bodied flask, probably 3rd–4th century AD; and a mould-blown barrel-shaped jug, 3rd century AD. All made in western workshops: the bottle and jug were found at Faversham, Kent, south-east England. H. of bottle 20 cm.

101 The base of the barrel jug in Pl. 100, showing the mould-blown inscription, FELIX FECIT or 'Felix made [me]'.

carried out by specialists in separate workshops. They, too, reached high standards of excellence.

Decorated mould-blown wares of the varieties first produced in the later years of the first century AD were still being made in the second. Among these were flasks in the form of dates or bunches of grapes, or with bodies in the shape of a human head, often facing two ways. By the third century new types of decorated mould-blown ware were being manufactured that were to remain popular for over a hundred years. Produced in great numbers were jars, jugs, bottles and sprinkler-flasks, which were first blown into decorated moulds which imparted intricate geometric patterns and then often further inflated. These are found all over the Roman world, but were particularly popular in the eastern Mediterranean. New and larger versions of older styles include grape- and head-flasks. While Syrian glasshouses were probably originally responsible for both these types, they came to be produced in the west as well, in the Rhineland (Cologne) and probably also in Gaul and Belgium, where one part of a two-piece mould for a grape-flask was found at Macquenoise. The western grape-flasks mostly have handles; some are unstable with pointed bottoms, but others have stemmed feet. Many different representations occur among the head-flasks, and occasional examples from eastern workshops carry Greek inscriptions. Besides Africans and others, usually with faces looking in both directions, there are representations of grotesques, probably modelled on the masks worn by comic actors. Instead of only a head, the body of the flask might be moulded in the shape of a figure of a deity or a monkey (itself perhaps a caricature of the god Mercury), or occasionally a fish.

As decoration on free-blown glass vessels, glassmakers continued to use trails and blobs but these were now applied in a somewhat different manner. In the Rhineland they used blobs and trails of different colours and so produced some attractive polychrome glass

102 RIGHT Inscribed head-flask, the body blown into a two-part mould. The head is that of a young man with curly hair; a Greek inscription above gives the name 'Eugen[es]', perhaps that of the glassmaker; another, around the base, reads 'May you prosper, Melanth[us]'. Probably made in the eastern Mediterranean in the 3rd century AD, and found in a tomb near Idalion, Cyprus. H. 19.7 cm.

103 BELOW Mould-blown bottle in the form of a fish, probably made in Gaul in the 3rd century AD. Perhaps from Arles, France. L. 27.8 cm.

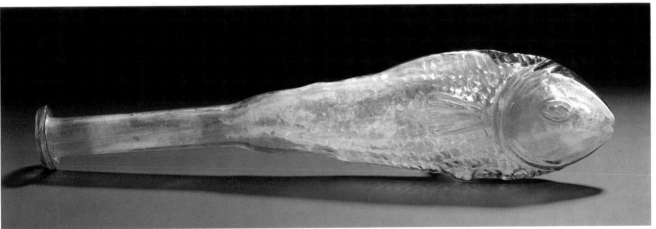

vessels. Intricate vessels decorated with polychrome blobs were also made in Italian glasshouses.

A new type of trailed decoration is described as 'snake-thread' because of the serpentine appearance of the threads. The majority of glass vessels with this decoration were made in the third century, but the first examples date from the late second century and the style continued into the fourth. Its origin may be connected with a new mode of ornament created in the east at about the same time. This involved applying polychrome floral decoration, sometimes including birds and snakes, to vessels. It continued into the third century, when some of the floral elements on examples from Syria and Palestine have a chequered pattern that seems to indicate local production. Most examples of this group have been found in the east. A few reached Europe, but so far none are known from the Rhineland. A connection with the 'snake-thread' trailed glass vessels is suggested by the inclusion of similar floral elements on a number of these. The main characteristic of snake-thread vessels from the east is that they are of monochrome glass, usually greenish or colourless, and the trails are of the same colour as the body. Dropper-flasks were popular, and there is one in the shape of a helmet (Cologne, Römisch-Germanisches Museum). Other flasks have taller necks with normal openings. The chequer pattern of the floral elements on the Syro-Palestinian group is also found on some of the eastern snake-thread trails. Colourless glass vessels with colourless snake-thread trails bearing similar chequer imprints are also abundant in Italy and known from other western provinces such as Spain and Britain.

Another western group of snake-thread glass vessels, which appears to have been produced in Cologne, includes a series with thick colourless or polychrome trailings, usually milled, on colourless or, less often, coloured bodies. A second variety has much finer polychrome trailing and includes patterns such as floral elements, spirals, swastikas and volutes. Among the more remarkable of this second group are two further dropper-flasks in the shape of helmets – one decorated with polychrome and the other (Cologne, Römisch-Germanisches Museum) with opaque white trails, thus differing in colour from the eastern example which is completely green – and a pair of flasks shaped like sandals. Popular in the Rhineland in the third century were pairs of jugs and saucepan-like vessels decorated with fine polychrome trails.

Glass vessels decorated with quite large applied blobs are also generally colourful. Rhineland workshops again preferred the polychrome, as did glassmakers in Italy. This style of decoration also originated in the mid-third century, but became particularly popular in the fourth, continuing in the west until the early fifth century at the latest but enduring for another seventy-five years or more in the east. Patterns of dark blue blobs occur throughout the Roman Empire, bowls and cups being common in the eastern Mediterranean, at sites on the Black Sea and also in the west, but in Egypt such decoration is found almost exclusively on bowl-shaped and conical vessels which probably served as lamps in the fourth, fifth and perhaps also the sixth centuries. Similar lamps are found on late Roman and early Byzantine sites in the east as well. Decoration of large blobs of various colours, usually blues, greens and browns, on more sophisti-

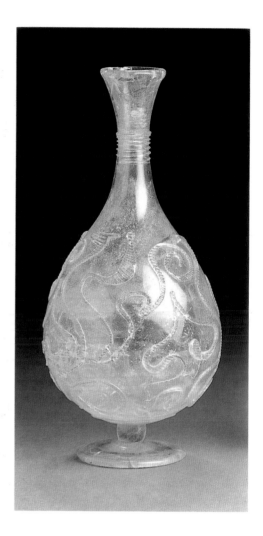

104 Flask decorated with snake-thread trails, tooled flat and milled. Found in a grave at Koblenz, in the Rhineland where it was probably made, late 2nd or early 3rd century A D. H. 19.5 cm.

105 OPPOSITE, TOP A handled dish and a jug, both with polychrome snake-thread trail decoration. Pairs of vessels like these were normally intended for hand-washing at mealtimes, but these glass versions are perhaps too small to have served this purpose. Found together in a coffin at Urdingen, near Düsseldorf, in the Rhineland where they were made in the 3rd century A D. H. of jug, excluding handle, 12 cm.

106 OPPOSITE Dropper-flask in the form of a helmet, decorated with blue snake-thread trails tooled flat and milled. The eyes are formed of coiled colourless trails with opaque white and blue pupils. On either side of the helmet is a bird made from colourless trails, standing on a coloured twig with red berries. Found at Cologne, where it was made in the 3rd century A D. H. 10.1 cm.

cated shapes was a speciality of western glasshouses in the Rhineland and Italy.

Cypriot workshops of the second century seem to have been responsible for a group of colourless glass bowls with lids on which a scene is 'painted' to be seen through the glass. It has always been supposed that the designs were cold-painted, since they are drawn with very fine lines and there is no obvious evidence that the pigment was fired on. In addition, the decoration flakes away easily. (The same observations apply to the much earlier 'painted' glass inlays made in western Asia in the eighth century BC; see Chapter 1.) If, however, that were indeed the case, it is unlikely that any of the decoration would have survived at all, and it therefore seems most probable that these lids (and the earlier inlays) were enamelled. It was in the late second century that the technique of enamelling was revived on a larger scale, initially in the east, and this may be one of several modes of decoration taken westwards by immigrant craftsmen. The eastern group, after its start in the late second century, centres on the third and continues into the fourth. The western group dates from the later second century until no later than a decade or two after the mid-third. The best examples of this last group have been found outside the political boundaries of the Roman Empire, in Denmark and northern Germany, but they were made in the Rhineland. The majority are

107

41

bowls of colourless glass on low bases, decorated in deep colours with wild beasts in the arena and, occasionally, gladiators in combat.

The enamelled scenes on glass vessels from eastern workshops, although not excluding animal motifs, are very different from those of the western group, indicating different tastes, whether of the craftsmen or the customers. Centres for their production were established in both Egypt and Syria. From Egypt come illustrations of human figures in both mythological and more mundane contexts, plant motifs and animals, and also more elaborate compositions – which are gilded as well – showing the worship of the Egyptian god Osiris together with inscriptions in Greek that read 'Drink and may you live'. Vessels with designs applied (no doubt by enamelling, since they have survived) on the inside to be seen through the glass were occasionally produced in Syrian glasshouses. These were probably also responsible for a number of remarkable enamelled glass vessels showing scenes from Greek mythology with the protagonists often named in Greek, though the inscriptions, in particular, are close to those of the Egyptian cut glassware. A close connection between enamelled glass workshops of west and east is illustrated by a bottle like those described below showing Italian landscapes, but whose decoration of a Greek mythological scene and a Greek inscription links it with our Syrian group. It may of course have been made in Cologne by a migrant Syrian glassmaker or for an eastern client, and an enamelled bottle of the same shape, but with a chariot scene and Latin inscription, has been found in the Rhineland (Bonn, Landesmuseum).

Turning now to the work of the artists responsible for cut decoration, we have already seen that fine facet-cut glass vessels were being made into the second decade of the second century; bowls with facet-cut decoration were evidently being made in the west in the later second century. To the last quarter of the second and the early third century belongs a large group of fragments of colourless glass vessels from Karanis in the Faiyum (Egypt), some of which are decorated with

107 Bowl with painted – or, more probably, enamelled – lid. The design, outlined in black, is on the inside, so that it is seen through the glass. It shows a naked winged figure with a bunch of grapes and vine leaves in his left hand, and a hook (perhaps a sickle) in his right. Found in Cyprus, where it was made in the 2nd century A D. H. of bowl 6.5 cm; D. of lid 7.4 cm.

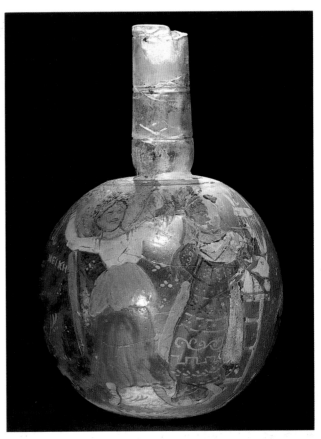

108 ABOVE, LEFT Group of enamelled bowls found in Denmark, showing wild beasts which would have been used in staged fights in the Roman amphitheatre. Probably made in the Rhineland between about AD 150 and 260/70. H. of example showing bull 9.15 cm. Copenhagen, National Museum.

109 ABOVE, RIGHT Bottle with gilded enamelled polychrome decoration. The main zone depicts the contest between the god Apollo and the satyr Marsyas over which was the better musician. Here is shown Nike (Victory), winged and named in Greek, and Apollo with his lyre. The subject and the use of the Greek language link this vessel with a group made in Syria, but similarly shaped bottles show Italian landscapes. It was perhaps made in Cologne by a migrant Syrian glassmaker, or for an eastern client, 3rd to 4th century AD. H. 14.6 cm. Corning, New York, Corning Museum of Glass.

fine wheel-cut and engraved designs. None of these fragments is inscribed and most show animals, birds and foliage, but three figured fragments (Corning Museum of Glass) with human figures, from elsewhere in Egypt, have names inscribed on them in Greek, including that of the mythological hero Orestes. Fragments of similar vessels have been found at Dura Europos in Syria, one showing part of the story of Artemis and Actaeon, with the latter's name inscribed in Greek (Damascus, National Museum). For complete or nearly complete examples we must turn to the western provinces: a number come from Cologne, while others are known from Saxony (also in Germany, but outside the Roman Empire), near Reims (France) and Britain. The style of cutting, engraving and lettering of all these examples is very distinctive and implies a single centre of production. That this was in Egypt, which perhaps came into its own at this time, is suggested by the finds from there and from further east, by the choice of Greek mythological subjects, and not least by the Greek language of the inscriptions. In addition, the motifs on an uninscribed cut-glass beaker of the early third century are so Egyptian that they confirm that such techniques were being practised in Egypt at this time. The principal scene shows a sturdy man with a chisel and a mallet, carving the Greek numeral 7 (the letter *zeta*) on a Nilometer, an instrument – shown here as a round-topped column – on which the height of the year's flood of the Nile was recorded.

These Egyptian bowls with figured scenes were the prototypes from which numerous cutting styles were evolved during the third and fourth centuries, not only in Egypt and Syria but also in Italy and the

111

110 Bowl with cut decoration of facets and deep-cut circles with projecting central knobs. From a late 3rd-century grave at Leuna in Saxony, outside the borders of the Roman Empire, but probably made in the Rhineland between about A D 175 and 200. H. 8.7 cm.

Rhineland and perhaps other western centres as well. Another Egyptian group consists of tall footed beakers, mainly of the late third century, which carry abraded Greek inscriptions in which the lettering is formed of double parallel strokes separated by diagonal slashes and combined with other patterns such as wreaths, palm branches and cross-hatching. Similarly decorated, but in a cruder style and of the fourth century, mainly the first half, is another group consisting of flasks, dishes and a few small bowls, made or at least cut in Asia Minor. Other glass vessels of the earlier fourth century, mostly jugs and two-handled bottles, from workshops in Syria, Palestine and particularly Egypt, as well as in the Rhineland, are decorated with simple abraded geometric patterns. The recent discovery in Egypt of bottle fragments with abraded lines in contexts of the late first or early second century suggests that this mode of decoration had a long history in that area. The continuation into the earlier years of the fourth century of close connections between glasshouses throughout the Roman Empire, at least through trade, is illustrated by a pair of jugs decorated in this manner. They are so alike that they seem to have been made by the same man or at least in the same place, but one was found in Egypt and the other in Cologne (now in the Römisch-Germanisches Museum). 112

Several of the styles of decoration that we have been examining continued into the fourth century and some for even longer. New types of storage and tablewares were introduced at this time in the countries bordering the Mediterranean Sea, a number of which continued to be typical in the centuries to come. The colours changed too. Colourless glass continued, mainly for luxurious glassware, and deliberately coloured glass, notably blue, became more common. Unusual, but reminiscent of an earlier (western) type, is a juglet of green glass with a thin outer white layer through which the green glass shows. Of the natural colours, those with a greenish or bluish tinge were still used, particularly in North Africa, but more pronounced shades were generally preferred: most vessels were now

111 Beaker with cut decoration. The principal scene depicts a man carving the Greek numeral 7 (the letter *zeta*) on a Nilometer, shown as a round-topped column. Made in Egypt in the early 3rd century A D. H. 8.6 cm.

112 Large jug decorated with abraded and wheel-cut geometrical designs, found in a tomb at Oxyrhynchus, in Egypt where it was made in the first half of the 4th century A D. A very similar jug was found at Cologne. H. 31.5 cm.

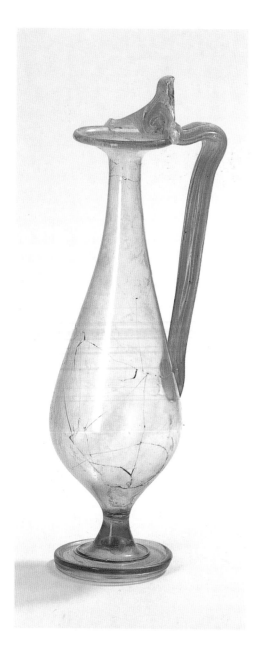

113 Large jug for which there are parallels in Late Roman silverware. From Syria, where it was made in the 4th century A D. H. 45.6 cm.

made of blue-green, olive-green, green, pale yellow or brown glass in shades that may occur naturally. Overall the number of different shapes was reduced and the decoration became sparser, consisting mainly of simple trails or dark blue blobs. Beakers, both cylindrical and conical, were very common in these areas in the fourth and succeeding centuries. Late Roman glass beakers normally had rough rims, achieved, no doubt, by 'cracking off'. There was also an assortment of jars, bowls (mostly with bases), jugs and flasks. A number of the flasks and jugs had long necks and pronounced funnel-shaped or circular mouths.

Figs 93

113

The essential unity of the Roman glass industry seems to have been broken by the middle of the fourth century, probably following the transfer of the Imperial court from Rome to Constantinople (modern Istanbul), since these new styles of tableware and storage vessels are found on sites in the eastern Mediterranean, North Africa and Italy but do not occur further north in central and western Europe. These divisions are also illustrated by the distribution of a distinctive form of perfume bottle with a bulge in the centre of the body, usually described as 'pipette-shaped'. It was introduced in the later third century, which may explain why until the middle of the fourth century it occurs as frequently on sites in the western provinces as in Syria and Palestine (but is so far unknown in Egypt).

There was divergence, too, among the products of the eastern provinces. In Syria and Palestine the glassmakers experimented with trailing and produced an imaginative series of perfume bottles with basket handles and often double bodies. These are unknown in the west, unlike the pipette-shaped variety introduced earlier. A local Egyptian industry which flourished from the fourth century at least until the coming of the Arabs in the seventh was responsible for some elegant tableware including bowls, oval and circular plates and dishes, and jars with collars, as well as conical lamps with blue blobbed decoration.

114

While there was evidently a common style for everyday glassware within the Mediterranean basin, there were disparate styles of cutting and other modes of ornamentation throughout the Empire. Certain of the late Roman glasshouses were responsible for some of the most remarkable and technically excellent, if impractical, decorated glass vessels of antiquity.

In Syria cutting and engraving to a high standard lasted for some time, even into the sixth century, but in Egypt by the fourth century good cutting had for the most part given way to abrasion. In the west, too, facet-cutting became less common in the fourth century, most of the designs being executed by engraving and abrading. A closely-knit western group, belonging mainly to the third decade of the fourth century, consists of open vessels, mainly shallow bowls, decorated with hunting scenes, stories from Greek mythology or biblical subjects. The designs are engraved, apparently freehand, with a sharp pointed tool in a series of short jabs on the surface of the vessel. Particularly ambitious is a series of bottles made in the later third or fourth century and engraved with waterfront landscape scenes. They carry Latin inscriptions which on some identify the places as Baiae or Puteoli, in Italy, both favourite watering-places of wealthy Romans. The scenes are distinguishable also by differences in details in the

115

114 Oval dish found in Egypt, where it was made in the 4th century A D, or possibly later. L. 23.7 cm.

115 Bowl with a scene of a hare-hunt and a Latin inscription engraved with a sharp-pointed tool. Found on Wint Hill, Banwell, Somerset, in south-west England, and made in one of the western Roman provinces between about A D 325 and 350. D. 19.2 cm. Oxford, Ashmolean Museum.

designs. Belonging to the years between about AD 330 and 370 is a group united by their crude workmanship. They show either pagan scenes such as a Bacchic dance or funerary banquet, or biblical stories. The drawing is competent but the designs are depicted by simply engraved, mostly straight, lines or shallow wheel-cutting with the hollows left unpolished. As they come from sites in Germany, France and Britain, they were probably made in the Rhineland, and perhaps in Gaul as well.

Not more than a generation or two before AD 300 the first of the principal series of cage cups, or *diatreta*, were made (their predecessors, made about 200 years earlier, have already been described). Most belong to the fourth century or the second half of the third, and represent the apogee of glass-cutting in antiquity. The majority are deep bowls (or 'cups'). A thick blank was blown, and then cut away to create an openwork design connected to the background wall by a minimum number of 'bridges' strategically hidden behind the decoration. Many, like those found in and around Cologne, where they were probably made, are decorated with a network of cages, usually of different colours contrasting with a colourless wall and often with an inscription in Greek or Latin at the rim. Others, more brilliantly conceived, show figured scenes. The most remarkable is a cup which illustrates the story of Lycurgus, the ill-fated king of the Thracian Edoni, who was strangled by vines after taunting the god Dionysos. The colour of the glass is very unusual in that in reflected light it is pea-green, changing to magenta in transmitted light. A similar colour change (pea-green to amber) occurs on a fragmentary cage cup from Termancia in Spain with network rather than figured decoration (Madrid, Museo Arqueológico Nacional), and on two more network fragments, one from Thessaloniki in northern Greece and the other without provenance but now in the British Museum. A few other glass fragments with cut decoration have similar properties. The change in colour might have happened by chance from the use of two gathers of glass on the blow-pipe and from the firing temperature. Alternatively it could have been achieved by the addition of minute particles of gold

116
117

116 Cage cup depicting the story of Lycurgus, the ill-fated Thracian king strangled by vines after taunting the god Dionysos. In reflected light it is pea-green in colour. The silver-gilt rim-mount, calyx, stem and foot have been added, probably in the late 17th or 18th century. Perhaps made in the Rhineland, 4th century AD. Max. H. 16.5 cm.

117 OPPOSITE The Lycurgus cage cup in transmitted light, when it appears a deep red, often described as magenta, and amethystine purple on the torso of Lycurgus.

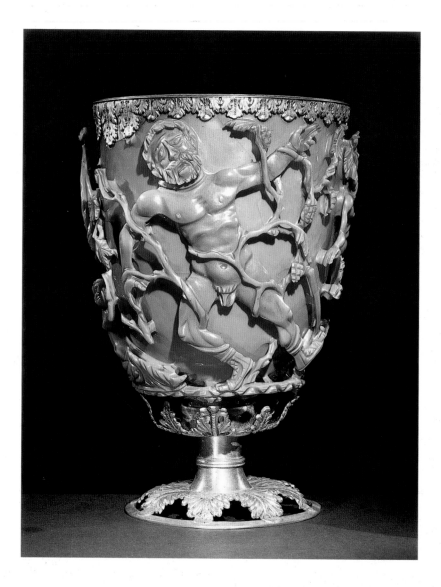

118 Replica made by George Scott of Edinburgh, Scotland, of a completely colourless cup decorated with a network of cages and used as a hanging lamp. The original, now in the Corning Museum of Glass, New York, was made around A D 300 and is said to have been found in Syria. H. 10 cm.

and silver to the glass batch, though exactly how this was done is not known. This latter technique seems to have produced the opaque tannish-pink colour of the occasional piece of early Roman cast glass tableware and in late Roman times the opaque flesh tones of figures in some *opus sectile* panels.

The best-known cage cups are those found in the west, where they were evidently made. However, particularly in more recent years, examples have come to light from further east. One of these, a bowl without figured decoration, now in the Corning Museum of Glass, said to come from the area on the modern border between northern Syria and southern Turkey, is of an unusual shape for this class, being broader than it is high, and is completely colourless with no coloured embellishments. Another recently discovered completely colourless example (also at Corning) of this hemispherical network type, but smaller, has metal fittings indicating that at the time of burial it was meant to be suspended. This suggests that the hemispherical cage cups, and perhaps also some others, served as hanging lamps rather than as drinking vessels – though a fragment of a rather shallower yet still hemispherical example (Trier, Rheinisches Museum) bears a drinking slogan.

118

The striking similarity in the technique of manufacture and the details of the design of all known examples with networks of cages has given rise to the suggestion that all were decorated by one family or even a single craftsman within a time-span of no more than fifty years. Other scholars maintain that a number of workshops, not only in the Rhineland, were responsible for these masterpieces, including the figured group. Late Roman metalworkers were also making open-work vessels with glass liners blown into the casings in the manner of the examples made perhaps some 200 years earlier when Pliny described the technique. Probably to the fourth century belongs an example from a hoard found in Scotland (now Edinburgh, National Museums of Scotland), whose silver casing forms a network of cages in apparent imitation of the completely glass series.

The delight of western glasshouses in colourful vessels is well illustrated by those decorated with applied blobs (or prunts) of coloured glass, which were being made in increasing numbers in the fourth century. Applied blue blobs remained popular (as in the eastern and Mediterranean glass workshops), particularly on simple shapes such as bowls and beakers that were still being circulated in Scandinavia in the fifth century. Some jugs, with distinctive ribbed handles folded over before being attached below the rim, are decorated with opaque white marvered trails forming festoon patterns, foreshadowing a Frankish style of decoration (see Chapter 3). Perhaps a corollary of these is an even more elaborate series of drinking vessels and bowls of colourless or greenish-colourless glass with applied decoration. This may take the form of self-coloured trails in an openwork design, just like the network patterns of the *diatreta* but the work of the glassmakers themselves. On one example the openwork trails are milled or plaited or decorated with moulded shells; on another the trails provide some protection for gilded decoration (both Cologne, Römisch-Germanisches Museum). Two large beakers with the usual rough rims are decorated with rows of lions' masks of the same green colour as the actual vessels. One was found in France and the other in Holland

120

119

122

119 Two small jugs: that on the left is decorated with white trails combed into festoons, in apparent anticipation of a Frankish style of decoration; the other is of two colours, the clear green showing through the outer opaque white layer, particularly in a vertical streak on the body. This is reminiscent of a much earlier western group of undecorated two-coloured glass bowls made alongside the better-known cameo-glass vessels. Both jugs were made in the 4th century A D; the undecorated example is said to come from Cyzicus on the Bosphorus. H. of undecorated jug 11.8 cm.

120 Plate of colourless glass decorated with green and yellowish-brown blobs or prunts. A yellowish-brown trail forms a small foot-ring. From Cologne in the Rhineland, where it was made in the first half of the 4th century A D. D. 22.8 cm. Cologne, Römisch-Germanisches Museum.

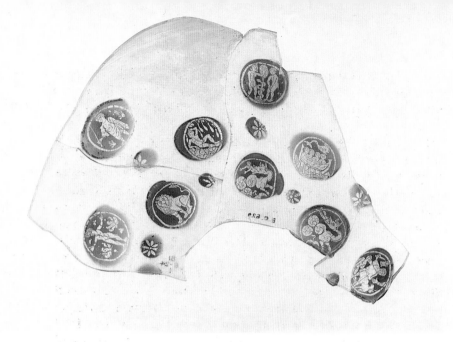

121 One of two surviving portions of a bowl of colourless glass decorated with applied blobs, under which are biblical scenes depicted in gold leaf. Found at Cologne in the Rhineland, where it was probably made in the second half of the 4th century A D. Max. W. 16.8 cm.

122 Large beaker decorated with rows of lion masks. To make the masks blobs of glass were applied in the required places on the body of the vessel and then mould-pressed *in situ*. Made in Gaul in the 4th century A D, and said to be from Reims, France. H. 22.9 cm.

123 Two gold-glass roundels originally at the bottom of bowls. The designs are rendered in gold leaf with added painted (probably enamelled) details sandwiched between two fused layers of colourless glass. The first shows a husband and wife with a small figure of Hercules between them, encircled by a Latin inscription; there are other inscriptions in the field. The design on the second roundel is divided in two: above are three figures between columns linked by a curtain-like garland, and below are three figures identified by the accompanying Latin inscriptions as Christ, in the centre, with the saints Hippolytus and Timothy. Both roundels were made in Rome in the 4th century A D. D. of top example 10.4 cm.

(Leiden, National Museum of Antiquities), while a smaller example (Copenhagen, National Museum) comes from a tomb in Denmark, indicating that they were made in a western, perhaps Gaulish, glasshouse.

The technique of applying gold leaf to the surface of glass, which provides a protective covering when the gold is on the underside, or sandwiching it between two layers seems to have persisted from at least the Hellenistic until the Late Roman period, but it was in Rome in the fourth century that glassmakers exploited it to the full with a series of roundels to be set at the bottom of bowls and normally known by the term 'gold-glass'. Portraits of couples, families or individuals, pagan deities, various legends, genre scenes, animals and Jewish and, above all, Christian motifs were depicted meticulously in gold leaf with added painted (or enamelled) details before being sandwiched between two layers of colourless glass. The roundels with Christian scenes have been found mainly in catacombs outside the walls of Rome. They had been purposely broken away from the vessels and were discovered mortared into the walls of the niches of the catacombs, perhaps to mark individual burials.

Possibly related to these bowl-roundels are a number made as medallions in their own right. These show portraits, in one case a family group, stylistically similar to mummy portraits from Roman Egypt. Another Egyptian connection is provided by inscriptions on two examples (one of which is the family group just mentioned) in the Alexandrian dialect of Greek (Brescia, Museo Cristiano, and New York, Metropolitan Museum of Art). However, these may reflect the nationality either of the craftsman or perhaps his client, and therefore provide no real proof that Late Roman gold-glass was originally an Alexandrian technique. It is, of course, also possible that the medallions were made by an Alexandrian craftsman living in Rome.

Another group of vessels uses small medallions showing biblical subjects set in blue and green blob-like roundels, connecting it with the series of glass vessels decorated with coloured blobs. A fairly well-preserved example comes from Cologne, but since similar medallions are known from the catacombs at Rome, it is difficult to determine precisely which glasshouses were responsible for this group. Not all gold-leaf decoration from Late Roman glasshouses in Rome was protected by an outer layer of glass, nor is it true to say that the entire Rhineland production of this time consisted of unprotected gilding. There are nonetheless some fine examples from the Rhineland, including a deep blue bowl (Cologne, Römisch-Germanisches Museum), in which the gold leaf is applied to the surface of the glass with no outer layer, although in the case of one vessel dating from the end of the third century the gilt decoration is partly protected by a network pattern of trails.

The story of Roman glass comes to an end around the beginning of the fifth century, which was to witness the final collapse of the Roman Empire in the west. Nonetheless, as we shall see, Roman traditions were to persist in the east for several hundred years, and in the west the products of Roman workshops in Italy, the Rhineland, Gaul and Belgium laid the foundations for glassmaking for centuries to come.

CHAPTER THREE

Early Medieval Europe

AD 400–1066

FOR SOME TIME after the end of the fourth century AD there were no fundamental changes in glassmaking traditions in either the east or the west. The west experienced major political reorganisation in the fifth century, brought about by the demise of the Roman Imperial power and the subsequent invasions of barbarian tribes (Germanic peoples from beyond the frontiers of the Empire), while in the east a more marked break occurred with the Arab invasions of the seventh century (see Chapter 4). Nevertheless, although distinct traditions emerged, common to them all was their Roman heritage.

The eastern part of the Roman Empire was bordered on the north by the River Danube and had included the whole of modern Turkey, Greece, the Balkans, the islands of the Aegean and the eastern Mediterranean, Syria, Palestine, Egypt and eastern Libya. This whole area remained under the control of the emperors, whose seat was now at Constantinople, the site of ancient Byzantium (hence the description 'early Byzantine' for the culture in this region for the years from the fifth to the seventh centuries during which Roman traditions of glassmaking persisted). Glassmakers in the rest of North Africa, despite an interval of rule by the Vandals (a Germanic people) in the fifth century, participated in these general trends, as did those in Italy, at least in Rome, where glass vessels are known to have been made in the fifth century, and to the south. Rather different glass was produced in northern Italy in the later sixth and seventh centuries, when it came under the domination of the Lombards (or Langobards), another Germanic people, from AD 568 until their absorption by the Franks in 774.

The changes in glassmaking in these eastern and Mediterranean areas around AD 400 were, then, for the most part only slight, and the existence of a common style in glass produced in the Mediterranean basin in the fifth to seventh centuries reflects the situation in the fourth. The Egyptian industry continued in operation at least until the coming of the Arabs. Long-distance trade routes remained open. Tableware from somewhere in the east, possibly though not necessarily from Egypt, reached Scandinavia in the fifth and sixth centuries, and fragments of similar glass vessels have been found in Cornwall in

124 Cone beaker with elegant trailed decoration, found in a grave at Kempston, Bedfordshire, England. Dating from the second half of the 5th century AD, it could have been made in Anglo-Saxon England, but is perhaps more likely to be a Frankish (or Merovingian) import from France, Belgium or Germany. H. 26.2 cm.

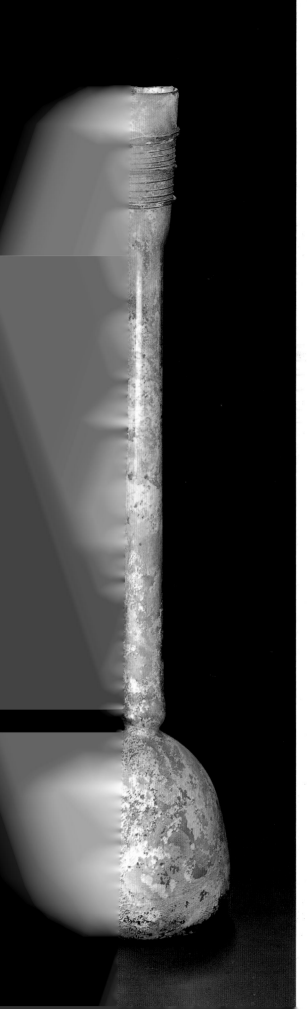

the far south-west of England. Stemmed flasks (sometimes described as goblets) of olive-green glass – one of which, showing a hound hunting two hares, was found in an Anglo-Saxon grave in Sussex in southern England (now in Worthing Museum and Art Gallery) – are finely decorated with abraded designs. The technique of the decoration, and perhaps the colour (though other eastern and Mediterranean glasshouses used olive-green glass at this time), point in particular to Egypt, suggesting that these vessels were made there in the late fourth or early fifth century. It seems that it was also in Egypt some time in the sixth, or possibly the seventh, century that lustre painting was first practised. This was to be a rare yet colourful technique used by certain Islamic glassmakers.

Elsewhere in the eastern provinces and also in North Africa and Italy, most vessels were made of thinly blown glass in different shades of green, most often bluish-green, as well as other pronounced natural colours that had been common in the fourth century. In North Africa yellowish- and greenish-colourless remained popular. Deliberately decolorised glass was rare. Newly or recently introduced shapes which became particularly common after AD 400 were flasks with exceedingly long necks and unguent bottles with tall manifold handles, rather more elaborate versions of the simpler single- and double-bodied varieties of the fourth century. Other flasks with broader bodies are also provided with very obvious handles. Conical and cylindrical beakers continued to be made in large numbers. Some had rough cracked-off rims as before, but often rims were now smooth, having been rounded and thickened in the flame of the furnace.

Stemmed goblets looking much like modern wine-glasses were very common. The stems were either plain and slender or, perhaps more often, beaded. They occur on nearly every early Byzantine site in Turkey, Syria, Palestine and North Africa, on islands in the eastern Mediterranean and also in Italy. Found in public buildings and private houses as well as in churches and synagogues, they evidently served both as drinking vessels and as lamps. These and other new shapes of glass lamps were to be popular in churches for many centuries. Many were shaped like a cup and had three small handles at the rim so that they could either be hung by chains from the ceiling or stood on a table or altar. A rarer version with triangular-shaped handles attached to the top or side of the rim so as to rise above it was produced in central Italy. Yet other lamps were bowl-shaped on long hollow or solid stems for insertion into candelabra. Coloured glass linings were probably used for openwork hanging lamps whose casings were made of silver or occasionally bronze, reminiscent of the Roman technique. A fine series dating from around the middle of the sixth century (Washington, DC, Dumbarton Oaks Museum, and Antalya, Archaeological Museum) comes from a hoard of ecclesiastical treasure found in south-east Turkey, perhaps originally belonging to the monastery of Holy Sion at Myra, about forty kilometres from the hoard's find-spot.

Most of the decoration on glassware of this period was carried out by the glassmaker. Trailing was very widely used on the tall-necked flasks and also on the elaborate unguent bottles. Blue blobs remained quite popular, adding some colour to an otherwise mainly monochrome series of vessels. A distinctive group of mould-blown jars, flasks and jugs with four, six or eight sides was made in Jerusalem for

125 OPPOSITE Tall flask with an exceedingly long neck, decorated around the top with an opaque red-brown spiral trail forming three thick bands dividing groups of thinner bands. Found in Syria, where it was made in about the 5th century A D. H. 36 cm.

126 RIGHT A jug and a hexagonal bottle, both mould-blown. The jug has a depiction of the *crux gemmata* (the jewelled cross erected in A D 420 on the site of the Crucifixion) with other motifs. The panels on the bottle show a cross on what may be an altar, and a monk or perhaps Christ, with panels with trellis designs between them. These vessels probably served as containers for holy oil, and were sold to visiting pilgrims. Made in Palestine, perhaps at Jerusalem, between about A D 675 and 725. The bottle was found at Aleppo, in Syria. H. of bottle 22.5 cm.

127 BELOW Cone-shaped vessel decorated with applied blue blobs and probably used as a lamp. Made in Egypt or the Near East, in the 5th or perhaps 6th century A D. H. 18 cm.

about fifty years from around AD 675. Glass of deep shades, deliberately coloured and therefore unusual in vessels of this period, was used for some examples. These were evidently made for visiting pilgrims, as containers for holy oil, since most are decorated with either Jewish or Christian symbols.

Glass-cutters were, however, still at work, decorating many simple forms with cut lines. We have already noted that fine facet-cutting probably survived into the sixth century in Syria. In Italy, too, some figured cut-glass vessels belong to the fifth or possibly the sixth century. Two chalices, one said to be from Syria and the other from Palestine (Washington, DC, Dumbarton Oaks Museum, and Amman, Jordan Archaeological Museum), bear deeply cut figured decoration which in each case includes a large cross with patterns on the arms.

Glass used for purposes other than vessels is found on early Byzantine sites and commonly includes window panes. Many, certainly blown, look like small dishes, for which they are sometimes mistaken. They were first made in the east in the fourth century but are more common in the fifth to seventh centuries, frequently being found on early church sites. At this time they spread to Italy as well. Glass tesserae (cubes) were often used in the mosaics that adorned the walls of churches and large secular buildings, but rarely occur in floor mosaics of this period.

A distinctive series of glass vessels belonging to the sixth and seventh centuries has been found in the north of Italy, which at this time was under the domination of the Lombards. The principal types were deep bowls, stemmed cups or beakers, drinking horns and

128 Deep bowl with polychrome enamelled decoration. Found in a Lombard grave in the cemetery of Santo Stefano in Pertica, Cividale, northern Italy; about A D 600. H. 9 cm. Cividale, Museo Archeologico Nazionale.

bottles. There are also two polychrome flasks with handles, but as these are the only examples known, and as they are unexcavated, their date has been questioned. The drinking horns are similar in shape to those made in Frankish glasshouses; stemmed cups and bottles also occur north of the Alps, but are not common. The bottles are largely restricted to northern France, but stemmed cups (or 'wine glasses') have been found in southern France as well. The latter are of course typically found on early Byzantine sites in the east and North Africa, but occur too at an earlier date in Rome. The bottles, particularly those with funnel-shaped mouths, are reminiscent of Late Roman forms, but the bowls seem to be wholly Italian.

It is the polychrome appearance of many of these vessels that sets them apart from most contemporary products of Frankish (and Anglo-Saxon) glasshouses (see below). A number, notably the drinking horns and most of the bowls, are of coloured glass – usually light or more rarely dark blue, or green – and some of the bowls have a trail of a different colour around the rim. Unmarvered opaque white trails decorating several of the bottles (which are mostly of bluish- or greenish-colourless glass) and the bodies of certain horns are reminiscent of the decoration on some of the Frankish series. In addition, the trellis pattern on the upper part of some of the horns, formed by trails of the same blue or green colour as their bodies or of opaque white glass, is similar to that decorating squat jars made perhaps in south-eastern England in the late sixth and seventh centuries. But on other horns the trellis designs are replaced with marvered red trails combed into two-way feather patterns similar to those in two colours which decorate some of the bowls, a design which has no close parallel except on beads of this period. As a whole, therefore, these glass vessels of Lombard Italy stand apart from their north-west European contemporaries in spite of the common Germanic origins of the people, but their delight in the polychrome heralds the return of colour to European glass vessel production.

At about the same time, a factory in the island of Torcello in the Venetian lagoon was making glass, starting, according to the excavators, after the beginning of the seventh century and ending in the eighth, though it has also been suggested that production began slightly earlier but had ceased by about AD 650, since it could not have continued after the completion of the neighbouring cathedral. The most important of the discoveries here were the remains of three glass furnaces which show that the annealing oven was placed alongside the actual furnace (rather than on top, as in early Roman illustrations). Among the finds were fragments of many stemmed beakers similar to those found in the Lombard graves, and some evidence of bichrome trailed decoration.

The chief inheritors of the Roman Empire in the north-west were the Franks, an amalgamation of Germanic barbarian tribes among whom were Teutons – hence the use by some authors of the word Teutonic to describe what is really Frankish glass (Teutonic has of course come to mean Germanic in a general sense). The Franks dominated the area of present-day France and western Germany until the disintegration of their empire in the later ninth century. One of their most important dynasties was the Merovingian, which took its name from the half-legendary Frankish king Merovech and which ruled much of France and Belgium from soon after the middle of the fifth century until AD 751. Meanwhile, Angles, Saxons, Jutes and other Germanic tribes came to England where, following the withdrawal of the Romans in AD 410, they founded individual kingdoms. These were not unified into a 'kingdom of England' before the tenth century, but the term Anglo-Saxon is often used to describe glass found in England in the whole of the period that concerns us.

The Roman glass industry in the cities of the Rhineland, Belgium and northern France continued to flourish under Frankish control. Most Frankish vessels were made of monochrome glass in pale and murky greens and browns. Colour was generally lacking, except for the use of opaque white in trailed decoration which was quite common until around the middle of the sixth century, after which the trails were normally of translucent glass similar to that used for the vessels. The range of shapes was very small, limited mainly to drinking glasses of different varieties, bowls, and a few containers such as jars, bottles, flasks and the occasional jug. Embellishments such as handles and appliqués that had adorned the more expensive classes of Late Roman glassware were for the most part lacking, except in the case of claw beakers, and decoration was restricted to what could be achieved by the glassmaker, such as mould-blown corrugations or ribs and applied trails. The technique of enamelling seems to have been forgotten, and cutting is noticeably absent.

The types of glass vessels in the Frankish repertoire are mostly called by names derived from their shapes; so we have, for example, drinking horns, 'cone' beakers, 'bag' beakers and 'bell' beakers. 'Palm cups' are small bowls which also served as drinking vessels and which, being without handles, had to be held in the palm of the hand. The most elaborate of the Frankish series were claw beakers, named after the claw-like projections on their bodies.

In the fifth century the number of different types of drinking glasses was already quite large and the debt to their Late Roman predecessors is often obvious. In Merovingian territory, principally in the region north of the Loire, flasks and bottles decorated with opaque white trails, sometimes forming patterns of festoons, were quite common for about a hundred years from the mid-fifth century. These, too, for the most part recall vessels of the Late Roman period.

Perhaps the best known of all Dark Age glass vessels are the claw beakers, whose elaborate decoration sets them apart from the rest. Their origin lies in a group of Late Roman beakers made at Cologne in the second half of the fourth century and decorated with polychrome appliqués added by dropping hot glass on the wall of the vessel and pulling part of the wall out and down so there is a hollow on the inside, a particular feature of the claws. These Late Roman cups usually had rough rims simply cracked off by the glassmaker and sometimes finished by grinding. The typical Frankish claw beaker stands on a foot and has trailed decoration under the rounded rim and near the base. An early claw beaker made around AD 400 (but buried as an heirloom in a tomb at Mucking in Essex, England, in the first half of the sixth century) clearly shows the Roman origin of the type. The rough rim and the corrugated or 'milled' trails with a horizontal zigzag border forming a panel style of ornament are all in the Roman tradition, and moreover the glass itself is of excellent quality. In the

129

130

129 Colourless glass cup decorated with schematic dolphins. Cups like this one were evidently the inspiration behind Frankish claw beakers (see Pl. 130), although the process was not entirely new at this time. From Cologne in the Rhineland, where it was made in the second half of the 4th century. H. 14.7 cm. Cologne, Römisch-Germanisches Museum.

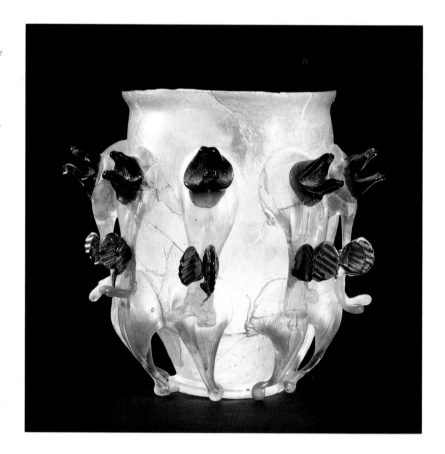

130 Two claw beakers. That on the left was found in a grave at Castle Eden, Co. Durham, in northern England; it appears to be an early Frankish import made in the second half of the 5th century, as it has close parallels on the Continent. The second, more elaborate, example was found in a grave at Mucking in Essex, eastern England, the other contents of which date from the first half of the 6th century. However, with its obviously Late Roman features, such as the cracked-off rim and milled trails, the beaker cannot have been made later than about A D 400 and must therefore have been buried as an heirloom. With no close parallels on the Continent, it may have been made in England, perhaps by a glassworker arriving with the Anglo-Saxon invaders. H. of Castle Eden beaker 26.2 cm.

For the making of a claw beaker, see pp.240–41, Figs 205–9.

fifth and sixth centuries claw beakers were no doubt made in the Rhineland around Cologne and in the area of the Meuse valley near Namur in Belgium, from where they were exported to other sites on the Continent and maybe to eastern England. It is, however, possible that glassmakers came over to Kent with the Germanic invaders, bringing with them glassmaking techniques which enabled specific types such as claw beakers and cone beakers to be produced locally from perhaps as early as the fifth century. Certain early types of claw beaker found in England, such as the Mucking example, have virtually no parallels on the Continent. As we shall see, by the seventh century glassmakers in Anglo-Saxon Kent had certainly acquired the necessary expertise to produce these remarkable vessels.

Cone beakers are among the earliest and most widespread of Frankish glass types. Their rounded rims distinguish them from the Roman, and their narrow bases meant that they had to be drained in one draught and stood upside down. The more elaborate versions include an elegant series each decorated with a trail, of the same colour as the vessel itself, applied in long vertical loops to form a

124

131 Drinking horn decorated with vertical looped trail patterns on the body and horizontal trails below the rim. Frankish, 5th century A D; found at Bingerbrück, Germany. L. 34 cm.

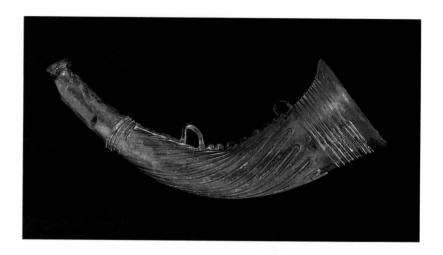

festoon pattern on the lower part of the body, and a second similarly coloured trail wound around several times in spiral fashion horizontally below the rim. Such beakers were made from the mid-fifth to the mid-sixth century and perhaps later as well. Their production centres were probably in France, Belgium and Germany and perhaps also in Kent in south-east England. Beakers of very thick glass with straighter sides and somewhat similar festoon decoration were probably made in Scandinavia, where most have been found, with occasional examples reaching Belgium and elsewhere. Some of these have feet. Mainly from Belgium and northern France (and very rare in the Rhineland) comes a distinctive group whose festoon patterns are formed of opaque white trails like those decorating flasks from the same area. Even a very simple shape of glass drinking vessel therefore reveals how different styles evolved in different areas of the region dominated by the Franks, while in places occupied by other Germanic tribes, such as Anglo-Saxon England, yet other kinds were made.

The drinking horn was another type of Frankish glass vessel with Roman antecedents: as we have seen, it also figured particularly among the glass vessels made in northern Italy under the Lombards. Unlike other Frankish drinking glasses, the horns had rough unfinished rims. They were first blown as cone-shaped beakers, and then bent and perhaps also twisted to imitate an animal horn. Vertical looped trail patterns already decorated horns of the third century from Cologne and from sites outside the Roman Empire in Sweden and Denmark. Frankish examples often combine this pattern with horizontal trails below the rim.

Bell-shaped beakers also made their appearance in the fifth century, but were produced in larger numbers in the sixth. Like shallow bowls, they are much more common on the Continent than in Britain. A particular type of bowl, found in the Namur district of Belgium and neighbouring regions of northern France, where it was prbably made from about AD 450 until the second quarter of the sixth century, was blown into patterned moulds creating a Christian symbol, usually consisting of the Greek letters *chi* and *rho* (standing for Christ), on the base, and vertical ribs or an arch pattern on the body.

In the sixth century claw, cone and bell beakers continued to be made, and palm cups were introduced. The first palm cups were decorated with mould-blown ribs. Of the sixth-century types, only the

132 OPPOSITE Cone-shaped beaker of thick glass standing on a small foot and decorated with spiral trails. Found at Hablingbo, Gotland, Sweden, it was evidently made in Scandinavia between about A D 450 and 500. H. (uneven) 20.2–20.5 cm.

133 Squat jar decorated with thick trails nipped together to form a lattice pattern. Anglo-Saxon; probably made at Faversham, Kent, south-east England, about 7th century A D, and part of a rich grave group found at Broomfield in Essex, eastern England. H. 7.3 cm.

claw beaker survived into the seventh, when it became taller and conical in shape. New at this time, the first examples being made in the late sixth century, were bag beakers, squat jars, plain palm cups and bottles with globular bodies known as pouch bottles. Of these, both bag beakers and squat jars are far more common in eastern England than elsewhere and were evidently made in Kent, perhaps at Faversham. One type of squat jar is made of blue glass and decorated with thick trails nipped together to form a lattice pattern. A bag beaker decorated with claws (Kent, Maidstone Museum) shows that this decorative technique was known to glassmakers in Anglo-Saxon Kent, who were therefore probably also responsible for the seventh-century taller conical variety of claw beaker found mainly in eastern England but also exported to the Continent. Some of these were made of blue glass like that used for squat jars. Probably to the seventh century belong bowls from Belgian or French glasshouses with mould-blown network decoration and sometimes nonsense inscriptions that seem to imitate Late Roman cage cups.

The blue glass of some of the Kentish vessels of the late sixth and seventh centuries provides a welcome return to colour in north-western glassware in a period largely represented by rather dull monochrome glass. Contemporary with these is a beaker found quite recently in Cambridgeshire of bluish-green glass with elaborate criss-cross trailing resembling some of the patterns that decorate pouch bottles. Most of the trails are of the same colour as the body of the vessel, but in the upper band a bluish-green trail partly overlaps one of pale yellow, and the lower zone of zigzag trails is drawn from a two-colour blob. However, although brightly coloured glass was not generally used for drinking vessels in western Europe in the immediate post-Roman period, except in Italy, coloured glass was plentiful in the form of beads, and it seems likely that it was being produced in England for use in jewellery from the first quarter of the seventh century.

In the ninth and tenth centuries England was subjected to attacks and some colonisation by the Vikings from Scandinavia. On the Continent in the mid-eighth century the Merovingian dynasty was succeeded by the Carolingian, named after Charles (in Latin, Carolus) Martel (*c*.688–741), who had been effective ruler of all the Franks from 719. The most famous ruler of the new dynasty was Charlemagne (Charles the Great), who was anointed 'Holy Roman Emperor'

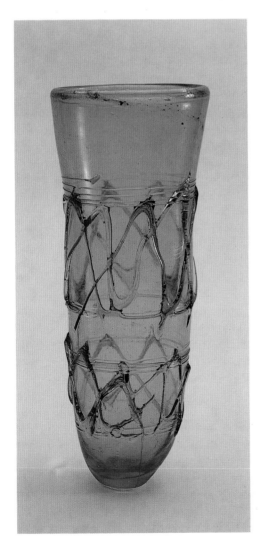

134 Beaker decorated with elaborate criss-cross trailing, mostly of the same colour of the body except that in the upper band a bluish-green trail partly overlaps one of pale yellow: this is an early example of the revival of bichrome decoration. Probably Anglo-Saxon, made in England in the late 6th or early 7th century A D. Found at Dry Drayton, near Cambridge, England. H. 18.8 cm. Cambridge, University Museum of Archaeology and Anthropology.

in 800 and with his immediate successors was responsible for a 'Carolingian Renaissance'. His empire embraced modern France, Belgium, Holland, most of Germany and northern Italy. However, western Europe, like England, was subject to attack by outsiders and from the beginning of the tenth century came to be made up of numerous different but interdependent principalities, lordships, counties and communities. Not until the twelfth century did consolidation get under way again.

The spread of Christianity meant that after the late seventh century goods were no longer buried with the dead in Britain, northern France and the Rhineland. In addition, in the ninth century the Church forbade the use of glass chalices at the Mass for fear that they might be broken. The prohibition seems not to have been strictly enforced, however, and glass was still used by the religious communities to make containers for sacred relics which were sealed with wax (itself impressed with a seal) and for dishes for oil lamps, as well as for windows. Nonetheless, pagan customs persisted in Scandinavia, meaning that the dead were still provided with gifts, and finds from there supply most information about glass vessels of our last period, which begins in the final decades of the seventh century, supplemented by important evidence from fragments of glass found on settlement sites in Britain and on the Continent.

In Britain, as we shall see, there is some evidence for glassmaking, notably in the north (by the monastic communities) and south-west; also, it seems, at the port of Hamwih (Southampton) in the eighth and ninth centuries and, at about the same time or perhaps slightly earlier, at Barking in Essex. In York two glassmaking sites of the Viking period of the ninth century have been identified. One was certainly making beads, of amber as well as glass; the other, in the Coppergate area, was re-using fragments, often of clear blue and green glass, as cullet, perhaps again to make beads or possibly window glass or simple vessels. On the Continent a glass factory of the ninth and possibly tenth century was excavated at Cordel near Trier in the Rhineland, and at about the same time glass windows and vessels were being made on quite a large scale at the Benedictine monastery of San Vincenzo at Volturno in central Italy. As in other periods, there must have been more European glasshouses in existence than have been discovered so far, since until the mid-tenth century some fine vessels were produced and a number of the older types survived, if in modified form. Coloured glass became more widely used.

The claw beaker degenerated into a type decorated with very few and flat claws, obviously later versions of the variety produced in Kent in the seventh century and now known mainly from Scandinavia. The most common glass vessels were squat jars and palm cups. The former occur nearly everywhere. The shape is usually the same, but the colour of the body and the decoration is varied. The palm cup became taller and more slender, finally developing into a funnel-shaped beaker. Various new types of bowls appeared, and bottles and goblets were also made. Glass drinking horns were rare after the seventh century, though they are occasionally shown in Carolingian manuscripts of the ninth and tenth centuries. Most of the illustrations in fact depict horns for ink, and a glass ink-horn was found in northern France in a context thought to be of the ninth or tenth century (Musée de Breteuil-sur-Noye). Made of translucent green glass that appears opaque black, it is decorated with an opaque rust-red trail wound all round the body, and two more twisted together under the rim.

A particular feature of this later period is the use of glass of different colours, often bright and vivid. The vessels themselves were made in blue, greenish-blue and bluish-green, dark red, dark green, red and a dark colour appearing black. A bicoloured effect was occasionally obtained from the end of the seventh century by red flame-like streaking, usually in blue or green glass. A polychrome result was more often achieved by the use of trails in colours which contrast with the body. The trails were quite often of single colours such as opaque yellow, white or light blue or occasionally red, but a more multicoloured effect could be provided by the use of trails of more than one colour in a manner which sometimes recalls the fine polychrome snake-thread trailing of Late Roman glasshouses at Cologne. Other vessels were decorated with fine canes, either of clear single colours or more often of spirally twisted threads of colourless and opaque white or yellow (like the 'network' canes of Hellenistic and early Roman glass and used even earlier by Mesopotamian and Egyptian glassmakers), normally placed horizontally or vertically on the body, although some fragments show them on the rim. This form of decoration is found on fragments almost exclusively from coastal sites in Britain, northern Europe and Scandinavia, although a few examples come from sites further south, including some on the Black Sea and in central Italy. More rarely, glass vessels were decorated with geometric patterns in gold leaf, which was evidently applied while the vessel was still warm as no adhesive was used, a technique reminiscent of Roman and earlier times. The majority of vessels were free-blown, but sometimes glass was blown into a mould to provide the decoration: a rare example of a flask in the form of a bunch of grapes shows a remarkable survival of a Roman type (Stockholm, National Museum of Antiquities).

The records of certain monasteries in north-western Europe in the ninth and tenth centuries mention a *frater vitrearius* who must have been responsible for the glass windows of the monastery, and the use of glass windows by the Church on the Continent is amply borne out by evidence from Britain. In 675 Benedict Biscop, the founder of the monasteries at Monkwearmouth and Jarrow in Northumbria, sent for glassmakers from France to make windows as well as lamps and vessels. To what extent the French glassmakers taught the Anglo-Saxons their craft is not clear, but almost a hundred years later, in 758, Cuthbert, the abbot of Jarrow, sent an urgent request to the Archbishop of Mainz in Germany, claiming that 'we are ignorant and helpless in that art'. Window glass is known from other churches of this time, mainly in northern Britain, but also from Winchester in the south. Evidence of glassmaking in the ninth or perhaps the tenth century has also been found at Glastonbury in Somerset (south-west England). Remains of at least three furnaces were uncovered there, one of which must have been for annealing, as at Torcello. The finds included fragments of window and vessel glass and a small mosaic cane like those used in some plaques found at Monkwearmouth.

All the actual glass that we have discussed so far, except for two fragments from the ninth- and perhaps tenth-century factory at Cor-

135

110

135 A palm cup of green glass streaked with red. Made in a Frankish – or, more accurately, Merovingian – glasshouse in France in the late 7th century A D, when brightly coloured glass was again being used for vessels. From Reims, France. H. 6.5 cm.

del in the Rhineland, was made using the naturally occurring soda natron as the alkali. This had been used since the seventh century BC and the same recipe had been dominant in the Roman period, although an older mixture using soda from saline plants found in the desert and around the marshy areas of the Near East had continued in use in Mesopotamia and some areas to the east. Egyptian natron is the alkali most frequently mentioned by the Elder Pliny and other ancient authors, and it was obviously in plentiful supply, though other sources are noted in northern Iran and in Macedonia and Thrace in northern Greece. A source of this natural soda has been identified in recent times in the western desert of Egypt, although even there the use of natron in glassmaking seems to have ceased no later than the tenth century. A significant change in the composition of glass made in the northern regions discussed in this chapter took place initially around the middle of the ninth century, when glassmakers came to rely on local supplies of potash for the necessary alkali. This came from the ashes of bracken and other woodland plants. It took some time, however, for the new recipe to be widely adopted, as is shown by the use of both mixtures.

From about the mid-tenth century, no doubt as a result of political turmoil, Continental glasshouses produced only very utilitarian vessels of few types and poor quality, and in the last century of Anglo-Saxon rule little glass is recorded from England. Nonetheless, eastern glass continued to travel westwards and reached Britain, Italy and Sweden in the ninth, tenth and perhaps eleventh centuries.

Until the ninth, if not the tenth century, therefore, glass vessels had remained quite plentiful and faithful to Roman traditions in both types and composition. Some western examples made in Continental or even British glasshouses, particularly in the later years dealt with in this chapter, are colourful and decorated, but all are generally functional. For ornamental and luxurious glassware from European glasshouses, of the quality of some of the vessels of earlier periods of antiquity, we must wait for the time of the Italian Renaissance.

CHAPTER FOUR

The Islamic Lands and China

WHILE China's contribution to the history of glass has never been of major significance, the glass of the Islamic world is as important as that of Rome. Just as Roman glass was widely distributed in the West and the industry established in many of the provinces of the Empire, so the glass produced in the central lands of the Islamic world was traded not only within the Muslim countries but also throughout the Mediterranean area, Scandinavia and Russia, East Africa, the shores of the Indian Ocean and even China. Like the Roman world, that of Islam was a unitary culture with shared social and religious institutions. At the same time there were manifold differences within its various parts, each of which made its particular contribution to a common culture. Like the other arts of the Islamic world, its glass, almost from the entry of Islam into world history, acquired a distinctive style determined in some mysterious way by the requirements of new patrons who introduced new styles of living.

Islamic glass production may be divided into three periods, the first being from the eighth to the eleventh century, when the unity of the Islamic world was more or less maintained under the successive rule of the Umayyad and the Abbasid caliphates, only to be disrupted in the tenth century by the rise of independent dynasties and rival caliphates. The centres of glass production in this period were the central lands of the Islamic world, that is, Syria, Egypt, Persia and Mesopotamia. The second period is from the twelfth to the fifteenth century, when glass production seems to have been confined to Syria and Egypt. In the third period, largely due to contacts with the glass industry in the West, there was sporadic production of glass in Persia and Turkey between the seventeenth and nineteenth century, and in India under the patronage of the Mughal court in the seventeenth and eighteenth centuries.

If the Islamic glasshouses developed distinctive styles and forms of glass, they also contributed to glass technology the technique of painting in lustre and the perfecting of gold painting and enamelling on glass. Another remarkable achievement was the carving of glass in relief, a technique known to the Roman glassmakers but not revived in Europe until the seventeenth century.

136 Miniature from the *Surname-i Humayun*, about 1582. Istanbul, Topkapi Sarayi Museum. This miniature is from a famous manuscript describing and illustrating the festivities in celebration of the circumcision of the sons of Sultan Murad III in Istanbul. The procession, which took place in the Hippodrome, consisted of floats representing the various guilds of the city. One of the miniatures shows the float of the glaziers, while this one is a vivid and detailed depiction of that of the makers of glass flasks. The furnace is in three parts: the lowest for replenishing the furnace with wood fuel, the middle containing the crucibles for the molten glass, and the upper part for annealing. A craftsman on the right is shaping a paraison by swinging, and another is working his paraison on the marver. Others are shown using the pontil and the pucellas.

Early Islamic glass

8TH–11TH CENTURIES

Our knowledge of Islamic glass in this period is entirely dependent on buried examples recovered either from controlled archaeological excavations or casual digging. Scientific archaeological investigation of Islamic sites was begun only in the present century and there are still many discoveries to be made. Significant finds from sites in Syria throw light on the glass produced in the period of the Umayyad caliphate, which ruled the Islamic world from Syria between AD 660 and 750. A rich and varied collection has been made at Samarra in Iraq, in excavations begun by the Germans and still continuing. Samarra, on the Tigris, was the temporary capital of the Abbasid caliphate from 836 to 892. Coming as they do from the seat of empire, the finds present a vivid picture of the range and quality of the glassware produced for the court in the ninth and tenth centuries. The same period has been covered by the British excavations at Siraf on the Persian Gulf. This seaport was an important trade emporium in the ninth and tenth centuries and, when published, the glass finds will no doubt provide an interesting picture of the variety of exports and imports both within the Islamic world and in the glass bound for the Indian Ocean trade. Fine examples of the luxury glassware of Persia have been revealed as a result of the American excavations carried out at Nishapur in eastern Persia just before the Second World War.

A particularly fruitful contribution has been that of the excavations carried out at Fustat by the American Research Centre in Egypt between 1965 and 1981. In the southern quarter of present-day Cairo, Fustat was the earliest Muslim settlement in Egypt and continued to be the administrative and military centre of the country until the foundation of the actual city of Cairo by the Fatimid caliph al-Mu'izz in AD 969. The excavations have produced a large mass of glass including domestic and luxury wares ranging from the eighth to the eleventh century and providing a firmer dating than has hitherto been possible.

Perhaps the most spectacular archaeological achievement, however, has been the recovery of the cargo of a ship wrecked off the coast of Turkey at Serçe Liman near Bodrum. The cargo consisted of many tons of glass cullet which were being exported to a northerly port. Tens of thousands of fragments have been patiently examined and matching pieces joined together to produce an astonishing number of more or less complete vessels. To judge from the evidence of coins and glass weights, the ship seems to have come to grief shortly after AD 1036. Its itinerary has so far not been ascertained; but we may tentatively suggest that the cargo was collected at a Syrian port and that the ship itself was destined for the Black Sea.

There are still many gaps in our knowledge of glass in this early period. Little is known, for example, of the glass production, if any, of the Maghrib, that is the provinces of North Africa and, more particularly, of al-Andalus, as Spain was called after the Arab conquest in the eighth century. Much glass has been found at Islamic sites in Spain as well as in North Africa; but it has yet to be determined whether these were local products or imports from the eastern Mediterranean, Persia or Mesopotamia. For it must be remembered that, in the Islamic as well as in the Roman world, craftsmen were mobile and it was no

137 Beaker of translucent glass. The honeycomb elements are here combined with two friezes of arcades; the columns or piers are rendered by horizontal cuts. The rounded base suggests that the vessel may have been intended either as a 'quaffing' cup or as a lamp for insertion in a candelabrum. Mesopotamia or Persia, 5th–6th century AD. H. 21.3 cm.

138 Bowl of green glass, partly iridescent due to weathering, made in Persia in the 5th–6th century A D and said to have been found at Amlash in northern Persia. The four rows of circular facets are arranged in a quincunx pattern, that is, two facets above and two below a central facet. A single large facet forms the base. A similar bowl, now in the National Museum, Tokyo, was recovered from the tomb of the emperor Ankan (*c.*A D 550–600). H. 7.5 cm.

139 An example of how the Sasanian glassmaker handled ordinary tableware. Trailed decoration is unusual, since prunts and applied ribs were preferred. This form of goblet continued into the Islamic period. 5th–6th century A D. H. 14.5 cm.

great problem for glassmakers to set up their industry in distant lands. Furthermore, there is need for caution in attributing a particular type of Islamic glass to a particular centre of production. But if a particular type of glassware is found in one region and nowhere else, that is sound reason for attributing it to that particular area.

With the Arab conquest of the Byzantine provinces of Syria and Egypt in the seventh century, artists and craftsmen were now working to satisfy the needs and taste of a new clientele. From the little we know, the quality and range of glass produced in these provinces on the eve of the Arab conquest was of no great account. In Persia and Mesopotamia, on the other hand, fine glass was being made certainly up to the sixth century AD, and it seems that it was these regions that contributed most to the resurgence of glass production in the first three centuries of Islam. Persia and Mesopotamia had undergone an artistic revival under the Sasanian emperors (AD 247–645), rivals of the emperors of Rome and their successors of Byzantium. The silver and bronzes and the woven silks of Sasanian Persia are justly famous, and it has become clear as a result of recent archaeological excavations in those regions that there was also a flourishing glass industry which continued without interruption into the Islamic period. The Sasanian glasshouses excelled in the cutting of glass on the wheel; closely associated with this craft was the carving of hardstones, in particular rock-crystal. This association was to continue into the Islamic period, and it is an open question whether the glass-cutters learned their craft from the hardstone carvers.

Characteristic of Sasanian decorated glass is facet cutting, resembling a honeycomb. Two or more rows of circular or oval facets, usually joined tangentially, form the decoration of a type of hemispherical bowl, a shape which seems to be unique to the Sasanian glasshouses. It is of almost colourless glass and thick enough to withstand the tensions of the cutting wheel. Such bowls must have been rarities, and they were much sought after in the lands beyond Persia: one such bowl reached Japan in the eighth century and was sufficiently esteemed to find a place in the Shrine of the Shosoin, where it is still preserved in its pristine splendour. This style of glass-cutting was inherited from the ancient world, for the carving of diamond-shaped facets had already been practised in Syrian (and Western) glasshouses in the first and second centuries AD. Facet

140

138

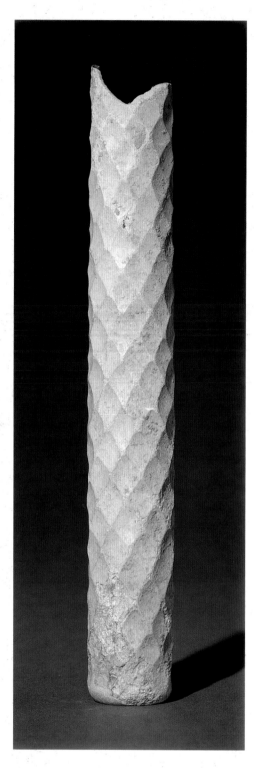

140 Scent or unguent container of green glass (the top missing), made in Persia or Mesopotamia in the 5th–6th century A D and found in excavations at Quyunjik, site of the ancient Nineveh, in Iraq. The buff-coloured patina is due to burial. Diamond-shaped faceting can also be seen on vessels found at Begram in Afghanistan and made in Syria in the 1st–2nd century AD. H. 22.3 cm.

cutting is found on other distinctive types of Sasanian vessels; in some, it was combined with incised linear decoration, such as arcades. 137

It is not surprising to find among the early Islamic glass vessels of Persia the continuation of the Sasanian style of wheel-cutting. There are examples of vessels with honeycomb decoration in which the facets are arranged in the same manner as those of the Sasanian period; oval facets are also combined with purely linear ornament. The hemispherical bowl no longer appears, having been replaced by quite novel shapes. One of these is the mallet-shaped flask, with a tall 144 tapering neck and broad horizontally outsplayed lip and a body curving outwards at the shoulder and then slightly inwards to a broad flat base; neck and body are generally of equal height. Another type is the bell-shaped flask in which a tallish funnel neck surmounts a body 141 with sloping shoulders and sides descending straight to a flat base. As in the mallet flask, the neck and body are roughly of equal height. The bell-shaped flask was evidently a popular form, since from the tenth century bronze versions were also made in eastern Persia. The necks of both types of glass flask were often cut with vertical facets so as to give a polygonal section. Yet another form of flask has a tall, slender, 144 straight neck on a globular body, with or without an added foot-ring. In some cases, more particularly in the smaller vessels such as toilet bottles, the whole shape of the vessel was obtained by facet cutting 142 and slicing. In such cases the rough form may first have been mould-blown.

A distinctive form of jug or ewer was a legacy from the Sasanian metalworkers, who developed it from a classical prototype. This has a pear-shaped body surmounted by a 'beak'-shaped mouth; the handle, attached to the back of the mouth and the lower part of the body, is in the form of a reversed L. The upper part of the handle is provided with a vertical thumb-piece. This form of ewer, familiar in rock-crystal as well as in glass, inspired some of the finest examples of relief carved decoration. One of the two examples in the British Museum is incised 143 with hatchings – possibly an attempt to simulate honeycomb faceting – and stylised flowers. In the other, a bird, highly stylised, is introduced as an ornamental motif.

Much of the incised decoration is rather summarily drawn; and more often than not the incised line, U or V in section, is left unpolished. Relief cutting, however, demanded considerably more skill, since in this technique the area surrounding the decorative elements was carved back to the ground, thus leaving the former in relief. The edges of the relief were cut either vertically or in a slanting or bevel cut. A popular form of decoration was the palmette, both whole and split, 146 which, combined with the continuous stem or stalk, was to become the arabesque, most typical of Islamic decorative motifs. Such was the fascination of these vegetal elements that even in the delineation of 145 creatures, parts of the body may terminate in a split palmette. Relief compositions are usually defined by raised bands, horizontal or arranged in festoons or arcades, and designed to enhance the form of the vessel.

The glass used in relief cutting is invariably transparent and colourless, with a faint yellowish tinge. Quite exceptional is a bowl of opaque turquoise glass in the Treasury of San Marco in Venice. The rim of this 147 famous vessel is mounted with Byzantine gold plaques, enamelled

141 TOP *Left*: the form of this flask of almost colourless glass was adopted by the metalworkers of Khurasan in the 10th century. The decoration consists of almond-shaped drops around the shoulder, and arcades below. The relief-carved effect is further emphasised by the vertical cutting of the edges of the decorative elements. *Right*: the decoration on this flask was inspired by a Sasanian type in which the circles and the bosses within them are in relief; in this Islamic version, the decoration is in a single plane and is defined by the rather broad linear grooves which add to the illusion of relief carving. There are patches of iridescence on the surface. Both flasks were made in Persia, 8th–9th century A D. H. of left-hand flask 15.2 cm.

142 CENTRE *Left*: this little bottle was probably intended for scent. Of colourless glass, it was probably blown into a mould in order to produce the square section of the body. The neck was then carved with hexagonal facets, and two opposite sides of the body carved in relief with two horizontal pointed ovals and the other two sides with a vertical pointed oval. The matt surface is possibly the result of abrasion during cleaning. *Right*: this small green glass flask is an example of the way in which the actual form of a vessel could be created by carving. It was probably free-blown and the octagonal faceting of both neck and body then carved on the wheel. Stepped horizontal faceting articulates the shoulder, and raised arcades on the side provide the modest decoration of the main field. Both made in Persia, 8th–9th century A D. H. of green flask 8.7 cm.

143 BOTTOM Two ewers of colourless glass with a slight yellowish tinge. The smaller is lightly incised with panels of hatching between bands of stylised flowers. The larger ewer has a bird between two diamond figures within larger ovals. The decoration of both ewers is confined to the front field of the body and is defined by a framing band on either side of the handle. This is a feature of all the known decorated glass ewers of this type, including the famous rock-crystal ewers of early Fatimid Egypt. Both made in Persia, 8th–10th century A D. H. of taller ewer 19.3 cm.

144 RIGHT Two flasks with linear decoration and faceting carried out on the wheel. That on the left was found in Persia, where it was probably made about the 10th century. Possibly intended for rose-water, the shape came into fashion in Persia at that time. The mallet-shaped flask was made in Syria or Egypt, 9th–10th century A D. H. of mallet flask 23 cm.

145 BELOW, LEFT The art of cutting glass in relief in the Islamic world seems to have originated in Persia or Mesopotamia, where there was already a well-established tradition of hardstone carving in the late Sasanian period. In this goblet, the glass, where cut back to the ground, is very thin and its carving must have been a delicate operation. Between raised horizontal bands are three birds, their wings in the form of split palmettes. Found and probably made in Persia, 9th–10th century A D. H. 10.1 cm.

146 BELOW, RIGHT Another example of relief-cut glass, with an unusual bluish tinge. Whole palmettes in trilobed arcades and paired split palmettes in the spandrels show how adept the artist was in suiting the composition to the curving surface of the bowl. Found and probably made in Persia, 9th–10th century A D. H. 9.2 cm.

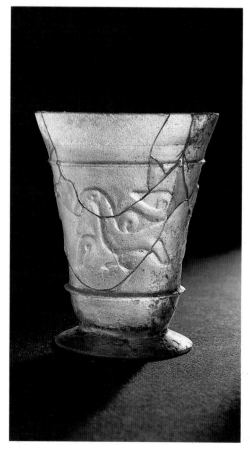

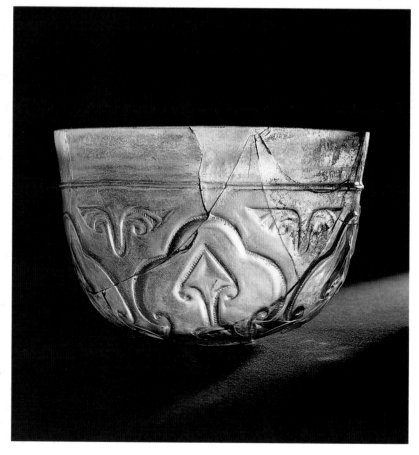

147 Opaque turquoise glass bowl, each of its five lobes carved in relief with a running hare. On the base is inscribed in relief in Kufic characters 'Khurasan', the name given in the medieval period to the region corresponding to eastern Iran and western Afghanistan. There have been several attempts, none satisfactory, to explain this enigmatic inscription: one that the bowl was made in Khurasan, and another that since Khurasan was the main source of turquoise this inscription would be taken as an indication that the bowl was made from the mineral. Opaque turquoise glass was rarely used in the early Islamic period. The bowl is probably Egyptian work of the first half of the 10th century AD: the style of decoration and of the inscribed Kufic characters can be closely paralleled in Egyptian cut glass and rock crystal of this period. The metal mounts consist of Byzantine gold plaques of the late 10th century on the inside, and Byzantine enamelled plaques of the 11th century combined with silver-gilt plaques with filigree work set with cabochons on the outside – these last probably dating from the 15th century. Venice, Treasury of San Marco. H. 6 cm.

and chased, as well as jewelled silver-gilt plaques of Western origin. The glass itself is carved in relief with running hares, each set within framing bands, and is Egyptian work of the tenth century. Glass of this colour is rare, but another example of certain Egyptian origin is a glass coin-weight of the Fatimid caliph al-'Aziz, who ruled in Egypt from 975 to 996.

A further development of relief carving was the introduction of colour by means of an overlay of transparent green or blue glass on the colourless body of the vessel. The decorative elements were then carved back to the colourless ground, leaving the composition in coloured relief. The technique is that of cameo glass practised in the Mediterranean region in the first century AD (see Chapter 2). Such pieces are rare in the Islamic world, but it seems that the technique was practised in both Persia and Egypt.

As far as we know, hollow and relief cutting was carried out by means of the bow drill. This consisted of a fixed spindle to which were attached the appropriate discs – a fine cutting edge for incised work and a broader edge for grinding. The drill was rotated by the backwards and forwards movement of the bow while the glass was held against the wheel, which was provided with the necessary abrasive. The final polishing was also carried out on the wheel.

Relief-cut vessels were costly rarities demanding highly specialised skills. Far easier to produce were moulded vessels. Blowing the gather into a mould of metal or pottery made mass production possible; and it is likely that such moulded vessels were a substitute for the more expensive cut glass. Thus honeycomb moulding was clearly inspired by cut glass, although it naturally lacks the sharp definition of the latter. Other forms of moulded decoration consisted of rows of rings

148

Figs 99–104

149

157

148 OPPOSITE The technique of cameo glass was practised in both Persia and Egypt. In this example, a rabbit is carved in a green overlay on two sides of the body of the flask, while a reversed stylised lily is carved on the colourless glass of the body in each of the two spaces between. Although the flask was found in Persia, it may be of Egyptian origin, since the rabbit is a motif found on other relief-cut vessels known to be of Egyptian origin, the finest of which is the opaque turquoise bowl in Pl. 147. H. 15 cm.

149 TOP Moulded vessels such as these two small jars were probably a cheap substitute for cut glass. To obtain the relief decoration, the vessel was blown into a two-part mould. The green glass jar is decorated with relief discs, a form of decoration used earlier by the Sasanian glass-carvers. It was made in Egypt in the 9th–10th century AD. The little unguent jar of colourless glass is of similar date but from Persia. Both the base and the sides are decorated with an overall composition of a four-petalled rosette within a five-pointed star; the points of the latter extend into the side which is decorated with five diamonds, each with a central depression. H. of green jar 7.9 cm.

150 In this small toilet flask of green glass the decoration is confined to crossing vertical and spiral ribs. Plain ribs, generally vertical, are a common mode of decoration; crossing ribs, however, are rare. Egypt, 9th–10th century AD. L. 16 cm.

or discs in relief, a type of decoration also used by the Sasanian glass-cutters, and vertical or spiral ribs, which had been a common feature of Roman glass. In a few rare pieces vertical and spiral ribs are combined to great effect; this required the use of two successive moulds.

Quite elaborate decorated moulds could be used. The body of a bell-shaped flask in the British Museum is moulded with a rather dense frieze of interlocking floral elements; and a tiny jar is decorated on the base with a rosette which is developed on the side into a star pattern. Simpler patterns consisted of plain stems formed into volutes.

Another method of manipulating the surface of the glass was the use of metal tongs with which designs could be impressed into the glass; one face of the tong might bear the negative design while the other remained blank, or one face might be negative and the other positive. The technique seems to have been used only in the Islamic world. This stamped decoration could be satisfactorily applied only to open vessels such as straight-sided bowls and beakers intended for daily use. Stamped designs usually consisted of rectangles or roundels containing simple geometric designs, or the name of Allah or good wishes to the owner rendered in Kufic, the characteristic Arabic script in this period. A bowl in the Islamic Museum, Berlin, is stamped with a roundel bearing a Kufic inscription stating that 'it [the bowl] was made in Misr' (Misr is the Arabic name both of Cairo and of Egypt, but in this context Cairo was probably intended). Judging from the great number of examples found at Fustat, stamped decoration was a speciality of the Egyptian glassmakers.

Yet another method employed for surface decoration was the application of trails of glass threads to form handles or embellishments, a common practice in Roman as well as in Sasanian glass. An extension of this technique was that of modelling. In Syria, for example, realistic figures of pack animals loaded with a large container were modelled in glass.

In this early period, then, the glasshouses seem to have been preoccupied with surface manipulation and less inclined to exploit polychrome decoration, which was to be the principal feature of the second period. Nevertheless, there was a revival of the art of mosaic glass, which had been a notable achievement of Hellenistic and Roman glassmakers. Islamic examples of glass mosaic tilework and a few small fragmentary bowls were found in the excavations at Samarra. The method was that of Roman mosaic glass. Canes of variously coloured threads were bound together, fused and then sliced to form 'beads' which were then placed on a plate in a decorative arrangement and fused before being slumped over a form. Finally, both interior and exterior surfaces were smoothed and polished on the wheel.

Another technique was that of gold-glass, in which the design was rendered in gold leaf and then 'sandwiched' between two layers of glass. As we saw in Chapter 1, the technique may have originated in the eastern Mediterranean before the third century BC but continued into the fourth century AD in Rome and the Rhineland (Chapter 2), to be revived some 500 years later in the Islamic world. It is only recently that a few Islamic examples, mostly fragmentary, have been found. Three fragments were recovered from excavations at Antioch; and

151 OPPOSITE, ABOVE LEFT This bottle of greenish glass shows how the glassmaker could enliven a simple form by adding touches such as pinching the mouth into a floral form and introducing a bulb into the neck. The moulded decoration is simple, consisting of broad volutes. Persia, 10th–11th century AD. H. 15 cm.

152 OPPOSITE, ABOVE RIGHT Bell-shaped flask of colourless glass which appears yellow owing to interior weathering. The main field is decorated with a dense composition of palmettes arranged in swags with foliate forms in the spaces between. This style of decoration is reminiscent of the so-called bevelled style which originated in the stucco work at Samarra, Mesopotamia, in the 9th century AD and was introduced into Persia and Egypt. The decoration is purely linear, each element being separated from its neighbour by a grooved line, bevelled in section, thus leaving no vacant background. Persia, 9th–10th century AD.

153 OPPOSITE, BELOW LEFT This figure of a pack animal with a pot roped to its back is an example of the glassmaker's skill as modeller. Such models seem to have been a speciality of the glasshouses of Syria. The pot was first free-blown and the animal and trappings added. The glass is green, but almost entirely covered by a brownish enamel-like weathering. Syria, 8th–9th century AD. H. 12.2 cm.

154 OPPOSITE, BELOW RIGHT In the early Islamic period glass lamps were usually of conical form, so that they could be inserted into a metal candelabrum. Another type was a straight-sided bowl with a candle-holder set in the middle of the interior. From this developed the hanging lamp, of which this is an example: in the bottom of the interior is a tubular candle-holder. With its wide flaring mouth and suspension handles, it anticipates the great enamelled and gold-painted glass mosque lamps of Syria and Egypt in the Mamluk period. Another example even closer to the Mamluk mosque lamp was recovered from the glass cargo of the Serçe Liman shipwreck and is therefore of the early 11th century AD (Bodrum Museum, Turkey). The lamp illustrated here is earlier, probably 9th–10th century, and of Persian origin. H. 14.2 cm.

155 Bottle with sandwich gold decoration. The neck is facet-cut and the walls of the body are double with the gold and blue painted decoration sandwiched in between. On the base is a dove in silver. The process is that of Roman gold-glass, but in the Islamic examples the gold was applied in suspension rather than in leaf form: the introduction of the blue dots is not known in Roman gold-glass. On the evidence of style, the bottle was probably made in Syria in the 9th–10th century A D. H. 15 cm.

156 A rare example of Islamic mosaic glass. Fragments of mosaic tiles were found at Samarra in Mesopotamia and also at Antioch in Syria; bowls such as this are most likely to have been made at Samarra or some other centre in Mesopotamia; 9th century A D. D. 7.4 cm.

judging from the homogeneity of the whole group, Syria seems the most likely place of manufacture. A novel feature in some of these Islamic examples is the introduction of blue enamelled dots. In a bowl in the David Collection, Copenhagen, there is a line of pseudo-Kufic punctuated by blue dots in the style of Qur'ans of the ninth and tenth centuries, where coloured dots indicate the vowels. The style of decoration also supports a ninth- to tenth-century date for the group. Possibly contemporary with these Islamic pieces are glass wall tiles rendered in the same 'sandwich' technique. These are decorated in gold leaf with crosses composed of triangles and squares of varying sizes laid on a ground of black mastic. Some of these tiles have been found in Syria, where they were associated with Christian churches and are thought to be of Byzantine origin (see Chapter 5). The existence of the Islamic examples, however, might equally suggest local production.

A technique of decoration that appears to be unique to Islamic glass

189

157 An example of the lustre-painted glass of Fatimid Egypt, here combined with moulded decoration. The base is moulded with a triangle within a roundel of tiny circles, from which is developed honeycomb decoration on the side wall of the bowl. The lustre-painted frieze below the rim consists of five cartouches formed of interlacing bands in each of which is an imitation Kufic character with foliate terminals. Egypt, 11th century. H. 10.7 cm.

is lustre painting. Many will be familiar with pottery in which the decoration is executed in a film of metallic lustre. The technique was applied to glazed pottery in Mesopotamia in the ninth century AD, but it had already been used on glass in the second half of the eighth. The method consists in painting on the glaze or glass in various combinations of sulphur, silver oxide and copper oxide in a medium of vinegar. The vessel is then placed in a reducing kiln, after which the painted decoration emerges as a yellow stain with a lustrous glitter. By using other metallic oxides it is possible to produce a variety of tones: polychrome lustre was used to great effect in the earliest lustred pieces, but by the tenth century it was replaced by monochrome lustre. Credit for its discovery must almost certainly be given to the glassmakers of Cairo, perhaps as early as the sixth or seventh century AD, and a goblet bowl found at Fustat bears a dedication to the governor of Egypt in 772. There is evidence, too, that lustre-painted glass was produced in Syria.

Among the finds from Fustat are vessels, often of manganese-coloured glass, with the partial remains of decoration executed in a greyish-white substance. This paint pigment, being unfired, does not adhere firmly to the surface of the glass, and this accounts for the fragmentary nature of the decoration, which was usually restricted to simple geometric designs. The pieces decorated in this way are not impressive, but they represent an attempt at painting on glass in a medium other than the demanding technique of lustre.

157

Islamic glass
12TH–15TH CENTURIES

Little is known about the glass industry in Persia and Mesopotamia in this second period; but Syria and Egypt continued production. These centuries saw many changes in the Islamic world. In the Mediterranean, sea-borne trade was falling into the hands of the powerful city-states of Italy, such as Pisa, Genoa and Venice. The Seljuq Turks and their successors, having secured Persia and Mesopotamia, conquered Syria from the Fatimid caliphs of Egypt and then Anatolia from the Byzantine emperor, while for two hundred years the Crusaders confronted the Muslims in Syria. The Latin kingdom of Jerusalem – the Outremer of medieval literature – was annihilated by the Mamluk sultans who ruled both Syria and Egypt. The decline of Mamluk power was due to the intrusion in the Near East first of the Mongols and then of Timur; and the final blow was dealt by the Ottoman Turks who conquered the Mamluk territories in 1516. However, this was far from being a period of economic decline; and the growth of urban centres increased the demand for luxury goods. The glass industry shared in this prosperity, and the glasswares of Syria and Egypt found their way to Europe and even to the Far East.

New forms and new techniques as well as new styles of decoration were introduced during this period. In particular, polychrome effects were now preferred to manipulation of the surface. Thus, on present evidence, wheel-cut glass was no longer in vogue, with one possible exception which calls for some discussion here. This is the group of so-called Hedwig glasses which has been the subject of controversy for more than a century. There are thirteen intact examples. The features common to the group are the 'bucket' form with the side wall rising more or less outwards from a foot-ring; the height, which ranges between 8 cm (3 in) and 14.7 cm (5¾ in); the glass, which is uniformly colourless with tinges varying from smoky topaz to yellowish green; and a distinctive style of carving. Moreover, eleven of the thirteen glasses share common iconographic elements, namely, the lion, the griffin and the eagle with outstretched wings, all presented heraldically; the remaining five glasses are decorated with palmettes or crescent designs. The surface of the exceptionally thick glass is carved back in a series of facets to a considerable depth from just below the rim to a little way above the base, leaving the composition in high relief. The surface of the relief elements tends to be slightly concave; and details such as fur, feathers and leaf veinings are incised.

Tradition has associated three of the glasses with St Hedwig, who died in 1238 and was canonised in 1267. The wife of Henry, Duke of Silesia and Poland, she led a life of exemplary piety and care of the poor, founding religious houses and a hospital. Legend has it that her husband, in his concern for her health, which he believed to be endangered by her abstinence from wine, came one day while she was at her meal. On examining the glass which she had just filled with water, he found to his astonishment that its contents were turned to wine. Three of the glasses are by tradition claimed to have been the receptacle used on the occasion of this miraculous transformation; and the designation of 'Hedwig glass' has been extended to the other ten. All are in public or ecclesiastical possession in Europe. Six, in Belgium,

158,159 Two views of one of the finest of the so-called Hedwig glasses. In size it is exceeded only by that in the Rijksmuseum, Amsterdam. Like all the other Hedwig glasses, the vessel is of bucket form. The ring foot has been broken away at three points, perhaps when a metal mount was forcibly removed. There is a pronounced pontil-mark on the concave base. The relief-cut decoration consists of an eagle with outstretched wings (OPPOSITE), flanked by a lion (BELOW) and a winged griffin which are separated at the back by a 'tree of life' composed of paired half-palmettes, one above the other. The ground has been sliced in a series of irregular facets, the top and bottom of the side wall retaining the original thickness of the glass. The profiles of the decorative elements are either cut vertically or bevelled. Inner details such as the lion's mane and the wing feathers of the eagle and griffin were incised with a smaller and narrower wheel. Byzantine or Islamic Near East, or southern Italy, 12th century. H. 14 cm.

158
159

Germany and Poland, can be traced back to the early thirteenth century. Fragments, too, of undoubted Hedwig glasses have been found in archaeological excavations at Pistoia in Tuscany and at Novogrudok in Byelorussia. The Novogrudok fragment is datable to the second half of the twelfth century and that from Pistoia to the twelfth or thirteenth century. Fragments have also been found in recent excavations in Germany: in the remains of Weinsberg Castle, Weibertreu, and on the site of the Castle of the Welfs in Göttingen.

There is no general agreement on the date and place of origin of the Hedwig glasses. Some scholars favour an Egyptian origin, relating them to the relief-cut glass of Persia and Egypt. Ascribing them to Egypt, they have dated them variously between the tenth and twelfth centuries. On the basis of the tradition of the miracle of St Hedwig, however, they cannot be much earlier than the twelfth century. The relationship with Islamic relief-cut glass is open to question, since there is no surviving Islamic relief-cut glass dating from as late as the twelfth century. Neither the 'bucket' shape nor the distinctive tinge occur in Islamic glass; and not a single fragment that can be associated with the Hedwig glasses has turned up in the Islamic world. The particular style of cutting – the high relief and the faceting of the ground – is also unknown. The decoration, too, is hard to parallel in Islamic art, for although individual elements such as the lion, griffin and eagle with outstretched wings and the various forms of the palmette may ultimately be derived from Islamic prototypes, their treatment and presentation do not entirely conform to the canons of Islamic art. Other scholars, pointing to Byzantine parallels for iconography and style, have sought a Byzantine origin in either the tenth or the twelfth century; but no glass remotely resembling this type has yet come to light in Byzantine lands.

There remains, however, a third possibility. In order to account for the generally admitted Islamic elements, an origin should be sought in a region open to, although outside, the mainstream of Islamic art. Sicily and South Italy under the Normans and Hohenstaufen would provide just such a milieu. From the eleventh to the early thirteenth century, Islamic art exercised a powerful influence on the architecture and the decorative arts of those regions. Muslim ivory-carvers worked alongside their Christian confrères in an undetermined centre in South Italy in the eleventh century; and a predominantly Muslim industry of painted ivories was also active in Sicily in the twelfth and early thirteenth centuries, supplying the needs of the Christians as much as those of the dwindling Muslim population. The Romanesque stone sculpture of these regions in its turn absorbed many Islamic themes, and perhaps the sculptured lion, eagle and griffin seen on the exteriors and interiors of the churches of south Italy might explain the figural elements of the Hedwig glasses. Admittedly there is no evidence of a glass industry in these regions, but it is now known that hardstone carving – and more particularly cameo cutting – was carried out for the court of the emperor Frederick II, and this could have favoured the development of a school of glass-cutters. No doubt other theories of the origin of the Hedwig glasses will be offered, and perhaps one day evidence will be found that will provide the key; but until then they must remain a fascinating enigma.

Among the new shapes that were developed in Syria and Egypt

160 Although opaque coloured glass was often used to create combed and marvered decoration on translucent glass, it seems to have been used only rarely for a complete vessel, like this handled jug. The relief-cut bowl in the Treasury of San Marco, Venice (Pl.147), which is Egyptian work of the 10th century A D, is of thick opaque turquoise glass. The glass of this jug, however, is thin and slightly translucent when held up to a bright light: it may have been intended as a substitute for porcelain. The shape is also found in the pottery of Persia, Syria and Egypt in the 12th–13th century, and this jug was probably made in Syria at about the same period. H. 11 cm.

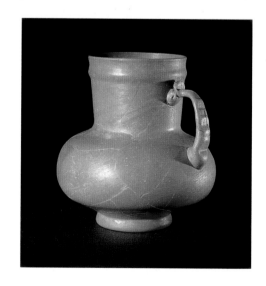

161 ABOVE, LEFT The ring body of this sprinkler of blue glass was made by flattening and then piercing the bulb. The trailed band of glass on the inside edge of the ring was intended to conceal any malformation that may have occurred when the bulb was pierced. While the zigzag trails at the base of the neck are decorative, the projection on the shoulder could serve as a thumb-piece. The high outsplayed foot, fashioned separately, became common in the 12th century. Syria, 12th–13th century. H. 25 cm.

162 ABOVE, RIGHT Combed decoration was common in Syria and Egypt in the early Islamic centuries and throughout the medieval period. This form of flask became the standard type of sprinkler in both glass and metal in Ottoman Turkey and in Persia as late as the 19th century. The indented trails at the base of the neck are the fantasy of the glassmaker. Made in Syria, 12th–13th century, and said to have been found at Adana in Anatolia. H. 20 cm.

during this second period of Islamic glass was the sprinkler. This was a flask with a long neck, narrowing to the tip, which acted as a dropper. A typical form has a globular body, slightly flattened so as to render it oval in section for ease of handling. An example in the British Museum is of transparent blue glass popular in this period. Also in the British Museum and of blue glass is another sprinkler, whose bulbous body has been flattened and then pierced to form an upright ring. The high outsplayed foot is also a novel feature common in this period. Both glasses are of Syrian origin and of the twelfth century.

Opaque glass is found both in white and in turquoise. The famous bowl of opaque turquoise glass in the Treasury of San Marco in Venice has already been described. Glass of this kind now becomes less rare: fragmentary vessels of opaque turquoise glass have been found at Hama in Syria; and it is to Syria, too, that a small glass tankard in the British Museum is attributed. The shape of the jug occurs in the glazed pottery of Persia and Syria in the twelfth to thirteenth century.

A technique which became popular in Egypt and Syria in the Ayyubid and Mamluk periods was that of combing and marvering. Threads of opaque glass were wrapped around the blown bubble usually of transparent green, blue or purple glass and then combed to form a series of parallel festoons. The technique is an ancient one and there are examples, mostly small bottles, from the early period. In the

163 This fragmentary flask must originally have had a tall neck. The decoration is executed in gold applied in suspension and then fired. In the upper frieze is a female dancer beside a pomegranate tree, holding a castanet in her left hand, and another female playing a harp. The middle frieze contains an inscription in Arabic cursive script, and the lower frieze an eagle with outstretched wings, between pomegranate trees. The inscription is in the name of the Seljuq Atabeg 'Imad al-Din Zangi, ruler of Mosul from 1127 and of northern Syria from 1130 until his death in 1146. The style of decoration is that of the Seljuq art of Anatolia. Syria, 12th century. W. 15.7 cm.

medieval period, however, it was used in the decoration of larger vessels, such as long-necked flasks and open bowls. Sometimes threads of several colours were used, such as in a bottle of dark purple glass, octagonal in section, where the combed decoration consists of opaque turquoise, white and red threads. Other examples, principally open vessels such as bowls, are decorated with vertical ribbings which heighten the effect of the combed patterns.

Lustre painting, on present evidence, ceased to be practised after the eleventh century and was replaced by gold painting. The technique should not be confused with that of the earlier gilded glass, in which gold leaf was sandwiched between two layers of glass. In the new technique gold, probably in suspension, was applied to the glass surface and then fired at a low temperature, producing a gold film barely perceptible to the touch. It is not known whether the technique was first used in Syria or in Egypt. An important example in the British Museum, however, can be dated to the first half of the twelfth century 163 since it bears a dedicatory inscription to 'Imad al-Din Zangi who was ruling in northern Syria at that time. Other fragments have been found in that region, so we may assume that some of these gold-painted vessels were made in Syria. In all cases the inner details of the decoration are scratched through with the needle.

Gold painting on glass was already being practised by Byzantine glassmakers who painted in gold or gold and polychrome enamels. The finest example is the silver-mounted glass bowl in the treasury of San Marco, Venice, which is described in Chapter 5. It now seems 187 generally agreed that this bowl is of the tenth to the eleventh century. Other examples, found in Cyprus, north Russia and Dvin in Armenia, probably date from the twelfth century.

Enamelling combined with gilding on glass was introduced into the 164

Islamic world towards the end of the twelfth century. It has not been determined whether the Byzantine glassmakers played any part in this development. In the technique of enamelling, ground glass mixed with colouring material was applied to the glass surface and then fired at a low temperature. It was precisely this technique which was used for the decoration of the so-called *minai* pottery of Persia in the late twelfth to thirteenth century. Its use obviously came from the need to find a suitably fluid medium for painting. Cold painting, as we have seen, had proved unsatisfactory on account of its impermanence. The earliest essays in painting in enamels and gold seem to have been made in Syria – possibly at Raqqa – in the late twelfth century. Typical of the early products is the beaker with trailed foot-ring and slightly flaring mouth. Examples are decorated with an inscription band in gold paint above a broad band of closely packed pellets or grains of coloured enamels, usually white. One explanation of this decoration may be that the enamelled 'beads' were first suggested by the turquoise enamelled pellets placed by the Syrian glassmakers in the centre of prunts which were of the same colour as the vessel itself.

The principal centres of glass production in Syria in the thirteenth and fourteenth centuries were Aleppo and Damascus. European travellers as well as Muslim writers attest to the high quality of Aleppo glass and its export to all parts of the Muslim world and the Mediterranean. An early reference relates how glassmakers at a centre near Tyre – itself the most ancient glassmaking centre in Syria – removed themselves to the vicinity of Aleppo from where they sent their blown glass vessels to the city for gilding and enamelling. In 1260 Aleppo suffered terrible devastation at the hands of the Mongols, and the local industries are unlikely to have revived. References to the glass production of Damascus are mainly of the thirteenth-century. That city, too, was attacked by Mongol hordes in 1300 but seems to have recovered. The final blow came precisely a hundred years later when the great conqueror Timur, or Tamerlane as he is known in the West, captured Damascus and carried off many of its skilled craftsmen, including the glassmakers, to his capital at Samarqand.

There have been attempts to distinguish between the gold and enamelled glass vessels of Aleppo and those of Damascus by means of a classification based on stylistic differences. It has often been assumed that the greater part of Islamic gold-painted and enamelled glass was made in Syria. It is true that only one small group of glasses of indifferent quality, decorated in enamels but lacking gold painting, has been found only in Egypt and may therefore be of Egyptian manufacture. Yet the quantity of high-quality mosque lamps donated to Cairene mosques and the numerous fragments of enamelled and gilded glass found at Fustat make it hard to believe that there was no local industry to supply these needs and so avoid exposing such vulnerable objects to the hazards of the long haul from Syria. On our present evidence it is perhaps wiser to resist any attempt to attribute pieces to particular centres and rather to classify and develop a broad chronology based on datable objects.

A striking feature is the close relationship between the decoration of the gold-painted and enamelled glass and that of the contemporary metalwork inlaid with silver or gold in regard to the disposition of the compositions and to their content. Both in Egypt and in Syria in

164 An early example of enamel and gold-painted decoration. The beaker with flaring mouth and added foot-ring came into fashion in Syria and Egypt in the 12th century. A number of such beakers are decorated with fishes and eels, the outlines and inner details rendered in fine lines of red enamel and the interiors painted in gold. The subject was considered particularly appropriate for a drinking vessel. Syria, about 1250. H. 11 cm.

the Ayyubid and the Mamluk periods, the glassmakers as well as the metalworkers, stone- and wood-carvers and potters were able to draw on a common fund of themes and decorative designs.

We can observe this relationship in the glass pilgrim flask in the British Museum, which is among the finest of the enamelled and gold-painted pieces. The enamels comprise no less than eight colours, and the decoration is particularly dense but leaves no sense of surfeit. The beautiful arabesque set in a trilobed cartouche on the front side of the flask is similar to the arabesque on a marble basin in the Victoria and Albert Museum which was made at Hama in Syria in 1278. Surrounding this cartouche are gold-painted scrolls terminating in human and animal heads. This is a known theme in Islamic art and represents the *Waqwaq* or Talking Tree which, according to the Islamic version of the legend of Alexander the Great, the hero consulted in the course of his adventures. The same theme can be seen in the silver inlaid decoration of the magnificent brass basin in the Freer Gallery of Art, Washington DC, made for the Ayyubid sultan Najm al-Din who ruled in Damascus and Egypt between 1239 and 1249. The female musician and the youth holding a beaker in his hand are also stock figures of the period. More original are the two splendidly accoutred horsemen on the sides of the flask. Their thrusting spears and wind-blown mantles, the prey at their feet and the herons flying overhead all make for a vivid scene such as is only possible with a medium as fluid as enamel. On the back of the flask, rendered in gold, is a roundel containing long pointed leaves radiating from the centre, all within an eight-pointed star, not unlike the *shamsa* or sunburst which adorns the opening page of Qur'ans and other manuscripts.

The glass of gold-painted and enamelled vessels is not of striking quality. It has a greenish or light brownish tinge and a rather high bubble content, although there exist rare vessels of transparent blue glass and of opaque white glass imitating porcelain. The forms of gold-painted and enamelled vessels include bowls with foot-rings and long-stemmed bowls with outsplayed foot, vases and beakers. A few are direct copies of the forms of contemporary metalwork, such as the candlestick with straight outward-sloping side and the flat-bottomed large basin with straight side and everted rim.

Perhaps the most familiar form is that of the mosque lamp, many examples of which have survived thanks to their preservation by the religious institutions for which they were made. The earliest is a lamp dedicated by the Mamluk sultan Malik al-Nasir to the *madrasa* (religious college) he founded in Cairo at the end of the thirteenth century. The rudimentary form of the mosque lamp had already appeared in the early period, but the canonical type was developed in Syria towards the close of the thirteenth century. Its essentials are a tall outspreading neck on a body that slopes outwards and then turns into the base, which may be of either ring or splayed form. Three or more loop handles are applied to the upper part of the body, since the lamp is designed to be suspended in the sanctuary of the mosque. It is not clear whether it was illuminated within or whether it was merely an object of decoration. Perhaps rather it had a symbolic meaning, since the opaque enamels are best seen with exterior lighting. Arabic inscriptions in a large cursive script are prominently displayed on the neck and upper body and occasionally on the splayed foot. The

165, 166 Two views of a pilgrim flask, one of the most splendid of the Islamic enamelled and gold-painted glasses. Derived from a leather form, the pilgrim flask was often reproduced in pottery but this and one other example (Vienna, Kunsthistorisches Museum) are the only known versions in glass. With its superb decoration it can only have been intended for show. On the front (OPPOSITE) is an arabesque set in a trilobed cartouche surrounded by scrolls terminating in human and animal heads, while on each side (BELOW) is a horseman and a roundel, in this case containing a female figure playing the harp. Syria (possibly Aleppo), 1250–60. H. 23 cm.

167 OPPOSITE, ABOVE LEFT A mosque lamp found in Damascus. The Arabic inscription, rendered in the cursive script known as *naskh*, consists of the verse from the Chapter of Light in the Qur'an; it begins on the neck, where it is executed in blue against a multicoloured scrolling ground, and continues on the upper face of the body, in gold outlined in red and set in a blue ground. The decoration of the narrower bands and the underside of the body is painted in gold with red outlines. The gold painting, as so often, has largely disappeared. The round disc below each of the three suspension handles is inscribed with a dedication for the mosque of the mausoleum of the vizier Taqi al-Din. Syria or Egypt, about 1300. H. 24.7 cm.

168 OPPOSITE, ABOVE RIGHT According to the bold inscription on the body, this lamp was made for Saif al-Din Shaikhu'l-'Umari (d.1357), a prominent Mamluk official and powerful supporter of Sultan Hasan. The lamp was probably intended for the mosque, monastery (*khanqah*) and tomb which he built in Cairo between 1349 and 1356. The three roundels on the neck contain Shaikhu's blason, a cup, which indicates that he held the office of cup-bearer. Syria or Egypt, about 1350. H. 35 cm.

169 OPPOSITE, BELOW LEFT The gold painting and enamels of this mosque lamp are unusually well preserved. The inscription on the neck is the verse from the Chapter of Light. The gold inscription on the body is in the name of Saif al-Din Tuquztamur al-Hamawi (d. 1345), an important amir of Sultan Muhammad b. Qala'un. His heraldic shield, an eagle above the cup – the heraldic device of the cup-bearer – appears three times on the neck. Syria or Egypt, about 1330–45. H. 33 cm.

170 OPPOSITE, BELOW RIGHT Except for the roundels on the neck and underside of the body, each containing an arabesque, this lamp is decorated overall with lotus flowers and foliage; there is no trace of gold painting. Similar decoration occurs on a number of mosque lamps destined for the great *madrasa* built in Cairo by Sultan Hasan (reigned 1347–51 and 1354–61). Syria or Egypt, about 1350. H. 38 cm.

inscriptions almost always include, usually on the neck, a Qur'anic verse from the Chapter of Light: 'Allah is the Light of the heavens and the earth. The similitude of His Light is as a niche wherein is a lamp. The lamp is in a glass. The glass is as it were a shining star. . . .' Other inscriptions contain the name and titles of the sultan or dignitary who dedicated the lamp, and sometimes the donor's heraldic device is included in the decoration. No figural element, however, is allowed. Most of the surviving mosque lamps were made for Cairene mosques as donations from the ruling sultans or high officers of state; others have been found in mosques in Jerusalem and Damascus as well as in Konya in Anatolia and in Yemen.

There is a large group of gold-painted and enamelled glass vessels in which 'chinoiserie' motifs form a large part of the decoration. The advent of Mongol rulers in Persia and China at the close of the thirteenth century stimulated trade between east and west Asia; and the exchange of merchandise was accompanied by the exchange of artistic ideas. It was largely through the import of textiles and porcelain, more particularly blue-and-white, that Chinese motifs such as the cloud scroll, the lotus flower and the phoenix attracted the attention of artists and craftsmen in Persia and Mesopotamia, Syria, Egypt and Anatolia. Such 'chinoiseries' were introduced into the gold-painted and enamelled glass of Syria and Egypt from about 1285 until about 1400, when production ceased with Timur's forcible removal of the glassmakers to Samarqand. The decline of the industry was not, however, entirely due to this calamity, since mosque lamps made in the second half of the fourteenth century show a marked deterioration in quality. None can be attributed to the following century when they began to be supplied by foreign markets. An enamelled mosque lamp now in the Islamic Museum, Cairo, bears a dedicatory inscription to Sultan Qa'it Bay (1468–96) and with its un-Islamic decoration can only be the work of the glassmakers of Murano.

Islamic gold-painted and enamelled glass vessels were eagerly sought in the West. Some were brought back by the Crusaders. A goblet known as the 'Goblet of the Eight Priests', now in the Museum at Douai (France), and another, the so-called 'Cup of Charlemagne', a bequest to the Cathedral of Chartres in 1329, are among the earliest examples of Islamic gold-painted and enamelled glass, dating from about 1190 to 1200. Another goblet of about 1250 is the famous 'Luck of Edenhall', now in the Victoria and Albert Museum, which reached England in the Middle Ages and was there provided with a leather case thought to be work of the fourteenth or fifteenth century. A surprising number of fragments have also been found in the countries of Europe, including England; and vessels and even a mosque lamp have been found in China, no doubt having reached there in the medieval period.

171 ABOVE, LEFT The precise function of this footed bowl is not known, but a number of other examples have survived. Below the rim is an inscription in cursive Arabic script which repeats the word *al-'alim*, 'the learned', common as a title of the Mamluk sultans and high officers of state; this inscription is anonymous. The upper surface of the foot is decorated with phoenixes amid flowers and foliage, drawn rather naturalistically in enamelled red outline. This bowl was acquired in China, and it is possible that, like other gold-painted and enamelled Islamic glasses, it found its way there soon after it was made. Syria or Egypt, early 14th century. H. 29.3 cm.

172 ABOVE, RIGHT The early Islamic mallet-shaped flask underwent a transformation in the medieval period when the ring base was added. The main field of this flask is decorated with an overall design of paired herons among flowers, all in red outline, the buds painted in polychrome enamels. In the lower frieze is the figure of a feline creature walking to the right – a popular motif in the contemporary metalwork. Syria or Egypt, about 1330–40. H. 27.5 cm.

Later Islamic glass
16TH–19TH CENTURIES

In the sixteenth century the Islamic world was dominated by three powerful states, the Ottoman empire, the Safavid kingdom of Persia and the Mughal empire of northern and central India. Court patronage in all three stimulated the development of architecture and the arts, but the glass industry was not to share in this prosperity. If Timur settled the glassmakers of Damascus in Samarqand, there has survived no single trace of their work. The glasshouses of Syria and Egypt may have continued to supply local needs, but produced no fine ware. By the end of the fifteenth century, the glass of Murano was already supplying the imperial court at Istanbul with its luxury products more or less adapted to Ottoman taste. In the sixteenth century Venice was exporting mosque lamps which adhered to the traditional form but with *latticino* decoration. A novel form of lamp, also exported to Turkey, was the *cesendello*, a long cylindrical vessel with suspension chains resembling the sanctuary lamp. Towards the end of the seventeenth century Bohemia entered the Turkish market to the detriment of Venice, and there is evidence for the import of Spanish glass in the fifteenth and sixteenth centuries and again in the eighteenth.

That there was also glass production in Istanbul itself, however, is attested by the description of the celebrations which attended the circumcision of Sultan Murad III's sons in 1582 when the city's guilds paraded before the sultan. In the manuscript of the *Surname-i Humayun* in the Topkapi Sarayi Library, this description is accompanied by illustrations which include those of the guild of glaziers and of the glass bottle makers. While the glaziers are shown inserting pieces of coloured glass into stucco panels, the bottle makers are busily engaged around the glass-kiln in blowing long-necked flasks and vases. Such vessels were presumably for domestic use and, perhaps not surprisingly, none has survived.

In the late eighteenth century a factory was established at Beykoz on the Asiatic shore of the Bosphorus and produced glass with pretensions of quality, supplying the needs of Istanbul as well as the provinces. Its products were clearly inspired by the glass of Venice and Bohemia; characteristic is the use of opaline and the Venetian *vetro a fili*. Other factories were founded in the nineteenth century, but none can claim to have escaped dependence on foreign techniques and forms.

In Persia there is no evidence for the manufacture of glass following the Mongol conquests until the reign of Shah Abbas (1587–1628), when the art of glassblowing is said to have been taught by an Italian, presumably from Murano. According to the French jeweller and traveller Sir John Chardin, who was in Persia between 1666 and 1677, glass was made everywhere in Persia but that of Shiraz was the best,

173 Although there was a glassmakers' guild in Istanbul in the 16th century, it seems that the glass industry in the Ottoman period was largely confined to coloured window glass and unpretentious wares. It was not until the 19th century that a glass manufactory was established at Beykoz on the Bosphorus, where the glass products went under the name *cheshm-i-bulbul*, 'nightingale's eye'. This ewer shows the strong influence of Venetian glass on the Turkish glassmakers. It is made from hollow tubes of opaque and turquoise glass inset into a colourless matrix. Turkey (Beykoz), 19th century. H. 25.6 cm.

while that of Isfahan – the Safavid capital – was of poor quality because much of it was made from re-used glass. The industry must have flourished, since exports to India, Sumatra and Batavia are recorded in the seventeenth century. Examples of that date are hard to identify with certainty, but some idea of the forms can be gained from the glassware depicted in Persian and Mughal miniatures of the period. Moreover, the industry has continued, probably without interruption, to the present century with little or no change in style. There are many examples in public collections, few of which can be earlier than the nineteenth century. Ewers, sprinklers and vases are rendered with the grace of the baroque – possibly the contribution of Murano glass – and the favoured colours are blue and aubergine.

Glassmaking seems to have been unknown in India before the Mughal period but, as in Ottoman Turkey, there was too great a reliance on the imports of Venetian glass to encourage native enterprise. Nevertheless, Indian glassmakers seem to have mastered the techniques of cutting, enamelling and gilding. Much of the glass which has been attributed to Indian glasshouses is now considered to be of Western origin. While there are examples of the *narghileh* – the type of tobacco pipe favoured in India – which are of native workmanship, cut-glass versions were being made in England for export to India in the late eighteenth and nineteenth centuries. Another type of vessel that seems to have been made in India is the small square bottle, often of blue glass with gilded and enamelled decoration of flowers or human figures, and possibly inspired by the Dutch gin bottle.

174 Four typical examples of Persian glass production from the 17th to the 19th century. The earlier centre was at Isfahan, but it seems that the later pieces were made at Shiraz. There is a strong preference for coloured glass and 'rococo' shapes. While the yellow sprinkler follows the traditional form, the neck of the other sprinkler is drawn up into a graceful curve terminating in an elongated mouth resembling some exotic flower. Another feature of both is the spiral ribbing on the neck, obtained by the process known as 'wrything' (twisting). The ewer with curving spout, vertical neck and mouth for filling, but with no handle, was a popular form. In the two examples seen here the tips of the spout are fashioned in the form of flower petals. Persia (Shiraz), 19th century. H. of green sprinkler 35 cm.

175 LEFT Glass ewer imitating a form in brass with flattened piriform body and curved spout, common in the Indian subcontinent from the 16th century. The gold painting is skilfully applied on the translucent blue glass, and the design of poppies framed by acanthus leaves, arranged in a diaper pattern, is reminiscent of textiles. India, 18th century. H. 28 cm.

175 BELOW, LEFT Square bottle decorated in coloured enamels. Bottles such as this are thought by some to have been made in Holland on account of the resemblance of their shape to the Dutch gin bottle; however, an Indian origin is more likely. The quality of the glass is poor, and the painting follows the Persian style as it developed in India. It has been suggested that these bottles may have been made in Ahmedabad or Surat, where the Dutch had establishments. India, 18th century. H. 13.3 cm.

177 BELOW, RIGHT The gold-painted decoration of this *huqqa* base belongs to the period of the Mughal emperor Aurangzib (1658–1707). The output of glass in India was inconsiderable, owing to a preference for European products. Tobacco was introduced into India at the close of the 16th century, and *huqqa* bases were made in metal, jade and glass. India, early 18th century. H. 19.1 cm.

Chinese glass

In the decorative arts, the Chinese have excelled in bronze work, ceramics and lacquer and the carving of hardstones, notably jade. They learned to make glass late in comparison with western Asia and Egypt, and the art of blowing glass reached China only some five centuries after its discovery in the Near East. In China glass seems never to have elicited the same response as in the Roman Empire, the Islamic world and Europe. This lack of aesthetic appreciation resulted in a very particular approach and treatment: the Chinese makers used glass in order to simulate other materials, such as hardstones, or as a vehicle for pictorial presentation. Until the seventeenth century, when glass production was organised on a larger scale, vessels and objects were unpretentious, little attempt being made to exploit decorative techniques. The Chinese seem to have relied rather on the import of glass from the Roman Empire, Sasanian Persia and the Islamic world.

Glassmaking reached China towards the end of the Zhou period (c.1122–249 BC). 'Eye beads' of Western origin have been recovered from tombs of the fourth and third centuries BC. Other beads clearly made in imitation of those from the West were also found in these same tombs, and are presumed to have been made in China on account of their distinctive constituents, notably barium. These are, therefore, the earliest glass objects of Chinese origin. The art of casting in glass was mastered in the Han period (206 BC–AD 220), when ritual objects such as the *bi* and cicada and objects for personal adornment, including earrings, were moulded in opaque glass in imitation of the jade original. Glass was also used as an inlay for bronze belt hooks and bronze mirrors. Two small vessels in cast glass have been found in a tomb of the second century BC. One is a bowl and the other an eared cup, a typically Chinese form commonly found in lacquer of the period.

For glass vessels, the Chinese depended on imports from the West. When the discovery of glassblowing in the first century BC made mass production possible, Roman glass from Syria began to reach China as early as the third century AD, Sasanian glass from the late third to fourth century AD and Islamic glass from Persia and Syria up to the fifteenth century. These imports were transported either by sea or overland by the Silk Route, where fragments of Roman, Sasanian and Islamic glass have been found.

In Chinese literary tradition glass was first manufactured in China in the fifth century AD, when according to one account it was introduced from India overland along the Silk Route to the capital of the Wei dynasty in the province of Shanxi; according to another, it was brought by a Syrian glassmaker, travelling by sea, to Nanking, capital of the rival Liu Song dynasty. But since, as we have seen, glassmaking had been known in China from the late Chou period, it has generally been assumed that this refers to the technique of blowing. This assumption is confirmed by the earliest finds of 'native' blown glass in an archaeological context of AD 481. These comprise seven small and unpretentious vessels of no great quality, suggesting that they are early attempts at glassblowing. Their shapes are distinctively

178

178 In the Han period the Chinese made glass imitations of burial jades. The ritual object imitated in this opaque cast glass version is the *bi*, a flat ring with a hole in the centre. The decoration is in the form of grains and may be connected with the festivals of the sowing and the harvest. China, Han period (206 BC–AD 220). D. 9.4 cm.

179 Three small figures cast in green glass. *From left*: a standing Buddha, a figure of a small child, and a seated figure. Tang period (AD 618–906). H. of seated figure 4.3 cm.

Chinese and, unlike the soda-lime glass of the West, the glass has a high lead content. Whether glassblowing was in fact taught by an immigrant Syrian craftsman or, as has been recently proposed, by immigrant glassmakers from Transoxiana, has not been determined.

Since the establishment of the People's Republic of China in 1949, Chinese archaeologists have recovered a number of specimens of early Chinese blown glass up to and including Song period (960–1279). Most are of lead glass and more rarely of soda-lime – the characteristic material of Western glass. On this archaeological evidence, glassblowing seems to have been well established by the Sui period (581–618). Vessels up to the Song period are types that can be paralleled in Chinese ceramics. An example of blown glass of the Tang period (618–906) is a small bowl in the British Museum. Its shape is known in contemporary Tang ceramics and the glass has a high lead content. During the Tang period, the casting of glass continued to be practised: objects such as animals and human figures were cast in opaque glass. These and a small standing figure of the Buddha in the British Museum have the same constituents as the small bowl.

180

179

The vessels produced in China up to the Song period are small and were used as *objets d'art* or as reliquary bottles for burial in Buddhist pagodas. Locally produced lead glass, however, was found to be brittle and it seems that for domestic vessels the Chinese still preferred foreign imports.

Little is known about glass production in China under the Yuan (1280–1368) and the Ming dynasties (1368–1644). The few attributions of known pieces to this period have been much questioned. Perhaps, as in the earlier periods, foreign competition discouraged the development of a native industry, since in the fourteenth and fifteenth centuries the gold-painted and enamelled glass from Syria was sought after in China. Mosque lamps were imported at the order of the Muslim community; other forms of vessels, mostly decorated in 'chinoiserie' style, may well have been intended for a wider clientele.

It was not until the Qing dynasty (1644–1912) that the glass industry was revived as a result of imperial encouragement; for among the ateliers established in 1680 in the Peking palace under the patronage of the emperor Kangxi (1662–1722) was one devoted to the manufacture of glass, working exclusively for the palace. But in the eighteenth and nineteenth centuries the principal centre of glass manufacture was at

180 This small bowl of green glass is an early example of a Chinese blown vessel. Small globular bowls of this type have been found in tombs of the Sui (AD 581–618) and the Tang period (AD 618–906), and are also found in ceramics of the Tang period. 7th century. H. 5.5 cm.

181 Moulded glass vase: the red glass is partly opaque and partly translucent, and mottled with various shades of yellow. It is probably a product of the imperial glass factory set up in Beijing under the patronage of the emperor Kangxi (1662–1722), and is an example of the Chinese predilection for coloured glass. H. 16.2 cm.

182 Two opaque glass vases dating from the reign of the emperor Yongzheng (1723–36): the turquoise example bears his reign mark on the base. By this period the imperial factory had mastered most of the glassmaking techniques and had overcome the earlier tendency of the glass to crizzle. H. of yellow vase 10.8 cm.

Bo Shan in Shandong. Its craftsmen mastered the techniques of moulding, relief cutting and cameo carving, and the preparation of monochrome and variegated glass as well as painting in enamels. Some of the glass produced in the reign of Kangxi suffers from crizzling. By the time of Yongzheng (1723–35) this defect had been overcome. Transparent colourless glass was used only rarely, and glass vessels are mostly opaque in imitation of monochrome porcelain or of hardstones. Shapes are commonly those of ceramics. If they have the appearance of porcelain under the mask of glass, at their best they are superb achievements of technical skill.

Typical of Chinese ingenuity is the snuff bottle. Tobacco was introduced into China at the close of the sixteenth century and from the seventeenth century it was taken in the form of snuff. The snuff bottle of uniform size and shape, designed to fit into the hand, became an essential for every gentleman. It was provided with a stopper to which a spoon was attached. Snuff bottles were made of hardstones, such as jade and realgar, of porcelain and of glass in all its varieties, including imitations of hardstones and lacquer and incorporating cameo cutting and painted scenes. Snuff bottles of transparent glass are painted either on the outside or on the inside. Interior painting demanded patience and skill: the surface of the glass had first to be rendered matt by means of acid; the painting was then carried out with a slender wooden pen. Such snuff bottles were particularly popular in the reign of the emperor Daoguang (1821–50), and it is doubtful if any are earlier than the nineteenth century.

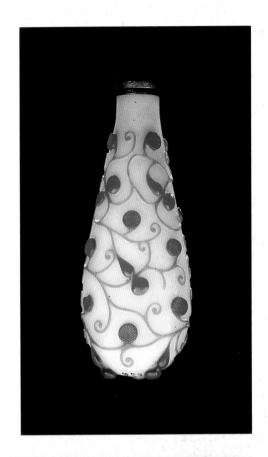

183 TOP RIGHT Glass snuff bottle with an overlay imitating cornelian. China, 19th century. H. 9 cm.

184 ABOVE, LEFT Glass snuff bottle painted on the inside with a cricket. China, 19th century. H. 5.7 cm.

185 ABOVE, RIGHT Frosted glass snuff bottle decorated on the front and back with floral designs on a gold ground. Blue trails on the narrow sides form handles. China, 19th century. H. 6 cm.

CHAPTER FIVE

Europe from the Middle Ages to the Industrial Revolution

Byzantium and medieval Europe
10TH–15TH CENTURIES

THE ROLE of Byzantium in the history of medieval glassmaking is still poorly documented and much disputed, though there can be little doubt that the products of the glassmakers of Constantinople, Greece and other parts of the Byzantine world in Asia Minor played an important role in both religious and secular art as well as in everyday life. By the end of the reign of the emperor Heraclius (610–41), the eastern Roman Empire, already being eroded by the new forces of Islam, had evolved into a distinctive, culturally heterogeneous, form of civilisation that was Christian and Greek-speaking – the civilisation that became known as Byzantine. For the next few centuries, its wealthy and efficiently governed lands were often under attack, though between 863 and the death of the Byzantine emperor Basil II (976–1025) a series of dramatic victories almost restored the frontiers of Byzantium to where they had been in the days of the Roman Empire. For another 150 years, especially during the brilliant reigns of Alexius I, John II and Manuel I, the illusion of Byzantine domination and wealth, with its patronage of the arts and learning, was maintained, but very few fine glass objects can be reliably associated with the Empire and its luxuriously endowed capital between the tenth century and 1204, when, after a long siege, Constantinople fell and was ravaged – not by the Infidel but by the military forces of the Fourth Crusade. The mainly French and German soldiery had been conveyed there in the fleets of Venice, the Empire's former vassal and now the emerging rival commercial and maritime power in the Mediterranean. Indeed, Venetians were in the vanguard of the looting and carried back home a large share of the spoils, including the many masterpieces that still adorn the Piazza and Basilica of San Marco.

A small group of extraordinarily fine cut-glass vessels, mostly mounted in silver-gilt (preserved in the Treasury of San Marco), may provide the most important insight into the finest achievements of Byzantine glassmakers, as many scholars believe. However, this

186 Two tall glasses of 'fantasy', both made in Venice: the taller, with the 'stepped' bowl, has a stem blown in the form of Punchinello, the famous character from the *Commedia dell'Arte*, later known in England as Punch; late 16th century. The other glass, which dates from about 1600, has a stem blown in the form of an owl. H. of Punchinello glass 30.5 cm.

For the making of complex objects, see pp.230–33, Figs 120–50.

187 Bowl of dark wine-red glass, with enamelled and gold-painted decoration, set in Byzantine silver-gilt mounts. Probably part of the Venetian booty seized during the sack of Constantinople by the Crusaders in 1204. Byzantine, probably 10th–11th centuries. H. 17 cm. Venice, Treasury of San Marco.

traditional interpretation is currently disputed by those who claim that their origin is much earlier and lies within the lands of the Sasanian empire (probably in modern Iraq or Iran) in the sixth to eighth centuries. Until new evidence resolves this controversy, these pieces – like the thirteen thick colourless glass beakers skilfully faceted and cut in high relief, the so-called Hedwig glasses (discussed in the preceding chapter) – will remain an enigma and will not be described here in case they give a false impression of the Byzantine contribution to medieval glassmaking. Certainly, the glassmakers of western Europe waited until the seventeenth century before they attempted to produce any form of cut (wheel-cut) glass and so there can be no disputing that – whether made in a Byzantine, Norman-Sicilian or an earlier Middle Eastern centre – the influence of this cut glass on European glassmaking was nil.

158–

In contrast, the most outstanding piece of Byzantine glass, about which there is general agreement, is an enamelled, dark wine-red, almost purple, glass bowl, delicately painted with figures from classical mythology. Also believed to have been part of the Venetian booty brought back to the Treasury of San Marco in 1204, this thin bowl has been afforded extra protection by the Byzantine silver-gilt mounts encircling the foot-rim and the neck, to which are attached the two openwork silver handles. Consequently, this masterpiece is now by far the best preserved of a small number of technically related works, all found within the Byzantine Empire and therefore all presumed to have a common origin – perhaps in some talented workshop within the capital, Constantinople. The enamelled colours used on this bowl include not only white and the subtle flesh-tones of the figures and profile heads but also red, yellow, greyish-blue and green. In addition, gold has been lavishly painted on and fired, not only to create a

187

background of intricate ornament but also within the figure-scenes to pick out such details as necklaces, headbands, a lance or a ceremonial staff, and similar accoutrements. Gold pseudo-Kufic lettering has been painted on to form a decorative band on the inner surface of the everted lip of the bowl and, again, around the foot-rim on the exterior. This kind of lighthearted imitation of Kufic seems to have been a special feature of the decorative arts in Constantinople under the new Macedonian dynasty of emperors (867–1056) and is one of the reasons why this glass bowl is now often dated as early as the tenth or eleventh century.

Furthermore, the way in which the bowl has been decorated would seem to be identical with the processes described by Theophilus, probably writing in Germany in the early twelfth century. In Book II, this monk, who may have been the metalworker Roger of Helmarshausen, describes the making of glass goblets which the Greeks (i.e. those living in the Byzantine empire) embellish with gold and silver:

. . . they take the gold, ground in a mill, which is used in books, and mix it with water – the same with silver. With it they make circles, and, in them, figures or animals or birds in varied work, and coat these with the very clear glass of which we have spoken above. Then they take the white, red and green glass, which are used for enamels, and carefully grind each one separately with water on a porphyry stone. With them, they paint small flowers and scrolls and other small things they want, in varied work, between the circles and scrolls, and a border around the rim. This, being moderately thick, they fire in a furnace in the above way . . . (*Theophilus: The Various Arts*, translated from the Latin by C. R. Dodwell, London 1961).

Unlike the beautifully preserved bowl in San Marco, the other specimens of this type have suffered from burial in the ground. The British Museum's bottle, for example, was originally a translucent purple glass that has become blackened by weathering, except in the base; and the gold-painted decoration has survived in only a few places, although it has left an almost complete blue-grey impression, revealing even the drawing of details (on the birds and animals) that were scribed with a point through the gold paint before the final firing. Because of the similarity with fragments found in a castle at Paphos that was destroyed in 1222, this bottle (along with several others) may have been made about the time of Theophilus's treatise. The artistic standard of the decoration of these pieces is high, even if it cannot rival the qualities of the slightly earlier San Marco bowl.

Less certain, however, is the date of the so-called Byzantine glass wall-tiles with gold cruciform decoration, a number of which are now scattered throughout collections in Europe and North America. In all these specimens the gold is well preserved because it was not painted and applied to the exterior surface. The glassmaker has taken gold leaf, cut it into triangles and small squares and, after placing them in position to form the cruciform pattern, has trapped them under a layer of hot clear glass. Confirmation that gold leaf was being used concurrently by 'the Greeks' can be found in the preceding passage of Theophilus's treatise, where he writes:

Taking gold leaf . . . they fashion from it the likeness of men or birds, or animals or foliage, and they apply them to the goblet with water in whatever

188 Bottle of translucent dark purple glass now darkened by weathering, with traces of muffle-fired gold-painted decoration (below). Byzantine, 12th century. H. 15.3 cm.

188

189

189 Wall-tile, with sandwich gold decoration, perhaps one of the many extant specimens thought to have been used to decorate a building in Maaret al-Nu'man, a cultural centre of ancient Syria. Byzantine, date uncertain (7th–8th or 11th–12th centuries). 9 cm square.

place they choose. This leaf ought to be somewhat thicker than usual. Then they take very clear glass, like crystal, which they make themselves, and which soon melts when it feels the heat of the fire [i.e. this specially prepared glass melts at a lower temperature than the glass being decorated] and they carefully grind it on a porphyry stone with water and lay it very thinly over the whole leaf with a paint-brush. When it is dry, they put it in the kiln . . . (Book II, section XIII).

If, as is widely believed, these tiles have a Byzantine origin, whether in the seventh to eighth or in the eleventh to twelfth centuries, then they not only illustrate an effective, albeit simple, use of gold leaf but they also reveal a knowledge of another Roman technique – the 'sandwich' gold glass technique – and, furthermore, an ability to adapt it to serve as architectural decoration. In the Islamic world, as we have seen, the practice was not to use gold leaf when gilding glass, although new evidence indicates that in the ninth and tenth centuries some glasshouses, perhaps in Syria, may also have revived the sandwich gold technique for a short period (see Chapter 4). However, in the main Islamic glass centres from the beginning of the twelfth to the end of the fourteenth centuries, the thickly enamelled ornament – on mosque lamps, bowls, basins and other large glass vessels – is almost always accompanied by a lavish application of painted gold, never gold leaf. Despite the inferiority of the glass itself with its numerous bubbles and amber or greenish cast, the results are spectacular and, throughout the Middle Ages, remained unrivalled, for it was not until the middle of the fifteenth century that Western Europe – in the pioneering glasshouses of the Venetian lagoon – was able to produce works of equivalent calibre, fired with richly enamelled and extravagantly gilded decoration. The Venetians, however, chose not to follow the Islamic method of gilding but to use gold leaf.

Figs 2

163–7

To what extent, therefore, did the Venetian glassmakers take over the technical expertise of the Islamic decorators of glass when political and economic circumstances brought an end to their industry in the late fourteenth century, as many writers have suggested? Or was the Venetian approach to enamelled and gilded decoration on glass more painterly, more in the manner of 'the Greeks' and, therefore, closer to the mythological scenes painted in the roundels on the Byzantine bowl that reposed in the heart of their city within the Treasury of San Marco? It seems that the Venetians were heirs to both traditions, but the answers – albeit very incomplete – lie in the events of the two centuries following the Sack of Constantinople in 1204 and, unfortunately, these have yet to be fully chronicled, though in recent years vital information found in the Venetian archives has helped to fill in some of the gaps and explain the phenomenal rise to supremacy of the Venetian luxury glass industry and the dominant position it occupied for so many centuries throughout Europe and the Eastern Mediterranean.

In laying the foundations of their great glass industry, the Venetians were unique in establishing strictly enforceable rules, regulating not only its members but the quality of its output. It was under state protection but also under state control. By 1268, the glassmakers of Venice were sufficiently well established to participate, along with craftsmen of other guilds, in the procession for the inauguration of the reign of the new Doge, and they appeared carrying 'water-bottles, and scent-flasks and other such graceful objects of glass' (according to the *Chronicle of Martino da Canale*). Three years later, the glassmakers' *Capitolare* was approved, laying down rules of conduct for the guild members but also creating for them a privileged position, prohibiting both the import of glass into Venice and the making of glass by any foreign glasshouse master (*padrone di fornace*). The rules governing the furnaces included a minimum of three working-holes to each furnace, a restriction on fuel (only willow or alder) and the maintenance of two watches every night – indeed, because of the fire hazard, the Grand Council of Venice decreed in 1292 the removal of all glasshouses from the city to the island of Murano – about an hour across the Lagoon in a rowing-boat. There, in relative isolation, the industry could be more efficiently nurtured and controlled. The *Capitolare* of 1271 had, for example, stipulated that the exporting of wares would take place every year only after the furnaces had closed down in August, and as early as 1282 the Venetian records indicate that glasses were being exported by German merchants. In this expanding export trade, the ships of the Venetian mercantile fleet played a crucial role, plying the Mediterranean and even venturing beyond Gibraltar to Flanders and England. Indeed, in 1399 there is confirmation that when two Venetian galleys were docked in the Port of London, glasses were among the goods being sold. Venice, the great trading centre between East and West, underwrote these long sea voyages which, even by 1500, were always estimated in weeks (about three weeks to Palermo, five weeks to Constantinople and nine weeks to Alexandria). Nevertheless, the Venetian glass industry, using a soda-lime formula, was dependent on vast cargoes of 'barilla', the alkali and main ingredient of soda-lime glass. 'Barilla', a soda ash with small percentages of lime, was obtained from the marine plants of certain salty marshes. Spanish 'barilla' from Alicante, regarded as the best in the Mediterranean, was probably much used in Venice but, from the beginning, stringent measures were taken by the Venetian authorities to prevent the use of inferior raw materials; for example, alum from Alexandria was forbidden by the edicts issued in 1306 and 1330 because its use lowered the quality of the glass – and hence the reputation of Venetian glass. During the last decades of the thirteenth century, edicts had been passed prohibiting the export of potash, broken glass and sand, stipulating that only the senior judges were to allocate the wood supplies and, most sinisterly, increasing the penalties to be imposed on glassmakers who wished to be reinstated after leaving Venice to work for others.

The end product of all this documented activity in Venice from the 1260s onwards was the creation of a finer glass, particularly for glass vessels, but what do they look like and to what extent do they reveal the influence of the Byzantine rather than the Islamic tradition? Little glass of this early period has survived; its chemical make-up may at first have been conditioned by the terms of the 1277 treaty between the Doge and the Prince of Antioch, in which there was provision for broken glass to be brought from the Near East for use as cullet in the glasshouses of Venice. The only type of glass specifically mentioned in the 1271 *Capitolare* are glass weights, bottles and beakers. Numerous clear glass fragments – mainly the long necks of bottles, the rims and sides of prunted or mould-blown beakers, together with their bases

189a Beaker of thin clear glass with small prunts forming a wide decorative band between two trails of glass thread. Found at Kerch in the Crimea, Ukraine, with a mixture of Mongolian coins, ranging between approximately 1313 and 1373. Formerly published as Islamic (Syria or Iran), but more probably European, 14th century. H. 9.4 cm.

189a

190 Medallions, mould-pressed using glass of many different kinds. *Top row, from left*: a bust of Christ; St John the Baptist; St Michael; and an equestrian rider with a falcon. *Bottom row, from left*: St Demetrius (with an inscription in Greek); the Seven Sleepers of Ephesus; Hercules (or Samson) and the lion. Venice, 13th century. D. of Christ medallion 3.5 cm.

with high kicks and pincered trailed-on foot-rims – were found not only in twelfth- to fourteenth-century contexts during the 1962 excavations on the island of Torcello (see Chapter 3) but also on the island of Murano (1975) and in Cividale del Friuli (1874 and 1959); however, few complete examples of these utilitarian vessels have yet been found, although pictorial versions survive, for example, in the frescoes at the Abbey of Pomposa and in Santo Stefano in Pinzolo/Trentino. Judging by these finds, there is little to suggest that the vessels were necessarily greatly superior to the best-quality glasses being produced in the decades around 1300 at a number of widely scattered glasshouses north of the Alps, particularly in France and Germany, and, indeed, in other parts of Italy and in Greece. Here, for example, in 1937 the remains of two glasshouses and their products were found in the Byzantine city of Corinth, which was sacked in 1147 by the Normans, who may have carried off the best glassmakers to Sicily. However, most recently, doubts have been cast on the validity of the early dating previously given to the Corinth finds and hence on the theory that they both represented the glass forms of the Byzantine world from the early eleventh to the mid-twelfth centuries and were probably the types that had a formative influence on the nascent Venetian glass industry of the late thirteenth century.

190 No such doubts exist about the thirteenth-century origin in Venice of a large homogeneous group of small coloured glass medallions and straight-sided plaques, nor of their direct links with the Byzantine world. Nearly 200 specimens have now been traced, many with a modern Venetian provenance, and some sixty or more different moulds – often with clear stylistic parallels in thirteenth-century Western art – were needed to produce the wide range of subjects depicted in relief. Although a few are secular, the majority have Christian religious subjects that, even when they contain markedly Byzantine features, would not have been out of place in Venice, a city where elements of the two strains – Greek Orthodox and Roman Latin – often met and mingled during this period. Thus, it is no surprise to

191 Knife-handle with elaborate moulded decoration, including six armorial shields relating to the family of Louis IX (reigned 1226–70) and a Latin inscription referring to a Frenchman, 'Jehan Deesenvil'. Found in 1981 in St Denis, north of Paris. L. 7.5 cm. Musée d'Art et d'Histoire de la Ville de Saint-Denis.

The line drawings opposite show the inscriptions on all sides of the knife-handle, and a section through it.

find on these medallions inscriptions in Greek as well as in Latin, or to find the images of saints who were especially venerated in the Byzantine world, like St Demetrius who was closely associated with Salonika (Thessaloniki). Indeed, the almost identical type of head and face has been used both for the early St Demetrius medallion and for the later, markedly Gothic, figure of St Michael killing the dragon, on a medallion which has been convincingly dated to the fourteenth century. The colours of these medallions include a translucent dark blue, an almost transparent yellowish-green, an opaque red and a black, whilst the unique, opaque light-blue medallion of St Michael bears traces of the original gold decoration.

These Venetian coloured reliefs in glass may not have been such isolated phenomena because, in 1981, the excavations taking place just north of Paris at St Denis (rue des Ursulines) revealed a medieval luxury object of exceptional interest: an opaque sky-blue glass knife-handle. Its surface decoration in relief, produced in a mould, consisted of six coats-of-arms alternating with four single fleurs-de-lys and a Latin inscription (now incomplete) but containing a French name, 'Jehan Deesenvil'. Although it is conjectured that he may have been a member of the local family, the Chevaliers d'Esanville (a village near St Denis), the heraldry of the six shields relates only to the family of the French king Louis IX (reigned 1226–70). A full and detailed interpretation of this elaborately moulded decoration has yet to be presented, but an origin before 1270, whether in Paris or in Venice (from whence it could have been ordered), is of great significance.

Finally, Venice possesses irrefutable – and unique – written evidence from the period 1280–1348 of the activities of 'painters of beakers' (*tintor de mojolis*). Three of these enamellers came to Venice from lands that were formerly within the Byzantine Empire; firstly, Gregorio da Napoli, a Greek from Morea (the region of southern Greece – the Peloponnese – in which Corinth lay), and, secondly, Bartolomeo and Donino da Zara (on the Dalmatian coast). There are also references by name to two others in this period, but they may have been Venetians: Zannus Totolus (*qui pingit mojollos*) and Petrus (*pictor*). Part of the output of these five named has convincingly been identified as the so-called 'Aldrevandin Group' of medieval drinking vessels – all beakers except for an armorial wine-glass with a shallow tazza-like bowl on a slender shaft-like stem and a high conical foot (dug up in Prague in many pieces in 1971) and two fragmentary shallow tazza-like bowls (London 1957 and Basle, Switzerland), both painted with figure-scenes (now very incomplete). All the pieces are of thin, clear glass, variously painted in enamelled colours with a combination of Latin inscriptions, Christian religious images, European secular scenes and Western European heraldry. The group takes its name from the celebrated beaker in the British Museum bearing the white-enamelled inscription: + MAGISTER . ALDREVANDIN . ME . FECI: (Master Aldrevandino made me). Not only is the family name, Aldrevandino, a Venetian one but there is recorded in 1331 a certain 'Aldrovandino, *fiolario*' (glassmaker) at Murano. This signed beaker – like the two unsigned beakers now in Frankfurt and in Chur, Switzerland – has never suffered from being buried but the other pieces in the group are fragmentary and often their decoration has been badly affected by acids in the soil. One cache of fragments dug up near St

191

192

151

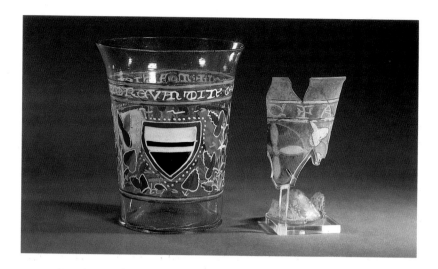

Paul's Cathedral in London in 1982 has the remains of six or seven beakers and, although incomplete, the inscriptions on two of them can be read as the signature of Bartolomeo – presumably the Bartolomeo da Zara mentioned in the documents – whilst those on two other fragmentary beakers found at Mainz (1976) and Tartu, Estonia (1988) seem to bear the signature of Petrus. Although there is still insufficient evidence to assign the glasses (or fragments) to different enamellers by name, nevertheless, within this large group two distinct subdivisions are discernible. The first has a more Islamic tapering form and all the enamel colours are painted exclusively on the outer surface (as on the fragmentary beaker found at Restormel Castle in Cornwall); the second type is more Western European in shape, but has no sign of gold decoration and the colours are partly on the inner and partly on the outer surfaces of the glass (as on the signed 'Aldrevandin' beaker). From the former group, the most compelling evidence came in 1982 when a fragmentary beaker bearing the enamelled and gilded coat-of-arms of the Scala family was found within their castle at Verona in an area that could be precisely dated between 1350 and 1364.

To receive the patronage of Europe's nobility and ruling families, the glassmakers of Murano had to compete not only with the traditional use of gold and silver plate but also with the fashion for Islamic enamelled glass – *verre de Damas* (as fourteenth-century French inventories often described it). They had not only to raise the purity of Venetian clear glass from the standard level of ordinary, plain functional vessels, but also to acquire the secrets of enamelling, gilding and artistic decoration in order to create a luxury commodity that would appeal to the courts of Europe. Even in this first attempt, the Venetians had a large measure of success, for the discoveries of recent years vividly demonstrate how widely these enamelled beakers travelled along the trade routes, either by sea or across the Alps and Germany, reaching as far as Ireland in the west, Sweden in the north, Palermo (Sicily) and Fustat (Egypt) in the south and the Caucasus in the east. Although none has yet been found in Venice itself, no other centre in medieval Europe had its 'painters of beakers', nor would the products of any other European glasshouses have carried the names of its craftsmen. For the first time in Europe, glasses were being made

192

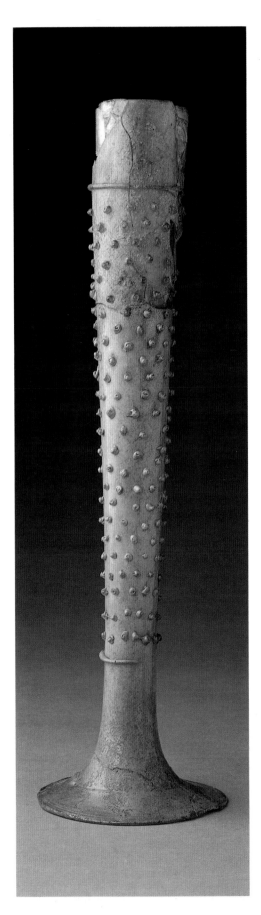

and signed – a clear indication of the sense of achievement – and the glasses of the 'Aldrevandin group' were Europe's first, if rather modest, step towards the production of glasses of individual artistic and technical merit. Little wonder, therefore, if Venice had to introduce penalties for those who deserted Murano.

Contemporary glasshouses in other parts of Italy, in France, the Low Countries and Germany, especially near the valleys of the Meuse and of the Rhine, were mainly centred near the great forests but, erroneously, their products have until recently tended to be dismissed as crude 'forest glass'. In this period, the vertically ribbed beaker but, more especially, the prunted beaker – universally popular in Italy, the former Yugoslavia, Switzerland and Germany – was often made of a thin, clear, almost colourless glass which, although neither entirely free of bubbles nor of a slight tinge of colour, usually had excellent proportions and finely manipulated applied details (such as foot-rims). As a form, the prunted beaker may have entered Europe from the Middle East (perhaps Iran) and, at present, the earliest datable finds are 189a from Italy. Fine glass bowls, flasks and, to a lesser extent, beakers were also being decorated with thin blue glass trails, often forming slightly haphazard geometric patterns, and were similarly very popular; they have been found in many parts of Europe, including Prague, the Rhineland and Winchester but also at Farfa (near Rome) and, more particularly, in southern France. Furthermore, the French developed from the late thirteenth and throughout the fourteenth century an elegant type of clear wine-glass on a tall slender stem. Although the bowl varies from a wide, shallow tazza-like form, as in the example found at Besançon, to a narrow tulip shape as on the famous 'verre des 193 Augustins' found in 1949 in Rouen among the wartime ruins of the church of that name, the proportions have a French Gothic quality – with the emphasis on the soaring, quasi-architectural, shaft of the stem. They can be seen standing on a white table in a miniature in the fourteenth-century illuminated *Bible historiée de Pierre Comestor* (Bibliothèque de la Faculté de Médecine, Montpellier, MS H.49). The numerous fragmentary finds from France suggest that from south to north they were mostly made of a thin, pure glass with only a pale greenish tint and there were almost as many variations to the form of the foot as to the bowl. However, some features were strictly regional: for example, the generally less exaggerated forms of the glasses made in the Argonne area of eastern France (near Verdun) were often decorated with extremely fine, mesh-like decoration in low relief produced by blowing into moulds of the highest quality.

Further east in Bohemia, where the silver mines were among the richest in Europe and brought exceptional prosperity and patronage, a similarly high-quality thin glass, sometimes almost colourless, was being made by the middle of the fourteenth century. Using a remarkably pure potash-lime-silica composition similar to that of the majority of northern European glasshouses, the Bohemian glassmakers created a range of some twenty different types of tablewares, of which the most dramatic innovation was undoubtedly the excessively tall, narrow, tapering flute, usually between 40 and 55 cm (16–21 in) high. 194 This slender form of glass, with its narrowing stem that curves imperceptibly to become the spreading foot, was usually decorated with a dense arrangement of tiny droplets or beads, rather than prunts. These Bohemian *Keulengläser*, as they are called, were occasionally made to look even more elegant by the application of milled trails, evenly spaced and gently spiralling.

The striving towards perfection and the impetus for imaginative innovations that characterised the decades around 1300 would seem to have deserted the glasshouses north of the Alps by the end of the fourteenth century; throughout the fifteenth and even into the sixteenth century there is little evidence that this fine colourless glass was being made, and even in France there is a dearth of good glass. Its place seems to be taken by a thicker form of pale glass ranging from a yellowish-brown to a dark green, especially in the Rhineland and Germany. Its crude decoration depends almost exclusively on trailing (often with quite elaborate tooled manipulation but without much finesse), on the simplest of mould-blown designs, and on the application of prunts – the latter even being added with virtuosity on the inside of the vessel. Perhaps in an attempt to give these tired old forms a new look, the glassmakers were increasingly tempted to resort to an excess of debased decorative features and, as a result, produced some of Europe's least attractive glasses, such as the late medieval *Stangengläser* embellished with 'claw motifs' reminiscent of the Frankish and Anglo-Saxon claw beakers of the fifth and sixth centuries AD. Even when the forms remain uncluttered, the beautiful and subtle proportions of the fourteenth-century Bohemian *Keulengläser* are not retained by the north German greenish versions of the second half of the fifteenth century, with their horizontal trails forming decorative rings around the glass. By the beginning of the sixteenth century the tall cylindrical *Stangengläser*, often encrusted with large obtrusive prunts, had become *de rigueur* in Germany and, together with the heavily prunted, thick beakers known as *Krautstrünke* and the single-handled cups known as *Scheuern*, tend to dominate the output of the

196

197a

197

195 Miniature from the 1425 copy of the famous manuscript *De Universo* by Rabanus Maurus, dating from 1023 and preserved at Monte Cassino, Italy. In this copy, ordered by Ludwig of the Palatinate, the miniaturist has omitted the lehr, or annealing chamber (at the top of the furnace), but has depicted a typical Rhenish double conical bottle (see Pl. 196). Rome, Vatican Library.

197 A B O V E , L E F T *Stangenglas* decorated with prunts on both the exterior and the interior, made in Germany about 1500, and a drinking vessel of the distinctive shape known as a *Berkmeyer*, probably made in the Netherlands or Lower Rhineland, about 1600. H. of *Stangenglas* 26 cm.

197a A B O V E , R I G H T View showing the interior of the *Stangenglas* in Pl. 197, with eight vertical rows of seven prunts. A similar feature occurs on the inside of a broken *Krautstrunk* found in Cologne and now in the Düsseldorf Kunstmuseum.

196 O P P O S I T E Group of 'forest' glasses from Northern Europe. *From left*: mould-blown cup, the so-called *Maigelein*, probably made in the Rhineland in the 15th century and found at Frankfurt-am-Main in 1872; bottle of double conical form, probably also made in the Rhineland in the 15th century and found near Bingerbrück; beaker with a chequered spiral trail, probably made in the Southern Netherlands in the late 16th century and found walled up in Culross, Scotland; and a *Stangenglas*, with octagonal rim and milled spiral trails, made in the Netherlands or the Rhineland in the late 16th century. H. of *Stangenglas* 20.5 cm.

forest glasshouses of Germany and to exemplify the change that had overtaken the glass industry in northern Europe.

Many of these wares would have been produced in the small and relatively primitive type of forest glasshouse that, fortunately, was meticulously recorded in the famous illustration painted about 1420, probably in Bohemia, to accompany a copy of the medieval manuscript *Sir John Mandeville's Travels*. Under the light wooden structure, the main furnace (perhaps oval in plan) appears to be built to provide the heat for the adjacent subsidiary oven or annealing chamber, which is on the same level – the typical 'northern' furnace construction as distinct from the 'southern' furnace (including that used in the Middle East), where the annealing chamber was built at the top, on a third level. Curiously, when in 1425 Ludwig of the Palatinate ordered for his library in Heidelberg a copy of the famous medieval manuscript *De Universo* by Rabanus Maurus, dating from 1023, the illustration of the scene at the glass furnace was brought up to date but the miniaturist has completely omitted to show the annealing chamber – neither depicting it at the upper level (as shown in the original eleventh-century manuscript at the Abbey of Monte Cassino) nor alongside on the same level (as was the standard practice in 'northern' glass-houses). However ignorant the miniaturist may have been about the construction of glass furnaces, he was evidently aware of their products and has introduced three typical contemporary German 'forest glass' vessels, one of which is the distinctive double-cone flask. This curious form, which was less vulnerable to damage, seems to have been most popular during the fifteenth century in the Rhineland area, where a number of examples have been dug up unbroken and almost unspoilt. They are always small, made of a thick glass, mostly with a strong yellowish-green colour, and typify the utilitarian glassware of the region at that time – and, indeed, the general decline of the medieval glasshouse tradition north of the Alps.

198

136

195

196

198 Miniature depicting numerous activities relating to a late medieval 'forest' glasshouse, which has its lehr built alongside the furnace. Painted to accompany a copy of the medieval manuscript *Sir John Mandeville's Travels*, it was probably executed in Bohemia between 1420 and 1450. London, British Library.

Venice and Renaissance Europe
15TH–17TH CENTURIES

In complete contrast, the prospects for the Murano glass industry seemed set to improve as the Islamic glass centres of Damascus, Aleppo and Egypt declined towards the end of the fourteenth century and more especially after 1380 when Venice emerged victorious from a lengthy and bitter struggle with its ancient rival maritime power, Genoa. With help from Hungary, the Genoese had lain siege to and all but penetrated the Venetian defences. Indeed, these troubles may help to explain the gap in the story of Murano's progress during the second half of the fourteenth century. Thereafter, Venice extended its dominion over a very large area of *terra firma*, including such rich prizes as Padua and Verona, then Brescia and Bergamo, until its frontiers were bordering those of the Duchy of Milan. The Venetian Republic, now one of the five most powerful states in Italy, went on to rule the Dalmatian coast and many parts of the eastern Mediterranean and, because during the fifteenth century economic expansion and wealth were concentrated in the Mediterranean, the importance of Venice as a commercial centre for Europe steadily grew. By 1500 Venice, one of only four great cities of Western Europe with more than 100,000 inhabitants, was enjoying her status as a major political power in Europe but had already become conscious of the destructive threat emanating from the Ottoman Turks in the east and of the commercial rivalry from the Portuguese in the west. By making certain adjustments and shrewd manoeuvres, the Republic was able to remain independent for many more centuries and during that time its talented glassmakers transformed man's perception of this strangely versatile, almost magical material that seemed in the hands of the men – and women – of Murano to possess such infinite variety.

Angelo Barovier, who died in 1460, is the Venetian master glassmaker credited with raising the art of glassmaking to a new artistic, as well as technical, level – rather as Nicolo Pellipario in the 1520s helped to elevate to an art the decoration of *maiolica* in the Duchy of Urbino. Angelo's name first appears in the archives of Murano in 1424, and thereafter he seems to have held official positions of increasing prominence, being one of the very few to travel abroad with the approval of the Venetian authorities. Having been in Milan in 1455, where he seemed to have impressed the Duke with his 'beautiful works of *cristallo*', Angelo and another glassmaker, Nicolo Mozetto, were in February 1457 granted by the *Podestà* of Murano a most favourable concession – to be allowed to use their furnaces for making *cristallo* during those times when it would not be possible to produce other glass. The full significance of this reference is hard to determine, though it may be taken to indicate that the production of *cristallo* was at this time in its infancy and that Barovier, with the help of Mozetto, was still perfecting his famous colourless *cristallo* glass; understandably, therefore, at this experimental stage, the Venetian authorities were perhaps only prepared to give encouragement to their venture so long as their normal regular production was not diminished.

Two years later Angelo Barovier is recorded in Florence and described as 'the most distinguished in the art of glass' and on his death a year later, in 1460, Ludovico Carbone described him as 'the best Venetian maker of cristalline vases'. Whilst it seems most likely that his achievements in the field of *cristallo* were but one aspect of his success, there is no precise information about his role in the development of the art of enamelling and gilding on glass. Nevertheless, he was praised extravagantly as one 'who knew the whole of the art of glass' and had won the respect of Alfonso, King of Naples, the French court and the Duke of Milan. Although the content of eulogies written upon the death of an outstanding man can rarely be taken at face value, there is little doubt that Angelo Barovier's fame was an historical fact; but whether it was well deserved is impossible to say, because today not one single glass can be identified as the work of this great pioneer. His *cristallo* was almost certainly neither as thin nor as free from bubbles and impurities as that of his successors in Venice after 1500.

212

Among his contemporaries, there is recorded in the Venetian archives of the mid-1440s a decorator of glasses who was a woman, Elena de Lando, and from among the next generation of Angelo's own family, another woman – Maria (Marietta) Barovier – was allowed in 1487 to build a little furnace ('*parvula fornace*'), perhaps for canemaking or for the firing of enamelled decoration on the glasses. Since the edict of 1469, the opening of a new furnace at Murano needed the approval of the authorities, and in 1470–71, for example, they gave

199 TOP Two early Renaissance beakers. The rims are no longer everted like those of the beakers in Pl. 192; the foot-rings are pincered or milled, and the imperfect gilding on the 'nipt diamond waies' below the rim and on the blue beaker has largely disappeared, but the soft colouring of the floral enamelling – perhaps intended for the Near Eastern market – is unspoilt. The elaborate pattern on the blue beaker has recently been found repeated on gilded glass fragments dug up in London. Venice, second half of the 15th century. H. of clear beaker 11.2 cm.

For the making of a beaker with 'nipt diamond waies', see p. 237, Figs 179–83.

200 CENTRE Two early Renaissance goblets. That on the left, which is slightly earlier, has a more tapering form and is enamelled with figures, including an equestrian group. The other glass, decorated with pairs of dolphins and mermen, is very similar to another late 15th-century example found beneath the foundations of the Campanile of San Marco, Venice, after its collapse in 1902 (Murano, Museo Vetrario). Venice, late 15th century. H. of left-hand goblet 13.4 cm.

201 BOTTOM Tazza on a low foot; on the exterior, twelve gilded ribs in high relief spiral outwards from the centre, where an enamelled scene depicts a doe lying under a sunburst (or 'glory') beside a stretch of water. Venice, second half of the 15th century. D. 27 cm.

For the making of a ribbed vessel by half-moulding, see pp. 235–7, Figs 162–78.

this permission to Pietro di Giorgio ('*perfetto maistro da dorar e smaltar lavorieri de vero*' – 'a perfect master of the technique of gilding and enamelling of glasses') but his work, like that of the two women, remains unrecognised. Between 1450 and 1525, a further eight decorators of glasses are referred to by name in the Venetian records, but not one of the magnificent surviving specimens can be assigned to them individually. 199–201

More hopefully, a correct identification of the artistic output of another contemporary enameller, Giovanni Maria Obizzo (active 1488–1525), may have been successfully established because of the evidence given in a legal dispute in 1490, when he was named as the painter of 'more than a thousand pieces of *lattimo* and other colours, all gilt and enamelled', which had been illegally fired by one Bernardino Ferro. If, as seems probable, Obizzo specialised in the decoration of this new opaque white (*lattimo*) glass, then the small group of less than twenty surviving examples, many of which are decorated with enamelled subjects in the manner of Vittore Carpaccio's pictures painted in Venice during the 1490s, may be from his workshop. For this reason, he is thought to have painted, as a special commission, the famous ring-handled *lattimo* vase of King Henry VII of England (reigned 1485– 202 1509), which bears both the King's portrait and his personal device, the portcullis and chains under a 'glory'. It is similarly conjectured that this vase was part of the gift brought to London in 1506 by Castiglione on behalf of the Duke of Urbino, on whom Henry had conferred the Order of the Garter. The vase's exceptional form could, in such circumstances, have been intended as a special compliment, because the shape was at that time very fashionable in north-west Europe, where it was being produced in painted tin-glazed pottery – the so-called early Netherlandish maiolica – and was often depicted in paintings and miniatures, especially in scenes of the Annunciation by Flemish artists like Gerard David. Another Venetian glass vase of identical size and shape, but made of emerald-green glass, was enamelled with Henry VII's portrait and 'the royal arms of England, as they were borne between 1405 to 1603, ensigned with a coronet'; whereas it was still in existence in 1897 in a private collection in England, the blue glass with 'the Kinges Armes gilt' which was listed in Henry VIII's inventory of 1542 had long since disappeared without trace.

Even before the end of the fifteenth century, therefore, the Venetian glassmakers had already been successful in winning the admiration of the most powerful princes with their masterpieces – monumental armorial covered standing-cups of gilded *cristallo* and betrothal goblets of sapphire-blue, emerald-green and turquoise, on which gold 203 and enamels have been lavishly applied. Fortunately, one or two of these prestigious commissions have survived, as at Breslau where the magnificent standing-cup with the arms of Hungary on one side and Bohemia on the other is thought to have been made for King Matthias Corvinus of Hungary (died 1490), while from the site of the royal palace in Budapest came fragments of a goblet with the arms of Matthias's queen, Beatrix of Aragon (1457–1508), who in 1486 had received gifts from Ferrara which included Venetian *cristallo*. Several glasses bearing the arms of Louis XII of France and Anne of Brittany (died 1514) have survived and were probably made at the time of their

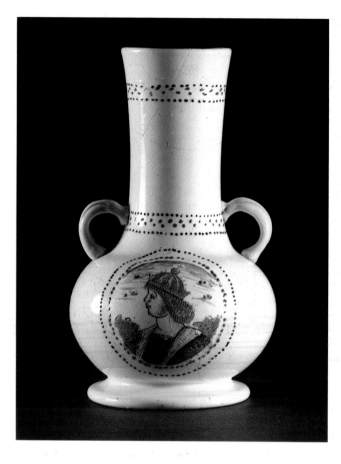

202 ABOVE, LEFT The 'ring-handled' vase of Henry VII of England (reigned 1485–1509), in *lattimo* (opaque white glass) with many traces of the original gilding. Within the two roundels are the enamelled bust of the King and (on the reverse) his personal device, the portcullis and chains in a 'glory'. Made in Venice and perhaps decorated by the enameller Giovanni-Maria Obizzo, about 1500. H. 19.8 cm.

203 ABOVE, RIGHT Betrothal goblet in two tones of blue: a lapis lazuli stem and a turquoise bowl and foot, reminiscent of the earlier Islamic bowl in the Treasury of San Marco (Pl. 147). Decorated with gold-leaf gilding, three circuits of applied *lattimo* and, above all, two delicately painted pairs of lovers within roundels. Made in Venice and, like the vase in Pl. 202, perhaps decorated by the enameller Giovanni-Maria Obizzo, about 1500. H. 18.9 cm.

marriage in 1499. In Spain, the monarchs Ferdinand and Isabella (1479–1516) set the fashion for building up collections of glasses, the Queen leaving hers to Granada Cathedral, where they were seen in 1526 by the Venetian ambassador Andrea Navagero, a gentleman of Murano. The inventories of Spanish noble families often contain references to these decorated Venetian glasses, as when the Marquis of Priego and Count of Feria died in 1528 and the list of his Venetian glasses included goblets painted with the arms of Portugal. One city in Spain, Barcelona, had a flourishing guild of glassmakers from 1455, and its leading members were by the end of the fifteenth century producing glasses that could rival those of Venice – albeit often using shapes and motifs of a Spanish character.

The technique of enamelling practised by these early Venetian glass artists is not recorded in complete detail, though a fifteenth-century manuscript, preserved in the Library of the monastery of San Salvatore in Bologna, seems to contain a reliable, brief account:

To paint glass, that is to say, cups or any other works in glass with *smalti* or any colour you please, take the *smalti* you wish to use, and let them be soft and fusible, and pound them upon marble or porphyry in the same way that the goldsmiths do. Then wash the power and apply it upon your glass as you please and let the colour dry thoroughly; then put the glass upon the rim of the chamber in which glasses are cooled, on the side from which the glasses are taken out cold, and gradually introduce it into the chamber towards the fire which comes out of the furnace and take care you do not push too fast lest the heat should split it, and when you see that it is thoroughly heated, take it up with the *pontello* and fix it to the *pontello* and put it in the mouth of the furnace, heating it and introducing it gradually. When you see the *smalti* shine and that

204 Spanish Renaissance glass: the plate, with its distinctive naïve enamelled decoration of foliage and birds, was made in Barcelona in the first half of the 16th century; the *façon de Venise* two-handled vessel is probably also Catalan, made in the second half of the 16th century. D. of plate 18.2 cm.

they have flowed well, take the glass out and put it in the chamber to cool, and it is done . . .

Most Venetian enamelled glasses of the Renaissance are richly decorated with gold – always using gold leaf. Frequently, the enamelling lies over the gilded surfaces, indicating that the application of he gold leaf was an earlier stage in the decoration of the glasses than the enamelling. The granular effect that normally results from applying gold leaf is often easy to detect, especially where the sections of gold leaf overlap or where an inscription has been incised through the gold leaf prior to firing. One contemporary eye-witness account, written by a Swedish priest, Peter Mansson, who was in Rome from 1508 to 1524, records:

The workman has also a second iron 56 inches long, shaped like the first, but not hollowed inside, called the *puntellum*. This has always a piece of glass on its end and lies in the fire. With this iron, fix the knob of glass on the base: it becomes attached at once, and is held in the oven to warm up. Then take it out and shape it with the pincers . . . When the glass is thus made ready, cut some gold leaf and lay it round the edge. Hold the glass in the furnace so that the gold is at once welded to the glass. Then lay the finished glass up in the other chamber to cool off, so that it does not get cold too quickly and break . . .

The gilded and enamelled glasses of Murano, whether using *cristallo*, *lattimo* or coloured glass, met with success not only at every European court but also, ironically, in the Islamic Middle East, where simultaneously the rulers and merchants were importing Venetian glass in large quantities throughout the fifteenth century. The Venetian export trade, mainly through Rhodes, to countries like Syria, continued even more profitably after 1516 when the Turkish sultan Selim I conquered Syria and Egypt and made Constantinople the capital of the empire of the Ottoman Turks. Its popularity in Northern Europe led skilled glassmakers to leave Murano, and, throughout the

205–8

220

206

207 RIGHT Tazza with a mould-blown lion knop on the stem and a highly exceptional 'sandwich' of clear glass in the centre of the bowl, trapping the enamelled and gilt roundel and armorial shield (see Pl. 208); its lozenge shape indicates that it was borne by a female, now identified as a member of a Flemish family, married in 1559 to Gilles Happaert of Antwerp. *Façon de Venise*, probably Antwerp. H. 15.2 cm.

For the making of a mould-blown lion stem, see p. 234, Figs 153–6.

205 FAR LEFT Mould-blown dish with applied blue and aubergine trails and, in the centre, a 'sandwich' of gold leaf between the *cristallo* and the applied disc of aubergine glass. Venice, beginning of the 16th century. D. 22.8 cm.

206 LEFT Goblet of enamelled glass, with a wide band of gold-leaf gilding below the rim, incised: IE.SVIS.A. VOUS.IEHAN. BOVCAV.ET.ANTOYNETTE.BOVC (lack of space cut short the surname, Boucau). The figures of Jehan and Antoinette (each with French expressions of love) are accompanied by a white goat attempting to drink from a bottle, forming the rebus BOUC *eau*. Possibly to be associated with the 'Jehan Boucau' reportedly listed in 1529 as a landowner at Beauwelz (near Mons). Northern France or perhaps Southern Netherlands, mid-16th century. H. 16.2 cm.

208 Detail showing the underside of the 'sandwich' decoration in the centre of the tazza in Pl. 207. It shows how the top of the stem was joined to the underside of the 'sandwich' without harming the elaborately enamelled armorial bearings, and, furthermore, that the white fleur-de-lys were not painted over the red, and that gold leaf was used to create this *tour de force*.

sixteenth century, to establish glasshouses in prosperous centres such as the Southern Netherlands, where in the city of Antwerp, for example, some of the finest *façon de Venise* glass was made after 1541. Their role in France, however, is less clear because they were in competition with rival Italian glassmakers from Altare, near Genoa, who enjoyed special patronage. The history of French Renaissance enamelled glass is sadly incomplete.

The Renaissance glassmakers of Murano were quick to experiment with ancient Roman glass techniques, often producing a highly individual result that was only distantly reminiscent of the Antique. Thus, towards the end of the fifteenth century they began to create a method for making *millefiori* glass, that is, glass in which thin slices of multi-coloured canes are embedded, creating the effect of a carpet of tiny flowers. The 'gather' of glass onto which the slices of canes were attached was not always a clear glass; it could, for example, be a light opaque blue glass – not unlike that used on the stem of the famous goblet with the two pairs of lovers which dates from about 1500. Although it is not known when Murano first started to make this rare *millefiori* glass, Maria Barovier was recorded in 1496 as a maker of the coloured glass canes needed for it. Furthermore, in the *Opera Omnia* of Marcantonio Coccio Sabellico, Book III, *De Venetae urbis situ* (1500), there is a passage that reads: 'But consider to whom did it first occur to include in a little ball all the sorts of flowers which clothe the meadows in Spring. Yet these things have been under the eyes of all nations as articles of export. . . .'

The colours of the embedded canes at this early date seem to be chiefly an opaque red, white, and a bright translucent blue, and are similar to those used by the Venetians in the making of that well-attested category of beads for export to the Near East. However, ordinary vessels of *millefiori* seem rarely to have been made and, on the whole, the extant examples are 'miniature' objects, apparently intended for a princely *kunstkammer* or a 'cabinet of curiosities' rather than for use.

The fascination of natural phenomena in its more unexpected guises led the Renaissance courts of Europe to collect not only carved rock-crystal but also beautifully coloured and veined hardstones (chalcedony, agate, jade, jasper, bloodstone, prase, topaz, lapis-lazuli, etc.). These, when polished on a wheel and fashioned to an elegant form, would become part of a goldsmith's *chef-d'oeuvre* with gold enamelled or embossed mounts and covers. This mania began in Italy, led by such arbiters of taste as Isabella d'Este at Mantua (died 1539) and was to spread across Europe, reaching its peak in the seventeenth century. The Venetian glassmakers, once again, seem to have kept in step with fashion and, by 1500, according to Sabellico, 'they began to turn the materials into various colours and numberless forms. Thence come cups, beakers, tankards, cauldrons, ewers, candlesticks, animals of every sort, horns, beads . . . there is no kind of precious stone which cannot be imitated by the industry of the glass workers, a sweet contest of nature and of man.'

Two rare and very early achievements in *calcedonio*, or 'chalcedony' glass, are the British Museum's famous monumental marbled jug of about 1500 and, perhaps even earlier, the shallow light bowl with 'nipt diamond waies' which, in contrast, is highly translucent and glowing

206

209

203

210

209 Venetian *millefiori* glass. *From left*: a miniature ewer formed from a clear glass gather incorporating sliced canes and set in silver mounts, a bead of opaque blue glass, and a goblet formed from a clear glass gather and mould-blown, all about 1500; a bottle formed from a dark blue glass gather also incorporating gold leaf, mould-blown and with an applied *lattimo* trail round the rim, 17th century; and a cup, also incorporating *filigrana* canes, 17th century. H. of ewer 12.6 cm.

For the making of a mould-blown *millefiori* bottle, see pp. 228–9, Figs 109–19.

210 Venetian *calcedonio* (or chalcedony) glass. *From left*: a bowl of mould-blown translucent glass (seen from the underside) with 'nipt diamond waies' and an applied trailed foot-rim, about 1500; a standing bowl of thicker, opaque glass, also about 1500; and a covered tankard incorporating 'aventurine spots' (copper powder inclusions), late 17th century. H. of tankard 18 cm.

with colour. Both these early Renaissance examples demonstrate the skill with which the glassmakers of Murano mastered the new material, and even in the eighteenth century when there was a great revival of interest in coloured vitreous pastes of all kinds, from 'malachite' to 'onyx' glass, each imitating the subtle variegations of these hardstones, the Muranese cleverly exploited their earlier invention, *avventurina* glass, to great effect. It became extremely popular and many examples have survived. Its chief characteristic is the eye-catching sparkle of the inclusions of copper powder within the marbled paste itself. It is said that the recipe remained the secret of the famous Miotti family of glassmakers in Murano, who had discovered it before the middle of the seventeenth century, and some of the surviving examples seem, on stylistic grounds, to be associated with their achievements before 1700.

Another stone that presented a challenge to the Venetian glassmakers of the Renaissance was the opal. Unexpectedly, the Venetians seem to have developed – by about 1600, at least – two solutions, because in the first European publication of formulae for coloured glasses – the great textbook of glass technology, *L'Arte Vetraria*, written by the priest Antonio Neri and published in Florence in 1612 – both 'opal' and 'girasol' are listed among the precious stones being imitated in glass. In early Italian, *girasol* was the name given to a milky precious stone, which with transmitted light turned a reddish fiery tint, rather like an opal; *girasol* was also the name for a sunflower. Furthermore, the term *vetri de girasol* was used consistently in eighteenth-century documents to describe the many pieces of 'opal' glass in that spectacular collection of Venetian glass acquired by King Frederik IV of Denmark during a visit to Venice in 1709 and subsequently kept in a specially designed 'Glass Room' in Rosenborg Castle in Copenhagen, where it can still be seen today. Without a doubt, these glasses at Rosenborg do not have the same 'opal' quality that can be observed, for example, in the two reliably documented 'opal' glass flasks of the sixteenth century preserved in the Dresden Grünes Gewölbe, the home of the historic treasures of the court of Saxony. From the beginning both these flasks had probably been treasured as 'rarities' and, at an early stage, had been enriched with fine Renaissance silver-gilt mounts, one bearing the enamelled coat-of-arms of the Abbot of Kempten (1571–84) and dated 1574. It might seem, therefore, that Neri's statement in 1612 could be accurately reporting the position in Murano but, as yet, there is insufficient evidence and, furthermore, it was not in Venice that Neri carried out his trials, including the testing of recipes for the colouring of glasses, but in Florence and Pisa, where the Grand Duke Cosimo I (1537–74) had established court glasshouses. However, even there, Venetian expertise proved indispensable to success and so one of the leading Venetian glassmakers, Master Bortolo d'Alvise, enticed by the prospects of lavish Medici patronage, had been working in Florence and since 1579 had been at the glasshouse used by Antonio Neri. Prior to the publication of his book, Neri had also been pursuing the subject in Antwerp, where since 1541 craftsmen from Murano had been producing a wonderful range of *façon de Venise* glasses. Consequently, Neri's awareness of traditional Venetian methods can scarcely be doubted, since by 1612 a working knowledge – if not a scientific under-

standing – of these recipes would already have been circulating in both Antwerp and Florence.

While Murano continued to excel in its production of both pure opaque-white (*lattimo*) and an impressive range of strong, clear colours – and in 1612 Neri recorded a number of recipes for 'aquamarines', 'emeralds' and 'blues' – the stylish uses to which these technical achievements were put by the artistic glassmakers of Venice were constantly changing. Thus, before the middle of the sixteenth century, a dramatic shift in taste led the workshops of Murano to abandon the production of enamelled and gilded glasses – except, perhaps, for export to their profitable markets in the Middle East and north of the Alps.

In Italy, for whatever reason, richly enamelled and gilded glass fell out of favour at precisely the moment that the glassmakers of Murano were bringing to perfection two fundamentally new types of glass, both of which succeeded in revolutionising the appearance of Venetian glass and winning for Murano the renewed admiration of its wealthy international clientele. Indeed, in 1550 an eye-witness left the following vivid description of the multitude of invention and fantasy being offered by the glassmakers of Murano:

Glassmen make a variety of objects: cups, phials, pitchers, globular bottles, dishes, saucers, mirrors, animals, trees, ships. Of so many fine and wonderful objects I should take long to tell. I have seen such at Venice, and especially at the Feast of the Ascension when they were on sale at Murano, where are the most famous of all glass factories. These I have seen on several occasions, but especially when for certain reasons, I went to meet Andreas Naugerius at his house there, in company with Franciscus Asulanus. . . .

The writer was Georgius Agricola (1490–1555), an aging scholar who in 1550 composed the preface to his great work, *De Re Metallico* (published in Basle in 1556) and who, in Book XII, describes in detail the technical processes of glassmaking, illustrating the furnace constructions, and so on. What had clearly impressed him on his visits to Venice and Murano had been the diversity of the shapes that could be produced in the newly perfected *cristallo*, a thin, almost weightless, pure and colourless material that permitted the glassmakers to blow and manipulate the most elegant and intricate of forms. Its featherlight quality combined with its stability provided the *virtuosi* of Murano's glasshouses with the ideal medium for expressing their own imaginative ideas as well as creating skilled interpretations of the fanciful designs for glass supplied by Mannerist court artists. The latter trend, fostered by princely patronage at various courts, can now be best observed in the numerous drawings that were produced for the Medici by Jacopo Ligozzi, Stefano della Bella, Jacques Callot, Bacchio del Bianco and others in the late sixteenth and early seventeeth centuries. With this new *cristallo*, the Venetians quickly realised how to emphasise not only the exciting Mannerist proportions but also the clarity and colourless quality by adding touches of bright blue glass – either by giving a vivid outline to the glass with a thin blue trail along the rim or by executing the intricate pincered details of a handle or a finial in a strong blue glass. Although this idea may have its origins in the fourteenth century, as mentioned above, the Renaissance craftsmen applied it with a precision and delicacy that was new and artistic, especially when it was combined with unusual or quasi-

211 ABOVE Covered beaker of 'opal' glass made in a three-part mould with a continuous frieze depicting a Marine Triumph in the Italian Renaissance manner. The unusual cover has three dolphins moulded in high relief. Venice, or *façon de Venise*, 16th–17th centuries. H. 23.5 cm.

212 OPPOSITE *Nef* (or ship) ewer of *cristallo* with added details in blue glass and two mould-pressed satyr-mask medallions. This is one of the few genuine specimens of this fragile Renaissance table decoration to have survived, although they were being made in Venice from 1521 by Ermonia Vivarini under a special privilege. Hitherto it has been universally accepted that they were also being made at the leading *façon de Venise* centre in the Southern Netherlands, the Colinet glassworks at Beauwelz, but the evidence – a sketch (with commentary) in the MS pattern book known as the 'Catalogue Colinet' (Rakow Library, Corning Museum of Glass) – can no longer be regarded as authentic. This sketch purports to be a record of the very large glass *nef* offered to the emperor Charles V in 1549. Venice, about 1525–50. H. 30.2 cm.

212

sculptural forms, like the owl or the *Commedia dell'Arte* figures that 186 form the stems of tall wine-glasses and the horses, dragons and grotesque creatures that form a strangely imaginative series of oil-lamps.

Alongside this new gossamer *cristallo*, the Venetians created an even more distinctive kind of glass – *vetro a filigrana*, an old term that encompasses all the varieties of thread-decorated glass. This new category of decorative luxury glass was composed of canes (threads or thin tubes) of opaque white (*lattimo*) or, occasionally, coloured glass (blue and red), that were embedded within a clear *cristallo* and could 217 be blown into patterns of remarkable complexity and fineness. There were, however, three main types, each of which has its own name derived from its chief technical characteristic.

In the first group, known as *vetro a fili*, the individual white canes Figs 1 99 are picked up on the 'gather' but, after blowing, remain separate and distinct from one another. On some examples, particularly some of the early versions, the canes remain in relief on one surface of the glass 216 and may seem, deceptively, similar to the freely 'trailed' threads of the older method. However, by marvering the canes into the 'gather', the canes become flattened and tend to sink more completely into the 214–1 thickness of the glass.

In the second type, *vetro a retorti* (or *vetro a retortoli*, as it sometimes appears in the documents), the embedded canes are composed of twisted threads, usually opaque white but sometimes also incorporating blue and red. These cable-twists can form a variety of patterns and, 213–1 when placed side by side or alternating with plain canes (*a fili*), they can be picked up and blown so that they mass together to form an extraordinarily complex patterned glass – an entirely new conception in the history of glassmaking.

In the third variation, *vetro a reticello* (literally, 'glass with small Figs 2C 204 network'), the canes – whether *a fili* or *a retorti* – are used to create the overall effect of a net. The glassmaker can, for example, embed single white canes (*a fili*) and blow the glass so that they spiral to the right, and then superimpose the cable-twist canes (*a retorti*) so they spiral to the left, thereby creating a criss-cross pattern. Other mesh effects can 214 be achieved in various ways, including the technique of blowing one paraison into another bulb with canes running in the opposite direction; as the two bulbs fuse together, the canes can, with skill, form a regular mesh with equal-sized diamonds between the points of intersection. *Vetro a reticello* is further distinguished by innumerable, almost imperceptible, air-bubbles trapped between the criss-crossing 204 of the threads. These minute air-bubbles catch the light, transforming the mesh-like effect rather as dewdrops glistening on a spider's web will illuminate its delicate linear construction. They develop unexpected shapes, becoming elongated or having a wavy outline whenever the spaces between the criss-cross canes are no longer the perfect, diamond-shaped areas of the regular mesh.

The Venetian glassmakers used elements of all three types in the most daring combinations – even trapping gold leaf between the *vetro* 218 *a reticello* – to dazzle their clients with their virtuosity. Indeed, large dishes – perhaps 20 inches (50 cm) across – would be blown with each of the three types clearly used in different zones but so designed that the overall unity of the pattern would create a masterpiece of *vetro a*

213 TOP Three Renaissance mould-blown vessels. *From left*: a *cristallo* vase with lions' heads between swags of fruit; a drinking glass of *vetro a fili* with grape-like bosses; and a sprinkler of *vetro a retorti* with a frieze of lions and double-headed eagles. Venice, second half of the 16th century. H. of sprinkler 17.5 cm.

214 CENTRE *Filigrana* vessels. *From left*: a tall-necked bottle of *vetro a retorti*, a vase of *vetro a reticello*, and a sprinkler of *vetro a fili*, probably made for export to the eastern Mediterranean. Venice, second half of the 16th century. H. of bottle 24.1 cm.

For the making of *vetro a fili* with closely spaced canes, see pp. 238–9, Figs 189–99.

215 Three Renaissance glasses in contemporary English silver-gilt mounts, each glass now being the only surviving example of its kind dating from the 16th century (the glass of the Parr pot in the Museum of London is a later copy). *Left and right*: a jug of blue and white *vetro a retorti* and a jug of *vetro a fili*, both with London hallmarks for 1548–9. *Centre*: Lord Burghley's Tankard, incorporating an open-ended tube of thin *cristallo* glass, probably made in London by the Venetian Jacopo Verzelini between 1572 and 1574 (see also Pl. 220); on the cover are the enamelled armorial bearings of Lord Burghley (1520–98) as borne by him after 1572, when he was made a Knight of the Garter by Queen Elizabeth I. He remained the Queen's Chief Minister until his death. H. of tankard 21.3 cm.

filigrana. Furthermore, extraordinary bold effects could be achieved
213   with these three types by blowing into cleverly constructed moulds,
which would then produce bizarre shapes and low reliefs, all rippling
with the zigzag lines of the white *filigrana*.

Perhaps the ultimate in daring *bravura* that became very fashionble
in the second half of the sixteenth century was the transformation of
these thin, and sometimes moulded, vessels of *cristallo* and of *vetro a*
219   *filigrana* into 'ice-glass'. The roughened, sparkling frosted appearance
of ice-glass is achieved by plunging the hot glass into cold water and
then, after reheating it gently so as not to smooth the fissured surface
caused by the sudden immersion and cooling, the web of tiny cracks is
slowly enlarged during the final blowing and the glass becomes
positively uncomfortable to the touch. It is no longer smooth and
transparent – indeed, it has become the very negation of *cristallo*. The
low reliefs of the moulded designs have been crumpled and distorted
whilst the symmetrical exactitude of the linear patterns of the *vetro a*
filigrana has been shattered. This wilful sense of confusion, superimposed on the most accomplished and disciplined of artistic craftsmanship, was wholly in the spirit of Mannerist art, especially as it too was
held in check and brought under control. Understandably, it was
greatly admired both in Italy and at the more sophisticated courts of
Europe: Philip II of Spain admired it so much that in 1564 he possessed
sixty-five examples from Venice in his palace of El Pardo.

Murano's mastery of the complexities of *vetro a filigrana* in all its
varied manifestations seems to have been achieved in the 1530s, after
a patent for a version of *vetro a retortoli* had been applied for in 1527 and
before the publication in 1540 in Venice of Vannoccio Biringuccio's
Pirotechnia, which seems to include a convincing description of *vetro a*
reticello, even though the term itself is not used. Biringuccio alludes to

216 LEFT Two glasses with *vetro a fili* in
relief. *Left*: a four-sided bottle using
alternating white and blue canes, the white
core of each cane being visible at the end,
especially on the blue. *Right*: a drinking glass
which also has two horizontal bands of *vetro a*
retorti and a knop and stem of smooth *vetro a*
fili. Venice, second half of the 16th century. H.
of drinking glass 15.2 cm.
For the making of *vetro a fili* with broadly
spaced canes and *vetro a retorti*, see p. 238,
Figs 184–8.

217 OPPOSITE, ABOVE LEFT Two beakers
of *vetro a fili*. The smaller incorporates red in
addition to the blue and white canes; the taller
has applied gilded bosses, three of which are
mould-pressed lion-masks. *Façon de Venise*,
made in the Southern Netherlands about 1600.
H. of taller beaker 21.5 cm.

218 OPPOSITE, ABOVE RIGHT Two
beakers of sandwich gold *façon de Venise* glass:
that on the left uses *vetro a retorti* with applied
bosses set with blue glass 'pearls'; that on the
right is *vetro a reticello*. Probably made in the
Southern Netherlands, perhaps in Antwerp,
in the late 16th century. H. 15.7 cm.
For the making of a beaker in sandwich gold
vetro a reticello, see p. 240, Figs 200–204.

219 OPPOSITE, BELOW Two Renaissance
'ice-glass' vessels. *Left*: a vase moulded in high
relief with gadroons (in the lower part of the
body) and two lion-masks on either side of
festoons and swags; gold-leaf gilding on the
stem and foot. Venice, mid-16th century.
Right: a beaker with some gold-leaf gilding,
four double bands of *retorti* canes and three
mould-pressed lion-head bosses. Probably
façon de Venise, perhaps made in Antwerp,
second half of the 16th century.

'large things, as well as small, that they make of white and coloured glass and that seem to be woven of osier twigs equally spaced with the greatest uniformity and exactness of termination'. Interestingly, he refers to coloured glass in this context and, although few, if any, mid-sixteenth-century examples incorporating coloured twisted threads are known, one specimen that was definitely made no later than 1548 has been preserved in England. It is one of two jugs blown by Venetian craftsmen and set in silver-gilt mounts made in London in 1548–9. Together, these two jugs offer irrefutable evidence of the production of both *vetro a fili* (opaque white) and of *vetro a retorti* (white and blue) before the end of the 1540s, whilst the 1542 inventory of Henry VIII's glasses listed 'bolles of glasse with oone cover to them all, wrought with diaper worke white' – probably a reference to the criss-cross pattern of the white canes in some form of *vetro a reticello*. As the documents record that in 1549 there were eight glassmakers from Murano working under contract in London and that some two and a half years of their contract had still to be completed, it seems very probable that these two jugs – so English in shape and so unlike any Venetian forms – were made by these Venetian craftsmen while they were staying in England and that the English patrons commissioned local London goldsmiths to make the handsome, protective silver-gilt mounts and hinged covers, which were then duly hallmarked in 1548–9 in the normal manner.

This evidence would suggest, however, that the demand for Venetian Renaissance glass was so great that within a decade or two of their introduction, the latest innovations from Murano would become available on the other side of Europe – and, indeed, might even be tolerably well copied at some northern glasshouse where itinerant Italians were engaged in the production of glass *à la façon de Venise*.

During the Italian Renaissance, therefore, the humble utilitarian craft of glassmaking had been elevated to a sophisticated courtly art,

220 The goblet on the left is very thinly blown and decorated solely with gold-leaf gilding: it is Venetian, or *façon de Venise* (perhaps made in Antwerp), mid-16th century. That on the right has two gilded applied bands of clear glass in relief, each flanked by thin white threads and three zones of diamond-engraved decoration often attributed to Anthony de Lysle, who lived in London: this includes the initials G S (in a love-knot), the date '1586' and the words IN.GOD.IS.AL.MI.TRUST. This goblet was made in the London glasshouse of Jacopo Verzelini, who was born in Venice in 1522, married in Antwerp in 1556 and arrived in London in 1571, where in 1574 he received a royal patent for twenty-one years. Having successfully run this Italian-style glasshouse in London, he retired to the country and died a prosperous merchant at his home in Kent in 1606. H. of Verzelini goblet 13 cm.

221 The acorn goblet on the right is in clear but greyish glass, with expertly trailed clear glass thread decoration, a mould-blown lion-mask stem and a detachable beehive-shaped cover resting over a plain high neck. This exceptional glass attempts to rival one of the rarest forms in the repertoire of the Renaissance goldsmith, and can be compared with a unique contemporary example made of gold (*left*) which was bequeathed to the parish church of Stapleford, Leicestershire, England, by the Earl of Harborough in 1732 and which has been preserved in the British Museum since 1957, and with a silver-gilt acorn cup (probably German, about 1500) in the Basilica of San Antonio, Padua. Probably made at the Palace glasshouse, Innsbruck, Austria, about 1570–90. H. 23.5 cm.

222 Plate from a Papal service, made of clear glass with two zones of gold-leaf gilding separating two circuits of white and two larger circuits of blue and white *vetro a retorti*. In the two remaining zones, the diamond-point engraving includes the crossed Papal keys. Two similar plates (Musée Curtius, Liège, and the Toledo Museum of Art, Toledo, Ohio) bear the arms of Pope Pius IV (1559–66). Venice, third quarter of the 16th century. D. 27.5 cm.

which led men of privilege, like Emperor Ferdinand I's son, Archduke Ferdinand of Tyrol (1520–95), and the ruler of Hesse-Kassel, the Landgrave Wilhelm IV (reigned 1567–92), to set up glasshouses not for commercial reasons but for their own personal use, curiosity and education. Glassmaking had become an accomplishment that a prince might enjoy in the same way that the emperor Rudolph II, for example, found lathe-turning a creative pursuit, almost an absorbing passion. Archduke Ferdinand's glasshouse, set up in 1563 near his palace of Ambras at Innsbruck, was manned by a tiny workforce, each craftsman being carefully selected, with the agreement of the Council of Ten, from whichever of the glassblowers of Murano had the most 'fantasy in him', as the Archduke's instructions expressed it. At least one glass – a very individual beaker – has survived, with its gem-encrusted gold mounts and cover, which is traditionally accepted as one of the Archduke's own personal creations. However, the Landgrave Wilhelm IV had many more difficulties in distant Kassel; soon after 1580 he engaged as collaborator in his scheme the glassmaker Francesco Warisco, who had been working in Sweden, and they brought in some Italian craftsmen from the Low Countries. Although glass was successfully made on the Landgrave's birthday – 22 June 1583 – harmony could not be maintained. At their own request, the Italians were released from their contract in August of the following year, leaving the Landgrave – and posterity – with several fine specimens of *vetro a retorti*.

This new recognition of the glassmaker's art and of the need to combine technical *bravura* with imaginative 'fantasy' had been brought about by the growing esteem in which the Venetian glass was held at every court throughout Europe. Furthermore, it relied for its success entirely on the glassmakers of Murano and not on other craftsmen, such as engravers, who play no part in the glassmaking process and need not live in the same town, let alone work in the same glasshouse. Although some Venetian glasses of the sixteenth century, particularly the splendid *filigrana* Papal plates with gilding, two of which bear the arms of Pope Pius IV (1559–66), have been decorated with truly fine quality diamond-point engraved motifs, this was a form of surface enrichment that failed to become popular in Italy. In complete contrast, it had a wide appeal in the Tyrol and north of the Alps. From the beginning the Elizabethan glasses made in the London glasshouse of Jacopo Verzelini (active 1574–1606) were frequently engraved with the diamond-point, and throughout the seventeenth and early eighteenth centuries it flourished in the Low Countries, where both men and women engravers, often amateurs, are recorded and their work reliably identified.

Perhaps the most extravagant use to which canes of spiral and twisted coloured glass were put by the Venetians – and by their imitators in the Netherlands – was to form the stems of wine-glasses and tall drinking glasses, the *vetri a serpenti*. These magnificent items of virtuosity, which were being executed in Murano from the end of the sixteenth century, are difficult to identify and distinguish from their northern counterparts – the seventeenth-century *verres à serpents* of the Colinet factory in the Southern Netherlands, for example. The light-hearted extravagance of drinking glasses of this elaborate form seems to have continued both in Venice and in those centres in north-

223 TOP Tall goblets with 'serpent' and 'flower' stems. *Left: verre à serpent* using a purple glass and incorporating *retorti* canes of white, blue and red within the stem. *Façon de Venise* (Southern Netherlands or Liège), mid-17th century. *Centre: vetro a serpenti* incorporating white *retorti* canes within the stem and terminating in two serpent-heads with blue cresting and eyes. A South German silver filigree mount with the arms of Baden has been added to the foot. Probably Venetian, first half of the 17th century. *Right: verre à fleurs* incorporating yellow and red retorti canes within the ring forming the stem and enclosing the individual flower sprays. Venice or *façon de Venise* (probably Liège), second half of the 17th century. H. of 'flower' goblet 27.9 cm.

For the making of a 'serpent' goblet, see pp. 232–3, Figs 137–50.

224 BOTTOM, LEFT Two Dutch flutes engraved with the diamond-point. *Left:* flute engraved with the coat-of-arms of the House of Orange above a sapling and the bust of a boy inscribed *Wilhelmus, Prince d'Orange, etc.* (the future King William III of England, who was born in 1650, shortly after his father's death. *Right:* flute engraved with the coat-of-arms of the Prince of Orange, who is depicted on the opposite side standing in military attire: this is assumed to be Prince Frederick-Henry (1584–1647), Stadtholder of the United Provinces (1625) and a successful general. Netherlands, mid-17th century. H. 40.1 cm.

225 BOTTOM, RIGHT Two covered standing goblets of the mid-17th century. *Left:* a distinctive form (with its numerous mereses on the stem and finial) associated with the late 17th-century Nuremberg school of wheel-engravers, although the thinness of the glass, the use of two colours and the raspberry prunt of clear glass on the finial indicate an early origin, in the third quarter of the century. *Right:* a late *façon de Venise* specimen with diamond-engraved Dutch inscriptions in the calligraphic style associated, in particular, with Willem Jacobz. van Heemskerk (1613–92), a cloth merchant of Leiden who was also a poet and dramatist. H. of blue goblet 40.6 cm.

226 Three German armorial enamelled glasses. *Left*: a beaker illustrating the continuing popularity of deep blue glass with gold-leaf gilding: enamelled with both the monogram and the arms of the unidentified owner, the date 1678 and sprays of exceptional flower painting incorporating gold. Made in Saxony, 1678. *Centre*: a 'Reichsadler *Humpen*' dated 1571, the earliest known example of this popular type depicting the double-headed eagle of the Holy Roman Empire with the crucified Christ and the fifty-six shields on the wings. Probably Bohemian, 1571. *Right*: goblet with the arms of Johann Georg II, Elector of Saxony, enamelled on a *filigrana* glass (made in imitation of Venetian *vetro a fili*) and, on the reverse, an arrow in the bull's eye of a target, with an inscription and the date 1678; made in Saxony for the inauguration of the newly built Schiesshaus (shooting gallery) in Dresden. Made in Saxony, 1678. H. of *Humpen* 26.8 cm.

west Europe, such as Liège and Brussels, where the tradition of glass *à la façon de Venise* was strong, despite the fact that (as the archival evidence proves) the cost of producing one of these fanciful creations equalled that of five ordinary wine-glasses. Rarely do the later versions of the *verres à serpents* or *verres à fleurs* measure up to the quality of the Venetian prototypes, which have a lively spontaneity in contrast to the flat, almost stereotyped monotony of the northern imitations.

A similar pattern of change can be observed in other areas too. The Venetian art of gilding and enamelling on glass was nowhere more lastingly admired than in Germany and Bohemia, but, again, local glassmakers gradually mastered the technique and, by the end of the sixteenth century, had begun to create a *genre* of their own, which was to have a flourishing history for at least another hundred years before sinking to the level of a minor peasant craft in the nineteenth century. Apart from the glasses made in France by Italians (partly from Venice's rival Altare), some of which were finely decorated with enamels and gilding during the second half of the sixteenth century, few major contributions came from France. However, Bernard Perrot, who was born in Altare in 1619 but worked after 1651 at Nevers and in the Loire region, received royal patronage, being granted letters-patent between 1668 and 1688 for his new methods of making glass, especially flat glass (for windows and mirrors) and certain colours, opal, opaque white and 'crystal'. He died in 1709, having introduced new forms of glass into the French market, but even his ingenious use

226
227

206

229–

7–8

of moulds to produce small-scale sculptures was an ambitious innovation that seems likely to have had only limited success.

During the eighteenth century, a new variation became popular in Venice: glass in which the white thread was given a feathered look by 'combing'. There are many delightfully coloured examples among the items presented in 1709 to King Frederik IV of Denmark during his visit to Venice and still preserved in the special Glass Room in the Rosenborg Castle. Slightly later, as the craze for porcelain swept Europe, Murano produced some of its finest enamelled painting on *lattimo*, like the set of twenty-four plates, each copied from etchings by Luca Carlevaris, which Horace Walpole brought back to England after his stay in Venice in 1741, two of which have been in the British Museum since 1868. However, such innovations were not enough to prevent the supremacy of Venetian glass from being toppled by the achievements of glassmakers in England and, more particularly, in Bohemia and Germany where, struggling to recover from the Thirty Years' War after the Peace of Westphalia in 1648, the glassmakers were similarly introducing major technological changes.

228

227 ABOVE *Passglas* painted in *schwarzlot* – a grisaille technique fashionable in Germany about 1650–1750 – with a triumphal procession on the occasion of the baptism in 1662 of Maximilian Emanuel, who became Elector of Bavaria and Governor of the Netherlands. The glass is divided into six zones or *Pässe*, which the drinker in jovial company had to observe, drinking down to the first *Pass*, but if he failed to hit it in one attempt, he had to continue onto the next. German (Munich or Augsburg), 1662. H. 22.6 cm.

228 RIGHT Enamelled armorial *lattimo* bottle. On the underside is the enamelled inscription *Murano Miotti 1747*. The Miotti family's glasshouse, at the sign 'Al Gesù', had been active for more than a century, and since 1700 had developed an ambitious line in enamelling on opaque white glass. H. 23.9 cm.

229 LEFT Figures of Louis XIV and a lady. Such figures – the so-called *verre de Nevers* – were made by flame-working and, often, building the glass around a base-metal armature. Similar figures of higher quality had been made in Venice; the French versions may reflect the influence of the many glassmakers from Altare who settled in Nevers in the 17th century. Nevers, France, late 17th or 18th century. H. of Louis XIV figure 10.9 cm.

230, 231 BELOW Ewer of a curious opal glass, more smoky than milky, enamelled in a subdued palette with a furnace and a man described in 1885 (E. Gerspach, *L'Art de la Verrerie*) as a baker kneading bread, but more probably a glassmaker melting and preparing his glass. The motto reads: *Vive la belle que mon coeur aime*. Gerspach records that this ewer was accompanied by a basin decorated not only with the same motto but also with the date 1625. Both pieces had been in the well-known collection of Jean d'Huyvetter (sold at Ghent in 1851). The ewer, which the British Museum acquired in 1863, is probably the earliest enamelled glass with a truly French origin and character, in which the Italian contribution is minimal. France, 1625. H. 20.3 cm.

North of the Alps
17TH–18TH CENTURIES

Whereas Venetian glass (and most of the *façon de Venise* glass) was a soda-lime *cristallo* – a soft material unsuitable for any form of deep cutting, such as wheel-engraving – the Bohemian glass had consistently been made of a slightly harder potash-lime-silica composition, using the ashes of local vegetation to produce the potash. Even before the end of the sixteenth century, Bohemian glassmakers were introducing new methods to purify the potash and other raw materials, using manganese as a decoloriser, and even creating a new design of oven called the 'Bohemian furnace' – so successful a design that it continued in use until the nineteenth century. The result of these efforts was a fairly clear glass, harder than anything produced in Murano, even if it lacked the lightness and clarity of the Venetian *cristallo*. Its hardness permitted the use of true cutting techniques in contrast to the 'scratchings' of the diamond-point. Consequently, Caspar Lehmann's only signed work, the famous Prague beaker with its wheel-engraved allegorical figures of Potestas, Nobilitas and Liberalitas, dated 1605, is a milestone in the history of European glassmaking. It is the first securely dated glass vessel to be decorated in this technique for hundreds of years, and it was the beginning of a vast new development that extends to the present day.

In 1588, Lehmann, an engraver of hardstones from Lüneburg, had arrived in Prague, where the court of the emperor Rudolph II offered lavish patronage to the finest craftsmen from all over Europe. By 1601 Lehmann had been given the title of 'Imperial Gem-engraver': however, in 1608 the title was expanded to 'Imperial gem-engraver and glass-engraver' and, without doubt, he was the first to be so designated, even though he may not have been the first in Germany to have used wheel-engraved decoration on flat panels of glass. 232 Lehmann's technique on the glass beaker of 1605 reveals a skilled understanding of how to achieve three-dimensional modelling by making cuts of varying depth, in the manner of the Italian Renaissance rock-crystal engravers. In 1609 he was granted an Imperial Privilege in respect of his skill as a glass-engraver and, after his death in 1622, this Privilege passed to his pupil Georg Schwandhart who, because of the political troubles, moved back to his native city of Nuremberg where a most productive school of glass-engravers grew up, contributing significantly to the history of German engraved glass during the next 233 hundred years or so. Despite the shortcomings of the metal of this so-called Nuremberg seventeenth-century glass, these glassmakers – not recorded as working in Nuremberg itself – produced a range of distinctive shapes, including those eye-catching covered goblets with 225 very tall stems made up of several hollow knops, each linked by a series of thin discs ('mereses'), and with straight-sided bowls that were just thick and strong enough to receive sophisticated wheel-engraved decoration.

The German and Bohemian enthusiasm for wheel-engraved decoration on glass, once kindled, seems not to have been extinguished either by the Thirty Years' War or by the lack of a fine, hard colourless glass that could be compared with rock-crystal. Apart from the talented exponents of the Nuremberg school, there were at least two

232 Panel wheel-engraved by Caspar Lehmann, one of a series executed either in Prague or in Dresden during the first two decades of the 17th century. It depicts Europa and the Bull (probably after Crispin de Passe's engraving of 1607); above is the crowned monogram of Christian II of Saxony and his wife Hedwig of Denmark (they were married in 1602; Christian died in 1611). In 1606 Lehmann left Prague and went to Dresden, where Christian appointed him *Kammeredelsteinschneider*, and in March 1608, before his return to Prague, he was paid for '5 engraved glasses of which the largest is engraved with the Saxon and Danish arms'. Probably Dresden, 1606–8. 23 × 18.2 cm. Private collection, on loan to the British Museum.

233 RIGHT Beaker in contemporary silver-gilt mounts bearing the Nuremberg mark. Signed by Paulus Eder (see below), the beaker is wheel-engraved with three large roundels, each bearing an inscription in German referring to the allegorical subject of the enclosed scene; the underside of the base is decorated with a large wheel-engraved sunflower. Active in Nuremberg between 1685 and 1709, Eder was a contemporary of the gifted Hans Wolfgang Schmidt, whose signed works are equally subtle. A tall covered standing goblet engraved with the arms of the City of Nuremberg (now in the Germanisches Nationalmuseum, Nuremberg) is perhaps Eder's best-known signed work, but the British Museum's example offers a far greater range of pictorial effects. Nuremberg, late 17th century. H. 11.6 cm.

contemporaries of Lehmann's in Prague – Georg Schindler and Johann Hess, who settled in Dresden and Frankfurt respectively – each of whom was responsible for the formation of a line of glass-engravers that stretched into the eighteenth century. Even in southern Bohemia the glass-engraving technique seems to have been tenuously kept alive after Lehmann's death in 1622 at the important glassworks on Count Buquoy's estates in Nové Hrady, re-emerging there in 1650. Consequently, there was mounting pressure from all sides in Germany and Bohemia to find a way of improving the potash glass of Bohemia. Finally, in 1683, their efforts met with real success in southern Bohemia, where a formula for adding chalk to the batch had been developed by Michael Müller (1639–1709), a very talented glass master at the Janousek (Helmbach) works. His recipe produced an excellent hard and brilliant crystal-like glass material that was ideal for wheel-engraved decoration. Under Müller's towering influence, southern Bohemia created baroque forms, including the distinctive Bohemian baluster-shaped goblet and cover, as well as introducing the exciting new gold-ruby glass.

Significantly, Michael Müller's 1683 chalk recipe for potash glass is not to be found in any form in Johann Kunckel's great book *Ars Vetraria Experimentalis* of 1679, but when Kunckel produced an enlarged second edition, published in 1689, he included two recipes for potash glass, both of which required the addition of sizeable quantities of chalk. Johann Kunckel was a gifted alchemist and chemist from an old glassmaking family who, having translated into German Antonio Neri's famous *L'Arte Vetraria* of 1612, was employed by the

Elector of Brandenburg to carry out scientific research at Potsdam, where he had a glass furnace specially built for his needs. Although he is frequently credited with being the first to produce a ruby-red glass by means of a precipitate of gold (a gold chloride), he may only have been the first to succeed in making a consistently good-quality ruby glass in large quantities to order. This wonderful colour that had eluded the Venetians was certainly being made by the turn of the century in many other parts of Germany and Bohemia, and the old ascription of every piece of early ruby glass to the Potsdam works is no longer tenable. Although many of the alternative attributions are still difficult to establish, the distinctive wheel-engraving on Potsdam glass is of great assistance in determining Kunckel's achievements.

Curiously, Bohemian engraved glass, which at first tended to be very simple, shallow and unpolished, was slow to improve though it became deeper on the new chalky 'crystal' glass. By the beginning of the eighteenth century a flourishing and highly profitable export trade from Bohemia had been built up with this relatively inexpensive and simply decorated wheel-engraved product. Because of its popularity, it was beginning to undercut the Venetian trade and Giuseppe Briati was among the leading glassmakers of Murano who in the 1730s attempted to produce a convincing imitation of the Bohemian wheel-engraved glass in a desperate move to recapture the market.

It must be remembered that until 1742 Silesia was part of the Bohemian kingdom and was an equally important region both for glassmaking and for wheel-engraving. Indeed, the three greatest exponents of the art, Martin Winter (died 1702), Friedrich Winter (died 1711) and their nephew Gottfried Spiller (died 1728) came from the same area of Count Schaffgotsch's estates in the valley of Hirschberg, close to the border of Bohemia, and all went on to work in Berlin. Nevertheless, the Silesian style of engraving remained distinct from the Bohemian for many decades, and Silesian glass, which seemed never to have been able to lose a noticeable trace of grey or pink, became more adventurous in design, the Silesian craftsmen often creating unusual shapes and relief carving that enhanced the novel forms of the vessels. With the proliferation of glasshouses in Germany in the eighteenth century and the wealth of wheel-engraved glasses being produced, it is important not to forget that in Bohemia and many parts of Germany and eastern Europe there remained a demand for glasses of the highest quality decorated with gold and enamelled colours. During the first half of the eighteenth century the Bohemian *Zwischengoldgläser* became very fashionable. This was a cold technique whereby etched or engraved gold- or silver-leaf was sandwiched between two layers of glass in the wall or base of a vessel – a laborious and therefore costly process, for which a substitute was found by Mildner of Gutenbrunn, Austria.

Venice suffered another blow when a revolutionary discovery was made in England – the invention of a remarkable lead glass with great powers of light refraction. An English translation by Christopher Merret of Antonio Neri's great textbook was published in 1662 and was part of a wider movement to promote research into the improvement of English glassmaking. Experiments brought to fruition by George Ravenscroft in London between about 1674 and 1676 as a result of his being granted a patent in March 1674 for a 'crystalline

236

238–40

237

235

234 Ceremonial goblet and cover of pure colourless lead glass, with 'nipt diamond waies' on the cover and base of the bowl and a Venetian-style stem and finial. English, late 17th century. The wheel-engraved decoration was added some sixty years later in Holland and signed in diamond-point (on the foot) *Jacob Sang Fec.: Amsterdam 1757.* It depicts a ship, the *Velzen*, launched on 30 June 1757. Jacob Sang and his brother, Simon Jacob, first advertised in the *Amsterdamsche Courant* in 1753, when it is conjectured that they may have recently arrived from Germany. H. 49.5 cm.

235 RIGHT *Left*: drinking glass of colourless lead glass, with a chain circuit in relief and, within the stem, a coin of King James II dated 1687. London, about 1690. *Right*: serving bottle or decanter of lead glass, with 'nipt diamond waies'. Below the neck-ring is an applied seal with a mould-pressed raven's head – a guarantee of George Ravenscroft's improved recipe. London (Savoy glasshouse), 1676–8. H. of bottle 20.8 cm.

236 BELOW *Left*: beaker and cover of wheel-engraved gold-ruby glass, set in silver-gilt mounts bearing the Augsburg hallmark and the maker's mark T B, for Tobias Baur (master in 1685; died 1735). Southern Germany, about 1700. *Centre*: miniature bottle of gold-ruby glass, wheel-engraved with two pairs of shields bearing the arms of Saxony and the monogram of Johann Georg, Duke of Sachsen-Weissenfels (1697–1712); probably Saxony (Dresden), about 1700. *Right*: covered goblet, wheel-engraved with the monogram S C R (Sophie Charlotte Regina, crowned 1701, died 1705), sister of George I of England and wife of Frederick I of Prussia. Made at Potsdam and engraved in 1701–5. H. of goblet 31 cm.

glass resembling rock-crystal' produced a heavy glass in which the fluxing element was supplemented by oxide of lead. Although the precise nature of Ravenscroft's recipe is still debated, it is likely to have been a mixture of roast crushed flints, red lead-oxide, tartar, borax and saltpetre. In the first years, Ravenscroft's new glass was prone to 'crizzling', a deterioration in the composition which caused it to lose its clarity and become unstable. Further experiments and adjustments to the recipe produced a metal that was both strong and wonderfully

234   clear and, unexpectedly, rang like a bell when tapped. For use on the table, the sparkling qualities of this modified heavy English glass became the envy of Europe. In keeping with the taste of English society during the late Stuart and early Hanoverian periods, the glassmakers favoured plain, massively bold forms with a minimum of decorative detail, though the German influence became more obvious after the Treaty of Utrecht (1713), which led to Western Europe being flooded with German and Bohemian glasses.

The Dutch were among the many who appreciated the virtues of English lead glass, and during the eighteenth century they were to apply a new decorative technique to its beautiful surfaces – the art of

242   stippling (Dutch *stippelen*, pricking). The diamond-point held in the hand is tapped on the glass and, depending on the size, density and depth of the dots, so the tones of light and shade vary and the pictorial composition is gradually built up. The highlights of the composition are achieved by concentrating the dots so closely together that they are almost touching, whereas the dark areas of a scene are scarcely touched by the diamond-point. At first the Dutch exponents of this art would combine their stippling with some minor additions of diamond-point engraving, but in its purest form and in the hands of professionals like David Wolff, the decoration was realised exclusively with stippling. David Wolff, the eldest son of Andries Wolff, a Swiss, and Alida (née van Dijk) was born in 's Hertogenbosch on 8 August 1732 but seems to have lived much of his life in The Hague. When he died, at the age of sixty-five, he had become renowned for his stipple decoration on glass. On one occasion, the Civic Officers of Leiden commissioned him to stipple a goblet using a

237 Two opaque white glass beakers incorporating medallions of gold leaf and ruby lacquer in a modified – and more commercially viable – form of the difficult *Zwischengoldglas* technique. The left-hand beaker has scenes of the Fürnberg establishment for floating timber, the owner's cypher and an inscription ending '. . . *Verfertiget Von Mildner im Jahr 1788*'. The other has a coloured portrait of a gentleman, half-length; on the reverse a coat-of-arms, and on the base a view of a large mansion. Both made by Johann Joseph Mildner (1763–1808) at Gutenbrunn, Austria. H. 10.8 cm.

238 RIGHT Goblet lavishly enamelled with foliate sprays (on the foot) and a landscape filled with fighting horsemen, largely drawn in grisaille but with details painted in strong colours and patches of yellow stain, produced with an oxide of silver as in window glass. From a yellow flattened bulb a ruby thread descends through the centre of the spirally ribbed stem. Bohemian, second quarter of the 18th century. H. 21.8 cm.

239 BELOW, LEFT Ceremonial goblet and cover, with a mould-blown stem and, most exceptionally, decorated entirely with applied gold in low relief, tooled and chased. On the cover boar and stag hunts flank the royal arms of Frederick Augustus, created Elector of Saxony in February 1733 and King of Poland in October of that year; on the bowl is his monogram, AR3. Made in Dresden, probably early in Frederick's reign (1733–63). H. 35.6 cm.

240 BELOW, RIGHT Ceremonial goblet and cover, engraved and heavily gilded, with gadrooning on both the cover and finial and the stem and foot. On the bowl are two convex medallions of coloured glass – gold-ruby and opaque turquoise – each engraved with the gilded monogram EP (Elizabeth Petrovna, daughter of Peter the Great; she seized the throne of Russia in 1741 and died in 1762). Potsdam, mid-18th century. H. 32.4 cm.

design specially drawn by the artist Abraham Delfos (1731–1820) and, interestingly, they paid Wolff five times as much for his stippling as they paid Delfos for his drawing, even though the glass had to be transported at their expense to and from Wolff's workshop in The Hague. Fortunately, at least nine reliably signed and dated examples of his work have survived and, as a result, more than 200 specimens have been attributed to his hand, though some of his contemporaries were producing equally fine quality stippling that is not always easy to distinguish from Wolff's work. Even the former view that all Dutch stippling of the eighteenth century had been executed on imported English lead-glass is now disputed, as it is claimed that at least one Netherlandish glasshouse succeeded in rivalling the best of English 'lead-crystal'.

241   The success of the 'lead-crystal' glass industry in the United Kingdom permitted the British Government in 1746 to levy a profitable tax on glass by weight, while at the same time prohibiting the export of any glass from Ireland – or, indeed, the import of foreign glass into Ireland. When in 1780 the Irish were granted free trade without taxation in this area, the glass manufacturers in Ireland were in a more favourable position than their counterparts in England. As a result, English capital and specialist labour flowed across to Ireland, where not only the Dublin and Belfast manufacturers benefited but in the new centres of Waterford and Cork glasshouses were quick to take root. The luxury glass industry at these four centres continued to flourish until 1825, when the imposition of a comparable tax on Irish glass heralded the industry's gradual decline. During that half-century, however, the brilliant light-refractive character of the 'metal' had been successfully matched by the introduction of sensitively designed wheel-cut decoration and by the skilful use of the press-moulded foot – a technique probably introduced from the Midlands – for many of the bowls and other similar tableware. The Anglo-Irish glass of the late eighteenth and early nineteenth centuries, distinguished by its purity of form and decoration, was renowned for its excellence of craftsmanship.

241 ABOVE Four English clear lead-glass wine-glasses of the first half of the 18th century: (*left to right*) with air-twist stem; with air-twist stem enclosing a coin of Charles II dated 1679 and with applied raspberry prunts and wheel-engraved Jacobite motifs; with a 'tear' bubble in the stem; and with air-bubbles in bowl and stem, enclosing a coin of George I dated 1718. The green wine-glass is Dutch, with air-twist stem and wheel-engraved baroque foliate ornament and birds.

For the making of an air-twist stem, see pp. 234–5, Figs 157–61.

242 OPPOSITE Two goblets of colourless lead glass, enclosing 'tears' of trapped air in the stems. Probably made in England (Newcastle) and decorated with diamond-point stippled scenes. Both are signed by Frans Greenwood (1680–1763), a gifted amateur of English descent who was born in Rotterdam and became a civil servant in Dordrecht in 1726, where most of his work was executed. The decoration on his earliest known glass, dated 1720, is entirely in diamond-point engraving, but during the early 1720s he introduced the art of stippling so successfully that throughout the 18th century other Dutch engravers, including at least one professional, followed suit. The left-hand glass is engraved with three putti, two fighting for a bottle of wine, while a third seizes and empties it. Signed *F. Greenwood f. 1738*. On the right-hand glass Bacchus and his companions encircle the entire circumference of the bowl; the design incorporates a short poem written and published by Greenwood himself. Signed *F. Greenwood fᵗ*. Not dated, but probaby mid-18th century. H. of left-hand glass 24.9 cm.

CHAPTER SIX

Europe and America

1800–1940

ONE CONCLUSION, based on the evidence of the glass that remains or is recorded from any earlier period, seems inescapable: the range and quantity of glass produced during the nineteenth and early twentieth centuries was greater than in any prior period in history. It is as if the entire inventory of almost 5,000 years of glassmaking had been compressed into 140 years.

Cut and engraved glass

During the last years of the eighteenth century, cut patterns on blown Anglo-Irish lead-potash glass were so highly refractive that they trapped light and turned it back into the viewer's eyes, and by 1800 the rich ringing tone of English lead glass had tolled the knell for traditional Central European cut and engraved lime-potash glass. So, as the nineteenth century began, Bohemian glassmakers struggled to imitate the Anglo-Irish style; but Bohemian strengths were soon to lie in coloured glass.

The prevailing Empire cut style was generic and international. As early as 1795, a cut-glass mausoleum approximately 2 metres square by 4 metres high (7 × 14 ft) was ordered by the Nabob of Oude from Mr Blades' London showrooms and shipped to Lucknow. In the first quarter of the nineteenth century, Blades fulfilled orders for large cut chandeliers, candelabra, tables and services from the rulers of Russia, Spain, Portugal, Egypt, Persia and India. A man usually went along to assemble the more complicated pieces *in situ*. For Russian palaces the Imperial Glass Works at St Petersburg produced clear and coloured luxury lead glass blown and cut in the form of large decorative objects with ormolu (*bronze doré*) mounts. A superb pair of toilet tables in amber and blue glass was cut about 1804 from a design by the architect A. N. Voronikhin. One of these is now in the Pavlovsk Palace Museum; the other is in the Corning Museum of Glass, New York. In 1824 the Imperial Glass Works supplied the Shah of Persia with a 'crystal' bed mounted on an iron frame faced with silver-plated brass.

France was not dormant during this time of imperial indulgence. In 1813, Charpentier, proprietor of 'L'Escalier de Cristal', the well-known glass and porcelain shop at 153 Palais-Royal, Paris, was granted a patent to market 'crystal' furniture. This was produced as blank parts by Aimé-Gabriel d'Artigues, then proprietor of the Belgian Cristallerie de Vonêche, and cut, assembled and mounted in ormolu at the workshops of 'L'Escalier de Cristal'. After Charpentier's death,

244

243 Lithograph showing the towering iron-skeletoned glass fountain, 27 feet (9 m) tall, with its tiers of alternate catching and shedding glass basins, designed by F. & C. Osler of Birmingham as the centrepiece of the Great Exhibition of 1851 in the Crystal Palace, London. By 1854 the fountain had been moved with the Palace to Sydenham, just outside London, where it stood in a pool of goldfish. It survived until 1936, when England's greatest glass building was destroyed in a gigantic fire, turning the goldfish black. Author's collection.

244 A new use of glass, not as a mere decorative embellishment of furniture but as its primary material and form, is evident from this one of a pair of massive yet graceful toilet tables made in 1804 at the Imperial Glass Works at St Petersburg from a design by A. N. Voronikhin and intended as stands for a basin and ewer. A single slab of blue glass is supported upon a spirally cut vortex of amber glass on a deep amber base. Ormolu mounts form the feet and unite the sections of glass. H. 87 cm. Corning, New York, The Corning Museum of Glass.

his widow, Mme Desarnaud, entered a selection of cut-glass furniture and accessories in the French National Exhibition of 1819, where it was awarded a gold medal, drew a constant crowd and was even illustrated a decade later in Julia de Fontenelle's *Manuel Complet du Fabricant de Verre et de Cristal*. From its foundation in 1825, Belgium's Val-Saint-Lambert glasshouse produced cut glass in both Anglo-Irish and Empire styles.

By definition, a fashion does not usually last very long, though eventually it may have a reprise. The elaborate earlier cuttings were soon replaced by simpler designs less strenuous on the eyes: broad fluted, reeded or flat panel cuts, or horizontal step cuts. Where

245 Lithyalin vase, designed by Friedrich Egermann (1777–1864) in about 1830–40. Egermann kept the production of Lithyalin a closely guarded secret. Its many-layered internally coloured effects in red, green, mauve, grey, brown and black, and in this case yellow, were achieved by repeated applications of metallic oxides fired in a muffle kiln. Beakers, vases, goblets and perfume flasks were cut with the broad convex and concave facets typical of other Bohemian glass of the period to reveal exciting inner patterns resembling marble or the grain of rare woods. The appeal of these patterns led to painted imitations. H. 30.5 cm. Corning, New York, The Corning Museum of Glass.

diamonds appeared, they were miniaturised to the status of textures. This panelled look, particularly in America, moved easily into bold Gothic Revival cutting, then in turn to be interpreted in pressed glass.

By the time of the Great Exhibition of 1851 in London, glass cutting had been both subordinated in its appearance to casing and strangled in the thickets of engraving. Nevertheless, a mid-century landmark was the cut-glass fountain by F. & C. Osler of Birmingham – over 8 metres (27 ft) tall and weighing 4 tons – symbolically placed in the axis of the incomparable Crystal Palace, where six million visitors took their bearings by it for rendezvous. But 1851 marked the beginning of a general hiatus in the production of cut glass that was to last a quarter of a century.

Meanwhile in Bohemia, following the Napoleonic Wars, glass styles had changed radically. Viennese glasses of the Biedermeier period (1820–40), superbly painted with miniature scenes in transparent enamel by the Viennese porcelain and glass painters Samuel (1762–1815) and Gottlob (1789–1825) Mohn and Anton Kothgasser (1769–1851) took the form of waisted beakers (*Ranfbecher*) on a thick cog-cut base. The Bohemians appropriated the form while enlarging the foot, cutting it into lobed and toothed shapes reminiscent of medieval chalices. They cut the bowls in broad flat panels faced with medallions, which were then enamelled with delightful chinoiserie.

However, it was not glass forms but the use of colour that saved Bohemia from playing a minor role in nineteenth-century glass. With the invention by Georg, Count Buquoy (1781–1851) in about 1803 of a sealing-wax red glass known as Hyalith, and a monopoly granted to him in 1820 to produce it for eight years, an era of coloured glass began that would set the styles for France, Britain and America. The complicated chemistry and firing of red Hyalith produced the effect of marbling. Count Buquoy's jet-black Hyalith of 1817, a shiny version of Wedgwood's Black Basaltes, provided a *soigné* surface for gilt chinoiserie and neo-classical motifs.

It was the marbled effect of red Hyalith that Friedrich Egermann (1777–1864) capitalised upon when in 1828 he received a six-year patent to produce his own Lithyalin glass. Lithyalin combined a variety of opaque and translucent colours achieved with stains; when cut in flat panels, patterns were exposed which resembled the grain of wood.

A vivid description of Bohemian coloured and cut production in 1844 is provided by the traveller Johann Georg Kohl:

Among the manufactures of Prague we must not forget to speak of the warehouses of glass goods. These have chemists and artists in their pay, who are constantly tasking their invention . . . by discovering new articles and giving new colours and forms to those articles which the glasscutters have looked upon as belonging to their legitimate sphere. Of each new discovery or modification a drawing is made, and a copy sent to the manufactory. The drawing and the copy bear corresponding marks and numbers, so that if a sudden demand comes to the warehouse for any particular article, all that is necessary is to send down an order to make up immediately so many dozens of B 288 . . . I was astonished at the immense variety of designs and invention for coffee, tea, and milkpots; at the endless modifications of form which so simple an article as a glass stopper was made to undergo . . . of a thing so unimportant as a lady's smelling bottle (J. G. Kohl, *Austria, Vienna, Prague, etc.*, Philadelphia 1844, p.48).

243

245

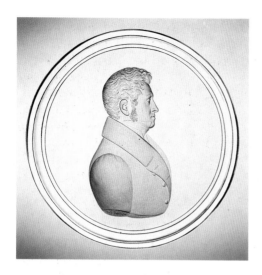

246 Wheel-engraved portrait medallion by Dominik Biemann (1800–1857), signed and dated 1834. Biemann spent his youth working in glasshouses in northern Bohemia and Silesia, where he learned to sketch designs for glass engravers. In Prague he studied with the famous engraver Franz Pohl. Biemann's speciality was engraved portraits, in which intaglio depth gives the illusion of sculptural relief. He had the uncanny ability to capture a sitter's features while conveying the volume of flesh, containing the subtlest of contours within precise outlines, as in the drawings of Ingres. D. 9.5 cm. Corning, New York, The Corning Museum of Glass.

These coloured and cut forms were already being copied in France and America.

As early as 1820, French Opaline glass appeared in the shape of urns, *flacons* (scent bottles) and jewel-boxes blown in wooden moulds, some with ormolu mounts. By 1830 Opalines were being produced in a wide range of colours rendered semi-opaque by the addition to the glass batch of powdered bone, oxides of antimony or arsenic. It is as if the pale rose, violet and greens of the new French Opalines were seen through a cloud.

In 1836, just as French glassmakers were visiting Central Europe to acquire for study examples of the rich, deep colours of Bohemian glass, and the Société d'Encouragement pour l'Industrie Française was offering prizes for the production of French domestic glassware imitating the Bohemian, Bohemia itself was busy adopting the French pastel palette. French Opalines of the 1840s were often gilded and painted in vitrifiable colours, and by the 1860s carried designs in relief. The finest Opalines were produced by the glasshouses of Baccarat, Saint-Louis and, until its closure in 1851, Choisy-le-Roi.

While the new Bohemian cut-glass forms were being developed, engraving far from disappeared. And with the cleanly delineated, telling portraits engraved by Dominik Biemann (1800–1857) on cast colourless medallions, beakers and goblets, a peak of refinement was reached in Bohemia. A Biemann portrait medallion (*c.*1840) of a lady seen in profile has the sparing, delicately incised features of an Ingres drawing. As it became fashionable to have one's portrait engraved by Biemann, he captured the likeness of many a prominent visitor to the famous spa of Františkovy Lásně (Franzenbad). A superb engraving by August Böhm (1812–90) of Mistrovice (Meistersdorf) on a colourless *pokal* (a tall goblet) depicts the overthrow of the Persians by Alexander the Great in 334 BC, painstakingly reproducing the composition of a painting by Le Brun, first shown in the Paris Salon of 1673 and now preserved in the Louvre. Böhm signed and dated the engraving on the goblet in 1840. In 1849 it came into the possession of the glassmaker Apsley Pellatt (1791–1863), who wrote: 'For depth of workmanship and artistic execution, as a modern intaglio engraving, this vase is unrivalled.' The goblet is currently on loan to the Broadfield House Glass Museum, Kingswinford, Dudley, England.

By the 1850s Bohemian engraving on coloured glass had progressed through the stages of staining, flashing and casing in two colours – usually cobalt blue or copper ruby over opaque white, sometimes with an acid-etched background. The engraving of beakers and especially tall goblets was a speciality of Karl Pfohl (1826–94), whose horses, subjects taken from paintings (including works by Raphael) and portraits were engraved to eerie perfection. Pfohl's portrait of Queen Victoria possesses the textural subtleties of a daguerreotype, from which it could conceivably have been engraved.

By the time of the 1851 Exhibition, Bohemian cased glass had established a lexicon of effective cut patterns: circles and ovals (printies), trefoils and quatrefoils, single and double-ended ogee arches. A few years later, however, the strong statement of these tactile motifs became camouflaged amid florid enamelling and gilding, apparently perpetrated for the flourishing Eastern market.

During the 1840s shiploads of Bohemian cased ('plated') glass had been arriving in Boston and New York, and by 1847 the New England Glass Company (NEGC) was parading its own 'plated' glass in Boston's fifth Massachusetts Charitable Mechanic Association exhibition, for which it received a gold medal. An advertising circular from the Union Glass Works, Kensington, Philadelphia, lists the colours Ruby, Canary, Turquoise, Opal, Victoria Emerald, Amber, Amethyst, Amarite, Black, White Agate and Chameleon. The Charitable Mechanic report of 1850 claimed that 'the NEGC Plated glass ware is all beautiful'.

Not enough stress has been placed on British cased glass, which was being produced from about the mid-1830s by Stevens & Williams of Stourbridge despite the restrictive excise tax levied on glass by weight. Following the repeal of the tax in 1845, W. H., B. & J. Richardson showed their cased glass at the Manchester Exhibition of 1849, to which the Birmingham firms of George Bacchus & Sons, Rice Harris & Son, and Lloyd & Summerfield also sent their latest examples. So international was the cased and cut repertoire that one tall and graceful vase has been variously attributed to Bohemia, England and France.

After 1851, as cut colourless glass went into fitful hibernation for the next twenty-five years, the vast international exhibitions became showcases for glass delicately engraved in a broad range of designs from recollections of mythology to design sourcebook transcriptions of classical and Renaissance motifs – even reproductions of seventeenth- and eighteenth-century Central European glass engraving. Apart from well-known manufacturers such as Pellatt & Co., engraving was done by the London decorating firms of Phillips, Dobson & Pearce, Naylor & Co. and J. G. Green; Green's 'Neptune' jug (now in the Victoria and Albert Museum) was shown at the 1851 Exhibition and was much illustrated at the time. Even the Staffordshire china manufacturer W. T. Copeland carried engraved glass; for example, at the Vienna Exhibition of 1873 he showed a handled vase finely engraved by Paul Oppitz, who came from Haida in Bohemia.

In America, internationally popular Germanic scenes of the hunt were exquisitely engraved through gold-ruby cased or flashed glass, many of these commissions being special orders. Outstanding is the cut goblet (Toledo Museum of Art) engraved about 1865–70 by Louis Vaupel (c.1812–1903), who came to the NEGC from Germany in 1852 and supervised the engraving departments until 1888, when the firm moved to Toledo, Ohio. Vaupel's hunting scene includes tiny figures of men on horseback, dogs hounding the stag at bay, a squirrel, a pheasant, an owl and a snake. Another hunting scene of equally high quality was engraved in about 1860 by Vaupel's prize student, Henry B. Leighton, an American of Scottish descent, on a jug now in the Corning Museum of Glass.

The term 'rock-crystal engraving' refers to deep intaglio wheel-engraving in which all the relief and intaglio cuts are polished so that the engraved design becomes one with the vessel's shining surface. Innumerable floral, Chinese- and Japanese-derived motifs gleam on bowls, decanters and jugs. Among the émigré 'rock-crystal' engravers and their disciples working in England from about 1880 to at least the early twentieth century, the best known were Joseph Kneller and John Orchard at Stevens & Williams, Brierley Hill (near Stourbridge), and

247 Kerosene lamp by the Boston and Sandwich Glass Company, Massachusetts, about 1865–75. This fine 'banquet size' lamp was blown in colourless glass, then double cased, first in opaque white and then blue, and cut back to reveal the clear inner glass. The ovals, quatrefoils and tracery were cut with a precision seldom seen in cased glass, leaving a thin, even, white line inside the blue. H. 81.2 cm. Norfolk, Virginia, The Chrysler Museum.

248 Engraved ewer by William Fritsche (1853–1924) for Thomas Webb & Sons of Stourbridge, England, 1886. It took Fritsche two and a half years to engrave this magnificent ewer, with its head of Neptune, its twisting convex curves suggesting rushing water, its fish and sea-shells. The oriental influences of jade and rock-crystal carving are obvious, but the flowing form of the piece seems to have been inspired by the swift mountain streams of Fritsche's native Bohemia. H. 38.5 cm. Corning, New York, The Corning Museum of Glass.

Frederick E. Kny (active 1870–1900) and William Fritsche (1853–1924), both of whom worked for Thomas Webb & Sons, Stourbridge. Kny's signed 'Elgin' vase (acquired in 1983 by the Broadfield House Glass Museum, Kingswinford) dates from about 1875, shortly after John Northwood had completed his famous 'Elgin' vase of 1873. It is remarkable for the high relief of its frieze of classical figures (based on the Elgin Marbles) and the polishing of some of its engraved areas). Fritsche's baroquely curvaceous jug of 1886 (now in the Corning Museum) was sold directly to the United States upon its completion.

Cutting returned in force at the Centennial International Exhibition of 1876, held in Philadelphia. At the Paris Exhibition two years later, the centrepiece of Baccarat's display was a massive cut-glass temple of six Corinthian columns supporting an open cupola of flying spandrels, the whole encircled by a glass balustrade topped by urns. By the early 1880s deep cuts into very thick lead glass blanks led to new design concepts based on intersecting parallel scorings forming a dense network of stars, octagons and other geometric patterns as intricate as an Islamic mosaic. First called 'rich-cut' and later 'brilliant-cut', like diamonds, the dense patterns resemble seat-caning, pinwheels or exploding stars. In America, Christian Dorflinger & Sons of White Mills, Pennsylvania, supplied highly refractive blanks to some of the hundreds of cutting shops, while their own cutting, though often dense, was always elegant.

At the 1893 World's Columbian Exposition in Chicago, the Libbey Glass Company of Toledo, Ohio (formerly the NEGC of Cambridge, Massachusetts) erected an impressive factory in the grounds of the Fair, where Adolf Kretschmann demonstrated cutting. Libbey exhibited not only the expected punchbowls but also a cut-glass lamp 83.8 cm (33 in) high; they went on to surpass this achievement at the St Louis World's Fair of 1904 with a lamp 146 cm (57½ in) high, as well as a large pedestal table, both of which are now in the Toledo Museum of Art. But by the end of the First World War it was all over. J. Hoare & Co. in Corning, New York, the oldest cutting shop in the United States, closed in 1920, and Dorflinger shut down the following year.

In 1916 and 1917 respectively, Simon Gate, an artist with a classical training from the Stockholm Academy, and Edward Hald, a former pupil of Matisse, were hired to design for Orrefors, the famous Swedish glasshouse, which had been turning out cased Art Nouveau glass and wanted something different. Each produced designs to be engraved in clear, colourless glass. Gate's designs called for deep sculptural intaglio engraving in neo-classical style, his lush nude figures choreographed around the vessels in mythological frolic; while Hald's thin, shallow lines and simplified, almost caricatured figures could have served for book or fashion illustrations. At the Paris Exhibition of 1925 their glass caused a sensation and put Orrefors on the international glass map. So much so that when Steuben of Corning achieved a chemical formula for 'crystal' (lead glass) of 'matchless purity and transparency', a sculptor, Sidney Waugh, was invited to become Steuben's first designer of the post-Frederick Carder era (for a discussion of Carder's work, see p. 209 below). Steuben's colourless glass is still being engraved today.

Pressed glass

Glass pressed by machine was the most technologically advanced and economically significant glassworking technique introduced since the invention of blowing. It made possible the unlimited duplication of plain or patterned glass; and skilled blowers could be replaced by unskilled, cheap labour, making more glass available at lower prices to a broader buying public.

In 1834 the Boston and Sandwich factory suprintendent William Stutson stated that between sixty and seventy presses were in operation at the factory, and that from one to four weeks was sufficient to train a good presser: 'I have taken labourers out of the yard . . . for that'; but 'to keep moulds in order requires a mechanic'. In his *Reminiscences of Glass-Making* (1865), Deming Jarves, founder and outspoken impresario of the Boston and Sandwich Glass Company, says of pressed glass:

Fifty years back [1815] the writer imported from Holland salts made by being pressed in metallic moulds, and from England glass candlesticks and table centre-bowls, plain with ['lemon-squeezer'] pressed square feet, rudely made . . . America can claim the credit of great improvements in the needful machinery which has advanced the art to its present perfection. More than three quarters of the weekly melt is now worked up into pressed glass, and it is estimated that upwards of two million dollars has been expended in the moulds and machines now used in this particular branch of glass-making. This leaves Europe far behind us in this process.

Inventions often evolve in stages. Fully-fledged mechanical pressing began on a small scale in 1825, with a patent by John P. Bakewell of Bakewell, Page & Bakewell, Pittsburgh, for the pressing of furniture knobs by means of a mould and plunger. Patents soon followed for Henry Whitney and Enoch Robinson of the NEGC, and for Deming Jarves of Sandwich; and by 1830 glass in both flat and hollow ware was being mechanically pressed, and even exported to Europe, the Caribbean and South America. Yet for at least the next twenty-five years American lamps combined blown fonts with pressed bases, and candlesticks were often composed of interchangeable pressed segments, creating a variety of design sources that today's glass experts are only just beginning to sort out.

In *Curiosities of Glass Making* (1849), under the heading 'American pressed glass', Apsley Pellatt showed a pressing apparatus and described the problems in its operation, which were initially many. The adjustable apparatus consisted of a table on which was mounted a mould containing a die. The mould was placed within a cap-ring below a plunger operated by a lever. Pressing was basically a two-man operation, requiring a gatherer to gather the glass to be pressed, and a presser to shear off the gather with one hand so that it would drop into the mould, while operating with the other the lever that lowered the plunger into the mould, thus pressing the glass. The mould had to be kept at an even temperature a little below red heat. If too hot, the glass would adhere to plunger and mould; if too cool, the surface of the glass would be marred. The gatherer had to gather the exact quantity of glass to be pressed, or the piece would be either incomplete or too thick.

The great glassmaker Georges Bontemps (1799–1884) wrote that the shear mark left when the glass was separated from the pontil did not disappear but was spread over the surface of the glass, and that joints between the sections of the mould were always visible. Pressed glass, Bontemps observed, lacks a surface comparable to that of blown or cut glass; and while a piece could be empontilled and reheated at the furnace to remove blemishes, reheating could also soften and distort the design. Bontemps noted that the Americans obfuscated these defects by stippling the interstices of the mould design, an effect he called '*sablé*' (sandy); Americans call it 'lacy'. Stippling gave a silvery sheen to the glass, which was quickly taken up by French, Belgian and British glassmakers and had for a time a great vogue. By the 1840s pressing comprised an important part of French crystal glass production.

Glass pressing had appeared at the time when Anglo-Irish cut-glass patterns and their cheap mould-blown imitations had largely run their course. It was a field day for glass designers and die sinkers. According to the complexity of the form, glass was pressed in simple or multipartite hinged iron moulds. American forms ranged from simple flatware to stemmed, handled and covered hollow ware; from cup plates – those small but necessary conveniences for holding the cup while the hot tea was poured into the saucer to cool – to covered sugar bowls, vegetable dishes and compotes, even a flowerpot. Pressed designs, with their hundreds of patterns which came to be named and sought after, were at first necessarily busy – and as enticing as lace valentines. Nevertheless, the designs were basically neo-classical, with an elaborate central patera surrounded by stippling, all within a border of floral or geometric cartouches having the authority of a Renaissance frieze. Scalloped rims more or less concealed the problem of producing a smooth rim, though in France pressed tumbler rims were often cut and polished. Pressed designs were copied from architectural pattern books and probably from imported English ceramics. The glass itself was usually clear and colourless, but was occasionally produced in rich amber, lemon, cobalt, green and amethyst. There are also opaque white (milk glass) examples, and some opal covered sugar bowls, probably from the Providence Flint Glass Works, Providence, Rhode Island, are the epitome of elegance in the French style. Some American pressed salts are even shaped like Napoleon I's sarcophagus.

In the years between 1830 and 1845, pressed glass window panes were produced in the Pittsburgh area, apparently meant for panels in or beside doors separating the dining room and parlour, though some have survived in cupboards and bureaus not only in Pittsburgh but also in West Virginia and Ohio. One made by Benjamin Bakewell bears the impress of an ogee arch above Gothic windows; another shows an Ohio River steamboat. Some Gothic Revival motifs are said to have been borrowed from cast-iron stove designs.

Colour appears in quantity after 1845 in architecturally composed candlesticks, celery holders and tall vases whose arched, boldly panelled and sometimes wrythen forms (swirled or diagonally twisted ribbing or fluting) rise to ruffled or scalloped rims. An American decorator filled a Gothic-arched window in his early twentieth-century house with Gothic-inspired amethyst pressed glass, and set a leaded door-frame with cup plates as roundels.

The speed of glass pressing was remarkable. Hunt's *Merchant's*

252 American pressed glass vases and a candlestick, about 1845–60. Because pressing techniques had not advanced sufficiently by this time to enable such complicated shapes as these to be pressed in a single mould, the top and the stem (with the base) were pressed in separate moulds and joined with a merese while hot. Both the vases were further hot-manipulated after leaving the moulds. That on the left was finished by tooling the bowl into a trefoil, while the upper portion of that in the centre was twisted to produce spiral flutes. H. of tallest object 24.2 cm. Norfolk, Virginia, The Chrysler Museum.

Magazine for October 1846 states that five workers – three men and two boys – could press 100 tumblers an hour, or one every forty seconds. This compared with four or five minutes for a blown tumbler. Advertisements and catalogues promoted the latest changes in pressed fashion, and by the middle of the century pressed table sets of a single pattern that included such accessories as celery and spoon holders, egg cups, sugar bowls, decanters and compotes in several sizes became a further inducement to buy. The family of lesser means could now furnish a dining table with an impressive array of glass.

A significant change in glass pressing took place in 1864. Up to that time, most American pressed glass had contained lead. But now William Leighton of Hobbs, Brockunier & Co., Wheeling, West Virginia, achieved a soda-lime glass in which bicarbonate of soda replaced soda ash. The new soda-lime glass proved less than half the cost of lead glass to produce and could be worked and cooled more rapidly. Furthermore, its optical clarity was good and it could be pressed more thinly than lead glass, all of which suggested new patterns and subject matter while promoting technological improvements in pressing.

An orgy of pressed forms followed. At the Centennial International Exhibition of 1876 in Philadelphia, Gillinder & Sons of that city set up a complete working branch factory on the exhibition grounds, where quantities of frosted and opal glass paperweight busts, toothpick holders and slippers were stamped out by mobile presses and sold as souvenirs. The Centennial constituted a sort of giant trade fair. In 1876, Doyle & Co. of Pittsburgh boasted of having sold 20,000 sets of glass toy miniatures. Libbey Glass Company's factory at the Chicago World's Fair of 1893 did a brisk business in souvenirs cut and pressed.

253 'Holly Amber' butter dish, made by the Indiana Tumbler and Goblet Company, Greentown, Indiana. The Indiana Tumbler and Goblet Company burned down in 1903, the year in which this butter dish (also called 'Holly Golden Agate') was pressed. In a single decade the company produced an astonishing variety of glass flora, fauna and patterns pressed into pitchers, mugs, cruets, bowls, toothpick holders and cakestands in a variety of colours, but notably in a mouth-watering café-au-lait. This unusual butter dish alternates transparent amber with opal panels on a cover that suggests a domed glass ceiling. H. 15.2 cm. Corning, New York, The Corning Museum of Glass.

In Britain, although 'press-moulded' glass was being produced in the Midlands from the 1830s, notably in the form of plates commemorating events in the lives of Queen Victoria and Prince Albert, pressed design appears not to have got into its stride until the 1870s and 1880s. In 1879, Sowerby's Ellison Glassworks, Gateshead, introduced the attractive 'Patent Queen's Ivory' patterned ware, and in 1882 it claimed to be the world's largest manufacturer of 'press-moulded' glass, the works employing 1,000 workers on a 5½-acre site.

From the 1880s, further colours were introduced, notably marbled colours, ruby-staining, the bicoloured 'Amberina' and, by the turn of the century, iridescent glass inspired by the glass of Tiffany and Carder (see below). Semi-automatic, electric-powered rotary presses appeared in the 1880s, and by 1920 the entire operation, from the gathering of the glass to its completion in the lehr, was automated without human labour. Some glass, such as the animals and patterns of the Indiana Tumbler and Goblet Company, Greentown, Indiana (1894–1903, destroyed by fire) in opaque Nile green, mocha and café-au-lait, and clear emerald, cool blue and amber, is both whimsical and delightful. But in general, automation produced more and more glass of lesser and lesser quality, until it came to be given away at carnivals and was thus subsequently referred to perjoratively as carnival glass. Today it is collectable.

Some special techniques and achievements

Nineteenth-century glassmakers developed an astonishing array of new and revived ways of treating glass. One of the earliest of these innovations was – to use the popular term – the 'sulphide'. Sulphides were generally isolated cut-out relief portraits of prominent figures, often in profile, reproduced in an opaque white silica-clay material from subjects by French medallists and enclosed in a deflated pocket of glass fused to the surface of tumblers, scent bottles, decanters, vases, jewel-boxes, candelabra and wall plaques. Among the first to

253

develop the technique were the former Sèvres sculptor Barthélemy Desprez, working in Paris between 1792 and 1819, and his son, who continued the enterprise until 1830. The Frenchman Boudon de Saint-Amans (1774–1858), who had made a special visit to the Staffordshire pottery factories, was the first to obtain a patent for the process, in 1818, followed in 1819 by Apsley Pellatt's patent for his similar *crystallo-céramie*. Pressed and cut tumblers bearing sulphides were produced in France, Britain, Belgium, Germany, Bohemia, Portugal, and in America, where profile portraits of Washington, Franklin and Lafayette (who visited America in 1825) appear in the bottom of Anglo-Irish-style lead glass tumblers made by Bakewell's of Pittsburgh. John Ford of Edinburgh encrusted sulphides of Wellington, Robert Burns, Gladstone and Prince Albert, among others. The popularity of sulphides was further enhanced by their inclusion in paperweights of the 1845–55 period in France. Sulphide production was revived in the late nineteenth century in Belgium, in Czechoslovakia (1918–35), and in France by Baccarat and Saint-Louis after the Second World War.

In 1827 the antiquarian and collector Heinrich von Minutoli used the then current Italian term *millefiori* (thousand flowers) to describe the contemporary revival of the old process of incorporating, during the process of manufacture, slices of glass canes bearing a variety of floral designs within the thickness of the glass itself. In the 1830s and 1840s, the Silesian and Bohemian glassworks of Carlsthal, Hoffnungsthal and others were producing millefiori snuff boxes, small vases and scent bottles; while in Murano, Domenico Bussolin (died 1886), Pietro Bigaglia (1786–1876) and Giovanni Franchini (1804–73) were turning out desk sets, cutlery handles and all manner of small baubles, many with remarkably detailed portrait and figurative canes.

By 1845 the Venetian *millefiori* ball had been sliced to rest without rolling, thereby creating the paperweight. These cheaply priced novelties containing *millefiori* or lamp-worked designs of fruits and

254, 255 Basket paperweight by Clichy, about 1850–55. Brilliantly patterned and coloured, Clichy *millefiori* paperweights epitomise the best in the art of decorative glass. This extraordinary basket, though now missing its red and white twist handle, is one of the most adventurously successful paperweights ever made. Unlike other paperweights, the design is not magnified by a dome of clear glass but lies just below the surface. The ground of grass or 'moss' canes becomes a parterre for roses and floral canes that could have been freshly planted at Versailles. D. 10.9 cm. Courtesy Sotheby & Co.

256 Lamp-worked glasses by the Venice and Murano Glass Company, 1878. These opalescent *tours de force* were shown at the Paris Exhibition of 1878. A hotter, gas-burning flame allowed lamp-workers to assemble coloured and opal elements borrowed from three centuries of Venetian glass in an acrobatic design. The old Venetian historicism was continued into the 1880s by the Rheinischen Glashütten (Cologne) at the same time as Emile Gallé was creating his entirely new glass decorating techniques. H. of tallest glass 51.5 cm. Corning, New York, The Corning Museum of Glass, Gifts of Jerome Strauss and of the Ruth Bryan Strauss Memorial Foundation.

flowers appeared simultaneously in Italy, Bohemia and Silesia, and in France, where examples were often signed and dated by Baccarat, Saint-Louis and Clichy between 1845 and 1858. The magnifying dome 254–5 of the paperweight enhanced the kaleidoscopic brilliance of the designs, and the *millefiori* repertoire was extended to include scent bottles, goblets, inkwells, vases and mantel ornaments. By 1849 the Birmingham firms of George Bacchus & Sons and Rice Harris were exhibiting *millefiori* paperweights, and in 1852 the vogue for paperweights jumped the Atlantic to Sandwich and the NEGC, where the finest examples were cased and cut like their French counterparts.

The European paperweight craze lasted about a decade, but in Murano it was only the prelude to a wholesale reinterpretation of Alexandrian, Roman, Renaissance and post-Renaissance glass, a 256 movement which lasted into the twentieth century. In 1861 Antonio Salviati (1816–90) had founded an enamel-mosaic factory which from 1866 was known as Salviati & Co.; it established branch offices in London, where important glass commissions were accomplished, including mosaics for St Paul's Cathedral and the Albert Memorial Chapel at Windsor Castle. The English fondness for Venetian glass was promoted by books illustrating 'historicising' Venetian glass, such as Charles Eastlake's *Hints on Household Taste* (1868) and Robert W. Edis's *Decoration and Furniture of Town Houses* (New York 1881); and

Salviati's share of the English market was competed for by such Venetian-inspired objects as the centrepieces and flower stands produced in the 1870s by Hodgetts, Richardson & Son, Stourbridge, the openly imitative glass of James Jenkinson's Leith Flint Glass Works, Edinburgh, and, from the 1880s, the delicately absorbed modulations of Harry J. Powell of Whitefriars in London.

Silvered glass, an innovation patented in 1849 by F. Hale Thompson of Berners Street, London, and licensed to Edward Varnish & Co., also of London, is double-walled glassware which to the eye appears to be made of silver. The effect was achieved by pouring a solution of silver nitrate through a hole in the bottom of the glass into the space between the inner and outer walls, draining off the excess solution through the same hole and plugging it with papier-mâché, cork or a lead plug sometimes bearing the manufacturer's name. Patented in 1866 by Thomas Leighton of the NEGC, the idea was soon taken up by the Brooklyn Flint Glass Company, the Boston Silver Glass Company and others, who produced silvered pitchers, vases, candlesticks, curtain tie-backs, gazing globes and presentation cups. Pretty but fragile and largely non-functional, silvered glassware became increasingly trivialised, and its production declined into a cottage industry during the 1880s, when in France, Belgium and Bohemia more elaborate, crudely engraved and painted forms were made.

Amidst the design overkill of the 1860s, the disciplined neo-classicism of an engraved glass masterpiece by John Northwood of Wordsley (1836–1902), the 'Elgin' vase of 1873 (Birmingham Museums and Art Gallery, England), which had taken nearly nine years to engrave, led inevitably to the prestigious commission to copy the famous Portland Vase. This talented English craftsman carved his version of the vase between 1873 and 1876; a second copy was carved by Joseph Locke in 1878 (both are now in the Corning Museum of Glass). Wedgwood had already made ceramic copies of the Portland Vase in 'jasper ware' in about 1790, but to undertake a copy in the hazardous and exacting cameo glass technique was another matter: a team of skilled workmen under the supervision of Northwood's cousin Philip Pargeter produced many two-colour blanks before one – thought to have been blown by Daniel Hancock – was considered acceptable. The two-colour blank was cased in the nineteenth-century manner, by making a 'cup' of opaque white glass and introducing a gather of blue glass, fusing this blue glass to the inner surface of the white cup; the cased result was then blown to the shape and size of the Portland Vase. After annealing, the shine was removed from the outer opaque white casing with Northwood's 'white acid', the design drawn upon it, then covered with an acid-resist varnish, and the vase placed in a vat of hydrofluoric acid which removed the extraneous areas of white from the blue body, leaving a design in rough matt relief. This then had to be carved away with engraving wheels and sharp-pointed steel burins set in wooden handles like leads in a pencil, creating a scene in subtlest relief and shading. Equally superb is Northwood's 'Pegasus' vase (1876–82), now in the Smithsonian Institution, Washington. The horses' heads at the sides and the Pegasus atop the lid were carved by Edwin Grice. Northwood became Art Director at Stevens & Williams, Stourbridge, in the early 1880s.

The next generation of cameo carvers included John Northwood II

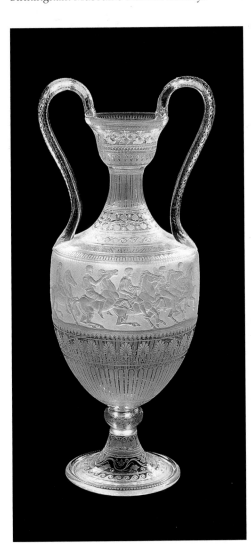

257 'Elgin' vase made in 1873 by John Northwood. In clear glass, the vase is engraved with a relief frieze of horsemen based on the Elgin Marbles. H. 39.4 cm. Birmingham Museums and Art Gallery.

257

75

(1870–1960) and the Woodall brothers, George (1850–1925) and Thomas (1849–1926). Both brothers had been apprentices of John Northwood I and were engaged by the Stourbridge firm of Thomas Webb & Sons, the chief rivals of Stevens & Williams. The Woodall team's cameo glass of the 1880s and 1890s is breathtakingly skilful in its subtle gradations of textures and depth of field: drapery falling over stairs, a fish seen under water. In George Woodall's plaque 'Moorish Bathers' (1898), in a New York private collection, the eight interior columns of the building in the background recede not only in perspective but in atmospheric distance. In the Woodalls' work, whether historicising or decorative, the floral and border carving is bold, almost timeless, while the figures reveal a late Victorian sentimentalised classicism, such as one sees in the paintings of Alma-Tadema. Late in the century the increasing popularity of both Webb's and Stevens & Williams's two-, three- and even four-colour cased and carved arabesque and floral vases, ginger jars, bottles and flasks encouraged a speeding-up of the cameo-carving process by using acid, and a consequent deterioration in the quality of the designs.

As the Aesthetic Movement of the late 1870s and 1880s spread throughout the decorative arts in England and America, glassmakers took advantage of glass chemistry to produce new colour effects, shown to best advantage on generally simple glass forms derived from historical or oriental prototypes; it was glass for art's sake, or Art Glass. A black 'Lava' glass collaged with coloured shards, produced by the Mount Washington Glass Company, New Bedford, Massachusetts, dates from 1878. Particularly striking were vessels in which one paler colour, usually in the lower part, transfused gently into a different, richer colour in the upper part, like a sky at sunset. The colour changes were achieved by adding gold oxide to the lead glass batch and reheating the upper part of the vessel, causing the metallic oxide to change colour, or 'strike'.

These colour effects were patented and given exotic names. 'Amberina' was patented in 1893 by Joseph Locke (formerly of Hodgetts, Richardson & Co., England, and now working for the NEGC); shortly afterwards it was licensed to Sowerby's Ellison Glassworks, Gateshead, England, as 'Pressed Amberina', and eventually produced by Mount Washington as 'Rose Amber'. Patents were infringed, companies sued, settlements reached and colour names changed because, as one advertiser put it in 1886, Art Glass was 'all the rage'. In 1886 a Chinese porcelain vase shaded the colours of a ripe peach fetched the unheard-of sum of $18,000 at the Mary Morgan sale in New York, immediately inspiring Hobbs, Brockunier & Co., Wheeling, West Virginia, to produce a 'fac-simile Morgan' 'Peachblow' glass mounted in an amber pressed glass stand with dragons. The same year Edward D. Libbey patented for the NEGC an opaque 'Peach-Blow' glass that shaded from cream to raspberry-sorbet pink. Mount Washington's 'Peach Blow' included cobalt, and shaded upwards from a pale evening blue to a soft rose. An Englishman, Frederick Shirley, patented his formula (developed at Mount Washington in 1885) for 'Burmese' glass; it fused from greenish or creamy yellow to rose or coral pink and contained oxide of uranium. This was made under licence in England from 1886 by Thomas Webb & Sons, who called it 'Queen's Burmese Ware'.

258 Cameo-glass vase signed by Thomas Webb & Sons, Stourbridge, England, and probably made in the 1880s. The tall neck of the vase and the hot colours of its arabesque pattern recall the Eastern designs so confidently transcribed in a variety of materials in the heyday of the British Empire. H. 40.6 cm. Courtesy Leo Kaplan Antiques Ltd.

259 Decorated satin 'Burmese' vases by the Mount Washington Glass Company, New Bedford, Massachusetts, about 1885–90. Uranium oxide had been used by the Bohemian maker Josef Riedel (c.1830–48) to achieve his colours 'Annagrün' (greenish-yellow) and 'Annagelb' (yellowish-green), the latter known at the Boston and Sandwich Company as 'canary yellow'. At the Mount Washington works, Frederick Shirley is said to have added to a glass batch of 184 pounds only 2 pounds of uranium and 1½ pennyweights of prepared liquid gold. In these delicately detailed pieces, the opaque and matte 'Burmese' is decorated in gold leaf and enamels with restraint and consideration for the form of the vessel. The ruffled rim of the central vase was achieved on a pegged or corrugated form. H. of tallest vase 35.5 cm. Norfolk, Virginia, The Chrysler Museum.

Other noteworthy American Art Glass included the delicately stained and acid-etched 'Pomona' (NEGC), Mount Washington's beaded 'Coralene', and the enamelled and gilded 'Royal Flemish' and 'Crown Milano' of the late 1880s and 1890s, the tableware frequently being silver-mounted by Mount Washington's adjoining Pairpoint Manufacturing Company.

In late nineteenth-century France, a basically new kind of glass, *pâte de verre*, emerged from experiments mainly carried out at the Sèvres Porcelain Factory, Paris. The artists Henri Cros (1840–1907), Albert Dammouse (1843–1926), Amalric Walter (1859–1942), Georges Despret (1862–1952), François-Emile Décorchement (1880–1971) and Gabriel Argy-Rousseau (1885–1953) created the semblances of marble, alabaster, ceramic, softly tinted wax or opaline glass by casting into sculpted moulds and fusing crushed and powdered glass coloured by metallic oxides. From 1883 to the mid-twentieth century, these artists exhibited signed sculptural works in *pâte de verre*, ranging from classical figural landscapes to Art Deco vases as precisely incised as the finest leather bookbindings of the period.

260

260 *Pâte de verre* vase by Gabriel Argy-Rousseau (1885–1953). While some of Argy-Rousseau's early *pâte de verre* is easy to confuse with that of François-Emile Décorchement, by the 1920s he had developed his own simplified Art Deco style of floral and figural subjects fitting into increasingly monochromatic geometric designs, as in this example. Apple-pickers in reddish-brown Grecian garb move among yellow and amber apples hanging from black trees in a translucent scene above a tall band of 'key' pattern. The opening of the tomb of Tutankhamum in 1922 inspired Argy-Rousseau to design vases in 'Egyptian style'. H. 24.2 cm. Courtesy Christie's, New York.

Five formative artists

The son of a Lorraine glassmaker, Emile Gallé (1846–1904) established his own glasshouse in Nancy at the age of 21, and in the 1880s became not only the central figure of the School of Nancy, designing furniture, faience and glass, but of the whole multi-media Art Nouveau style. At first Gallé decorated the surface of his clear, colourless glass with raised enamelling, champlevé and engraving of flowers, figures, lines of verse and personal or patriotic inscriptions. But he soon began thickening the body of the glass in a sculptural way, building up the inner body with cased layers enclosing naturalistic elements (*intercalaire*), while adding carving in high relief and preformed coloured elements to the surface, and flattening and marvering other elements into it (*marqueterie de verre*). Gallé applied to glass a thorough knowledge of flora and fauna, from weeds to orchids, bats to butterflies, seahorses to octopi – all subjects that he introduced onto or within the glass in a naturalistic style, eschewing the writhing distortion generally considered the hallmark of Art Nouveau design. The results were time-capsules of natural growth and decay, a three-dimensional life-cycle revealed alternately in reflected and transmitted light.

261–2

Gallé's best work was shown in both major and local exhibitions between 1878 and 1900, and also in Siegfried (Samuel) Bing's Paris shop 'La Maison de l'Art Nouveau'; while some 300 workmen produced vast quantities of more affordable lamps and vases in pale yellow, amber or grey bodies over which are silhouetted landscapes, flora and fauna in browns, reds and blues which have been thinly cased, engraved and cut back with acid to the inner pale glow. Less often, brilliant sunset and subtle twilight effects were achieved. After Gallé's death, his friend and chief designer, Victor Prouvé, continued the enterprise until 1913; it finally closed in 1931.

Louis Comfort Tiffany (1848–1933), the scion of the famous New York family of jewellers, had studied painting with George Innes after the Civil War. In 1869 he travelled to Spain, where he met Samuel Coleman, a pupil of the painter Asher B. Durand. Together they went to North Africa, where Coleman interested Tiffany in Islamic textiles. Later Coleman, the textile designer Candace Wheeler and Edward C. Moore, Tiffany & Co.'s silver designer, steered the young Tiffany towards decorative arts and orientalia. With these three as partners, Tiffany formed in 1879 Louis C. Tiffany and Associated Artists, the first of several Tiffany decorating firms, studios and factories.

Even more the multi-media master than Gallé, Tiffany turned a well-stocked imagination to interior design: no material escaped his transforming influence, especially glass. His leaded windows, many designed and all produced by staff artists and craftsmen, are collages of flowing passages of naturalistic effects achieved through colour lamination of folded, pulled, fractured, splattered, wrinkled, rumpled opalescent and impure pot-metal glass manipulated while hot – the leading and copper foiling following the naturalistic design. Tiffany conceived and designed, though he did not himself blow, his favourite Favrile (hand-wrought) glass, but he supervised its progress, quick to take advantage of chance blowing or tooling errors or glass defects that could be turned to novel effects. Aside from the delicate, long-stemmed floriform glasses and such *tours de force* as the iridescent

263

'Jack-in-the-Pulpit' and 'Peacock' vases, most Favrile vessels follow classical, oriental (e.g. gourd), bulbous or robust shapes whose colouristic effects do not interrupt the surface of the glass. Tiffany owned ancient Roman glasses that had become iridescent through burial, and reproduced the effect by treating the hot glass with metallic oxides.

Using a broad range of materials, Tiffany decorated the mansions of wealthy clients such as the H. O. Havemeyers, whom he eventually persuaded to donate some of the earliest pieces he had made for them to the Metropolitan Museum of Art – the first 'modern' American glass acquired by that museum; and in 1923 he lent to the Metropolitan and other museums a range of Tiffany glass from his own collection. Tiffany's eminence in the decorative arts was established at the Paris Exhibitions of 1878 and 1900, and at the Chicago World's Fair of 1893. Like Gallé, Tiffany exhibited at Bing's Paris shop, 'La Maison de l'Art Nouveau'.

For over half a century as a designer, first of jewellery and later of glass, René Lalique (1860–1945) managed to avoid becoming a

261, 262 Vase by Emile Gallé (1846–1904), about 1900. Of all Gallé's adventurous techniques for decorating glass, the most ambitious and arresting was his exploitation of the tricks of light played through collaged layers of glass. In reflected light (LEFT) the engraved and textured surface of this vase shows a screen of leaves, while in transmitted light the eerie ghosts of these leaves are revealed, together with shards of bark or the detritus of a forest. H. 16.9 cm. Paris, Musée des Arts Décoratifs.

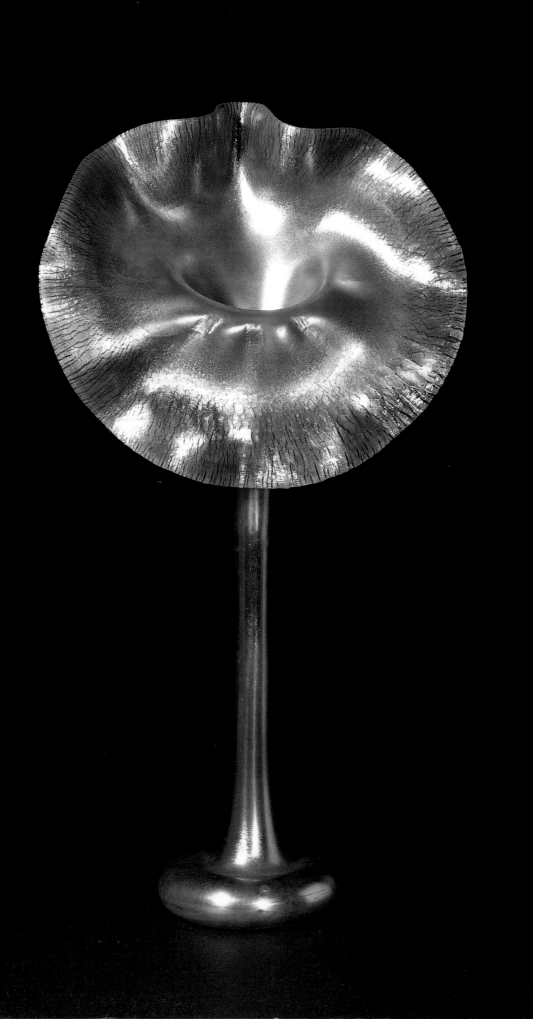

263 'Jack-in-the-Pulpit' vase by Louis Comfort Tiffany (1848–1933), about 1912. Apart from his lamps, Tiffany is best known for his 'Jack-in-the-Pulpit' vases, which came with a purplish-blue-green sheen or a golden sheen, according to the colour of the glass blown (blue or amber). From the 1890s Tiffany's glass chemists simulated the iridescence caused by weathering on some ancient glass (which Tiffany admired and collected) by spraying the hot glass with tin chloride in a reducing flame. A lawsuit brought by Tiffany Furnaces in 1913 against Steuben Glass Works, where Frederick Carder's 'Blue Aurene' and 'Gold Aurene' were causing stiff competition for Tiffany's 'Favrile', was soon aborted, and years later it was determined that the two glassmakers had used different formulas to arrive at a similar result. H. 47.6 cm.

prisoner of both Art Nouveau and Art Deco by adapting the raw material of each style to his own uses. Regardless of the intended material, but especially for glass, he borrowed whatever was suggestive or inspirational from architecture, theatre design, fashion and the decorative arts, transforming it into a seemingly free-flowing suite of designs. The human figure, flora and fauna were observed directly, then reinterpreted to cover flat and curved surfaces, sometimes in relief, more often incised.

Working with Coty from 1907, Lalique's glass and packaging of perfume bottles emphasised the varied appeal of fragrances and modernised the perfume industry. His designs were applied to mould-blown and pressed glass from 1910 to 1945 in over 4,500 different examples, decorating every sort of glass from perfume bottles to fountains, candelabra to clocks, bracelets to bookends, lighting fixtures, liquor cabinets, tables, panels, windows and sculpture for churches, table glass sets, paperweights, and radiator caps for cars; not to mention the 300-foot-long (91 m) walls and lighting for the largest interior space on any ocean liner – the first-class dining room of the *Normandie*. Lalique's titles for his glass nearly always name the decorative subject, but for some dramatic vases the title of subject or place is only latently apparent in the abstraction of the design. Lalique's achievement was to have given volume to linear design.

264

It was the sight of John Northwood's copy of the Portland Vase that set the 16-year-old Frederick Carder (1863–1963) on an eighty-year career in glass. Working under Northwood at Stevens & Williams in the 1880s, Carder designed popular cameo vases, vessels engraved in rock-crystal style, Venetian-inspired threaded glass, and the stylish 'Matsu-No-Ke' bowl. He was to become by far the most knowledgeable and versatile glassmaker-designer in the history of glass; he knew the chemistry and was skilled in every branch of the industry from building a furnace or making a mould model to designing, producing and marketing the finished product. Inspirations for his designs came from everywhere, including museums – he was the great glass eclectic – but whatever he borrowed he transformed into his own.

Sent on a fact-finding tour of the American glass industry for the South Staffordshire County Council in 1903, Carder 'jumped ship' and teamed up with T. G. Hawkes, president of the successful Corning glass decorating firm, to co-found the Steuben Glass Works. Carder designed and managed everything at Steuben from 1903 until 1918, when owing to wartime material priorities Steuben became a part of Corning Glass Works, with Carder reinstated as manager of the Steuben Division. He continued to produce a bewildering variety of new designs in a range of colours and textures that is probably unmatched, even by Tiffany. But then, in 1932, a new lead glass of high optical clarity developed by Corning scientists led to a management decision to produce only clear, colourless glass, thus ending Carder's era of colour. Carder was 'kicked upstairs' with the title of Art Director, but fortunately retained the freedom to design and make whatever coloured or uncoloured glass he wished. For the next twenty-seven years, including a decade during which Paul V. Gardner was his assistant, Carder turned to sculpting and casting, *pâte de verre*, *millefiori*, architectural glass and, finally, to *diatreta* glass produced by the *cire perdue* (lost wax) process, casting his last *diatretum*

266

264 ABOVE, LEFT 'Tourbillons' vase by René Lalique (1860–1945), 1926. The name 'Tourbillons' (French for whirlwind or whirlpool) aptly describes this vase, which was mould-pressed from a model, leaving a surface texture like a fingerprint. This example, with the exterior outline of the vortex enamelled in black, is in uncoloured glass; in other examples the glass is amber or blue. The design, typical of the volatile energy of Art Deco, perhaps suggests the spin of propellor blades on the French ocean liners that churned across the Atlantic in the 1920s and 1930s. H. 20.4 cm. Corning, New York, The Corning Museum of Glass.

265 ABOVE, RIGHT Acid-etched vase by Maurice Marinot (1882–1960), 1934. Apart from its bucket shape, this thick vessel with its bosses standing in high relief suggests a familiarity with Sasanian vessels of the 6th–7th century (see Chapter 4). But Marinot's form was achieved by eating away the glass blank with repeated immersions in hydrofluoric acid. The layers of attack can be counted like layers of erosion, and the brutally bold result suggests a melting ice sculpture. H. 17 cm. Corning, New York, The Corning Museum of Glass, Gift of Mlle Florence Marinot.

at the age of 96. Just below its rim is the inscription: LIFE IS SHORT, ART IS LONG.

The major early twentieth-century modernist figure in glass was Maurice Marinot (1882–1960), a well-known exhibiting Fauve painter (c.1905–13), who experienced an instant passion for the material of glass in 1911 during a visit to the Viard glassworks at Bar-sur-Seine, France. Initially he learned the basics of glassblowing from a Viard gaffer, while enamelling the glasses blown for him by others with decorations in the prevailing lighthearted Parisian illustrative styles. But he soon began to approach glass as a sculptor concerned with its body and form. From about 1920 Marinot's glass underwent three transformations: massively thick glasses deeply acid-etched to sculptural form; equally massive glasses in simple forms suffused with bubbles; and small, ball-stoppered bottles with coloured inner casings mottled, swirled and cracked to suggest tree bark, melting ice, river beds and other natural phenomena. For Marinot every piece was a contest: 'the blowing acting on the interior while the tooling pressures, the solicitations of tools work on the exterior, these two forces alternating'.

Marinot's glass received broad recognition at the Paris Exhibition of 1925, but poor health forced him to cease glassworking in 1937, after which he continued quietly to paint. The influence of Marinot is evident in the sculptural glass forms of Henri Navarre (1885–1971) and in the bubbly, melting forms of Henri Thuret (born 1898) shaped at the fire. But Marinot's glass stands alone as the most creative, forceful statement made in glass in the first third of the twentieth century.

265

Epilogue

THE pioneering achievements of that giant among modern glassmakers, Maurice Marinot, inspired succeeding generations – and, as so often in the past, new technology was soon to become the handmaid that enabled his revolutionary approach to glass to become universal. No painter or artist of standing before Marinot had abandoned his easel in order to work directly with hot glass. Glass became Marinot's new-found, chosen artistic medium, as his writings vividly confirm. He not only had to learn the skills of the glassmaker from the most basic processes to the most sophisticated techniques, but also how to produce his artistic creations in glass single-handed. This break with tradition was perhaps the most revolutionary change introduced by Marinot. Suddenly, the historic evolution of the 'chair' (or team of people making glass) had been halted and, in its place, the artist – working on his own – was there, seeking to create 'the unique piece'. Thus, Marinot's approach made the fundamental spirit of cooperation and swift interplay among the members of a glass team as irrelevant as the salutary consequences of the 'chair's' traditional anonymity.

However, in those days, not even Marinot or any like-minded artist could operate without an active glasshouse and, whereas Marinot enjoyed the exceptional good fortune of being able to work for more than a quarter of a century at his friends' glasshouse near his native city of Troyes, not all his contemporaries were as lucky or as free to pursue their creative impulses. Only in the early 1960s, with the American invention of a small tank furnace which not only could be installed in a comparatively tiny space but also had the potential to cater for all the needs of the individual glassblower working on his own, was glass brought within the orbit of the more typical artist.

Its development by one of the glass industry's most talented technicians, Dominick Labino (1910–87) in collaboration with the potter Harvey Littleton (born 1922), aided by the resources of the University of Wisconsin and the Toledo Museum of Art, resulted in improvements to the design of the small furnace and annealing oven as well as a significant advance in refractory technology. In parallel, the marketing of standardised materials (compatible colours and rods of glass with the same coefficients of expansion, etc.) was organised and, as a result, glass could be treated by artists as yet another medium – rather as they had been accustomed to treating oil-paints or, more recently, ceramics. Both Labino and Littleton went on to become prominent glass artists, but stemming from their joint contribution in 1962–3 – and aided by an affluent educational system in Western countries – a vast new movement of glass experimentation outside the glass factory spread from America to many other parts of the world.

The fruits of this 'studio glass' movement, as it is called, have been regularly shown at exhibitions and seem to have greatly outnumbered the products of new industrial design. Many are sculptures of too introverted and personal a character ever to serve a wider public, but among these 'unique pieces' by studio artists are some that have subsequently become prototypes for industrial production. The once fashionable theory that only studio glass realised by the artist himself can express his ideas and aims should no longer prevent industrial design from being enriched by the stimulus and originality of the glass artists. Time alone will show how the achievements of the last fifty years in glassmaking will be viewed by our descendants – and certainly we are far too close to be objective about the contribution of the studio glass movement – but frequently it seems that the more versatile artists make the greater contribution. Artists who have both designed excellent utilitarian glassware for large-scale production and created their own unique pieces of sculpture, understandably command the respect of a wider public.

The future of the story of glass can only be the richer if the next generation of talented artists similarly seeks to reach that larger audience, many of whom in their everyday use of glass value its incomparable qualities and appreciate the merits of originality in industrial design. With the greater intensity of worldwide communications – publications, conferences, 'workshops' and exhibitions – artists and designers are even less isolated than before and the results of this global interchange may be counter-productive. Most probably, the glass artist will need, more than ever, to find individuality and inspiration by drawing upon his or her particular heritage within the last 5,000 years of glass's resilient history.

266 'Prong' vase by Frederick Carder (1863–1963) for the Steuben Division, Corning Glass Works, New York, about 1930. Although Carder is said to have disliked the prevailing Art Deco style, he designed refreshing glass examples with apparent ease. The idea for a multi-part vase undoubtedly came from the branching arms of an épergne, but Carder's Cubistic sharpening of the jade green forms springing from an opal base called unmistakably for fresh-cut flowers. H. 26 cm. Corning, New York, The Rockwell Museum.

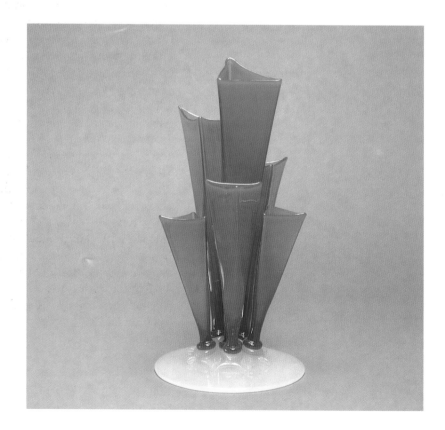

Techniques of Glassmaking and Decoration

T HE EMPHASIS throughout this survey has been on the glassmaker's creativity at the furnace, rather than on the skills of craftsmen who subsequently embellished the surfaces of objects by means of cold techniques, such as engraving with a diamond-point or a wheel. Cold-worked decoration, however impressive, is secondary to the art of glassmaking itself.

Consequently, a clear understanding of the behaviour of glass when it is heated to different temperatures is essential if the craft of the glassmaker is to be fully appreciated. Even the temperatures at which glass will react in particular ways are not constant, for glass is easily affected by small changes in the quality of the raw materials and, in most cases, the empirical approach of the master glassblower remains a necessary ingredient for success.

The skills required by a gifted glassblower were probably learnt while young, when the hands had not become set or rigid. Manual dexterity gave the glassblower confidence to handle at speed the intensely hot and easily destroyed forms created at the end of the blowpipe. With the acquisition of that confident control, the glassmaker could concentrate on using his 'fantasy' and so create works of originality and beauty.

The sequences that follow were photographed in the New York Experimental Glass Workshop while Mr Bill Gudenrath was demonstrating the techniques which are now thought to have been used by glassmakers in the past to create some of the magnificent specimens that are today the treasured possessions of renowned collections in Europe and America. Bill Gudenrath's intensely close examination of many of these precious survivals has revealed important microscopic evidence that now sheds light on the way in which certain pieces of glass were made, enabling him to demonstrate the probable stages and movements involved in each technique.

Vessel core-forming

FIGS 1–15

Sixteenth to first centuries BC; Mesopotamia, Rhodes, Western Asia, the Mediterranean world.

Other techniques shown Trailing, combing (vertical), adding, manipulating.

Equipment A glass-melting furnace, a lehr, a marver, metal rods, pincers.

Materials Animal dung and clay (for the core), glass for coating the core, and a smaller quantity of glass of various colours for decoration.

Notes Vessels made by core-forming are necessarily of limited size and their walls are unavoidably somewhat thick. The nature of the core material and the way in which it was covered with glass have in recent years been the subject of much research and experimentation. It was long thought that the core was made primarily of sand, and that it was covered with glass by trailing (see Figs 6–7). However, the results of analysis of surviving cores as well as experiments at the furnace suggest otherwise on both counts.

1 Mediterranean core-formed *alabastron* (perfume flask), probably made on the island of Rhodes, 6th–5th century BC. H. 8.8 cm. British Museum.

2 Making the core. A mixture of horse dung and clay is kneaded with a small amount of water to the consistency of bread dough.

3 The material is shaped around an iron rod (approximately 3 ft (1 m) long and ⅛ in (3 mm) in diameter) in the form of the inside of the object to be made. The core is then thoroughly dried or fired.

4 Covering the core with glass. The core is immersed almost to its upper edge in a crucible of molten glass in the furnace. Turning the rod ensures an even coating.

5 The core is lifted out of the glass and any excess allowed to drip back into the crucible. This continues until the desired amount of glass is left on the core.

6 Applying the trailed decoration. Soft glass of a contrasting colour is attached to a spot near the bottom of the vessel, then pulled slightly to form a thread.

7 As the rod is turned and the mass of soft glass is moved gradually towards the top of the vessel, the thread covers the vessel in spirals.

8 **Combing the trailed threads**. After reheating to soften the glass and threads thoroughly, a pointed instrument is dragged alternately up and down across the threads.

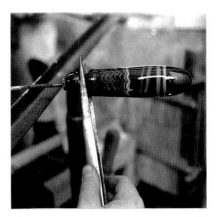

9 **Manipulating to form the shoulder, neck and rim**. After reheating, the glass just below the upper edge is constricted with pincers, thus forming the neck. The glass displaced to the right forms the shoulder.

10 The glass displaced to the left becomes a horizontal rim: as the vessel is slowly rotated, pincers are used to squeeze this glass flat.

11 **Manipulating to form suspension loops**. For each loop, a bit of soft glass from the furnace is added to the side of the vessel and then separated from its pontil.

12 Using pincers, a portion of the glass is drawn down along the side of the vessel towards the bottom.

13 The remaining portion is squeezed flat, then rolled into a circle to form a closed loop. The finished vessel, with rod still attached, is placed in the lehr to cool gradually.

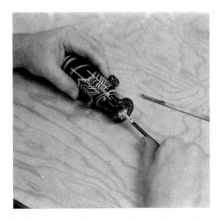

14 **Removing the rod and core**. The rod is given a few sharp blows to break up the core immediately surrounding it. Then, using a bending and twisting motion, the rod is withdrawn from the vessel.

15 A long-handled instrument with a hook at one end is used to break up and scrape out the remains of the core.

Bead-forming, using the core-forming or the so-called 'rod-forming' technique

FIGS 16–21

From earliest times. A particular group made perhaps initially on the island of Rhodes and later, it seems, in the eastern Mediterranean and at Carthage dates from the late seventh to the third century BC.

Other techniques shown Flame-working.

Equipment As for core-forming (see above), and a device for flame-working, later known as a glassworker's lamp.

Materials As for core-forming.

Notes While the core was probably covered in glass in the same way as for vessels (see Figs 4–5) and served the same purpose, as a separating agent to prevent the glass sticking to the metal rod, it was used on a much smaller scale at the tip of the rod (see the Glossary, under CORE-FORMING, where the use of the term 'rod-forming' is discussed).

Many early beads also show evidence of flame-working, a technique which permits the worker to achieve great detail on a small scale by the intense localised heating of the glass at a lamp separate from the furnace.

16 Core-formed head pendant, *c.*600–400 BC, of a type perhaps first made on the island of Rhodes at the end of the seventh century BC. Toledo, Ohio, The Toledo Museum of Art.

17 After the bead has been made on the core, an area of the surface is heated in the flame, then pulled downwards to form the chin. Glass of a contrasting colour is applied and fused to make the face.

18 Making the eyes. A large gob of black glass is applied and heated until it becomes flat.

19 A smaller amount of opaque white glass is added in the centre of the black glass but melted and fused to a lesser extent, so that it remains in relief. Finally, a dot of black glass is added to form the pupil.

20 Adding the remaining features. Softened black glass is drawn along the bead to form the eyebrows. Two bits of black glass are added and pincered to become flat ears.

21 The lips are also formed by adding black glass which, after reheating, is divided lengthwise by pressing and squeezing with pincers. Finally, the bead, with the rod still attached, is slowly cooled.

Cane-making

FIGS 22–35

Fifteenth century BC to the present. First practised in Mesopotamia, and thereafter in the classical world; after the medieval period it was revived and greatly developed in Venice in the sixteenth century and has been in use ever since.

Other techniques shown Fusing sandwich gold; combing (horizontal).

Equipment A glass-melting furnace, a marver, metal rods, pincers, shears.

Materials Glass of different colours; gold leaf.

Notes During the long history of this process, a virtually inexhaustible variety of canes – and bands – have been made. There are, however, only two basic types of canes: those intended to be sliced and viewed in cross-section from the end (e.g. mosaic and *millefiori*), and those intended to be viewed from the side (e.g. spiral-patterned (or 'network' canes, single-coloured and polychrome bands). In addition, the principle of manufacture of all canes, however simple or complex in appearance, is the same: a relatively compact mass of glass is stretched to become long and narrow.

22 Perfume flask (*alabastron*) of gold-band glass. Made in the eastern Mediterranean, probably on the Syro-Palestinian coast, 1st century BC. H. 11.2 cm. See Pl. 66.

23 **Making a polychrome band**. A strip of opaque white glass is attached to the side of a substantial mass of soft dark glass on the end of a pontil.

24 After reheating to fuse the two glasses thoroughly, the mass is flattened against the marver.

25 The end is held with pincers while the pontil is slowly drawn away. The mass is stretched to form a relatively narrow band. The greater the length, the narrower the band.

26 **Making a gold band**. While still hot from the pulling process, a band of clear glass (made in the same way as the previous one) is covered halfway down one side with gold leaf.

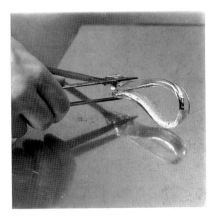

27 This is immediately folded in half to form a loop with the gold on the inner surface.

28 Following reheating, a point on the loop opposite the pontil rod is held with the pincers, then pulled firmly, thus trapping the gold as the two halves of the loop touch and fuse together.

29 Attaching the bands to the core. The core, having just been coated with glass (see Figs 4–5) is pressed against one end of a tightly packed row of heated bands lined up on a ceramic surface.

30 The core is rolled over the canes until it is completely surrounded by them. By reheating and marvering, the canes become fully fused and the surface completely smooth.

31 Horizontal combing. As the core is slowly turned, the glass is squeezed with rough pincers, pulling the canes out of parallel.

32 The process is repeated at intervals along the length of the vessel, the direction of rotation being reversed at each new location so that a zigzag pattern results.

33 Smoothing and finishing the vessel. Following thorough reheating, the deep furrows resulting from the horizontal combing are smoothed by further marvering.

34 Alternate reheating and marvering continues until the surface is completely smooth.

35 The tip of the vessel is held with pincers while the core is turned to produce a twist at the end. After cutting off any excess glass, a final reheating and marvering of this area produces a smooth tapering end.

Fusing and slumping

FIGS 36–58

First practised extensively by Hellenistic glassmakers in the third century BC and thereafter in the classical world, the technique seems not to have been revived until the nineteenth century.

Other techniques shown Mosaic cane-making; twisting canes.

Equipment A glass-melting furnace or a kiln (optional), flat ceramic plates (for fusing), contoured ceramic forms (for slumping), pincers, shears, spatulas, a long-handled tool for transporting the plates and forms into and out of the furnace or kiln.

Materials Glass canes.

Notes To make complex patterned glass vessels of the mosaic type, two separate processes are involved: fusing and slumping, often practised in quick succession. A flat slab of glass is made by fusing cane sections together; this is then slumped over (or into) a form to produce the required shape.

36 Mosaic glass bowl, probably made in the eastern Mediterranean. From Vulci, central Italy, *c.*2nd century BC. H. 6 cm. See Pl. 56.

37 Making the network cane for the rim. A thick thread of opaque white glass is applied to the side of a conical mass of dark glass attached to the end of a pontil.

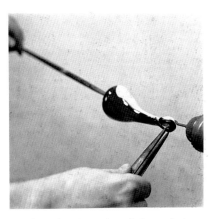

38 After reheating, a loop is formed at the tip of the cone and then attached to a hook.

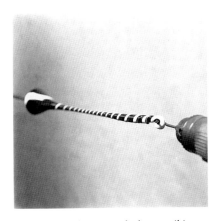

39 As the hook is turned, the pontil is slowly pulled away, drawing out a cane.

40 Making mosaic sections. A flattened mass of soft opaque white glass thinly coated in clear glass is stretched to form a band.

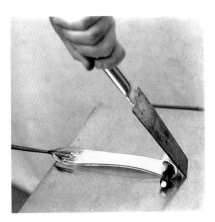

41 A cane of opaque white glass thinly coated with glass of a contrasting colour is attached at right angles to the end of the band. The band is then rolled up around the cane.

42 The band is rolled up until it surrounds the cane in two or three layers. This is then cut free of the pontil, and turned on its end.

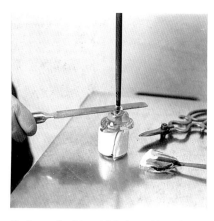

43 A pontil with a thick disc of hot glass on its end is attached to the centre of the roll.

44 After reheating and marvering, the roll is coated with more glass, then attached to a second pontil.

45 The roll is stretched by pulling it in opposite directions simultaneously, until a cane of the desired diameter is produced. This is then placed in the lehr.

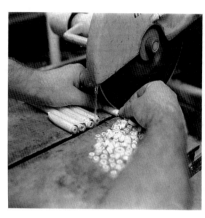

46 After cooling, the cane is cut into sections about ¼ in (6 mm) thick.

47 Fusing. The sections, perhaps with others of different patterns and colours, are placed side by side on a ceramic plate to form a disc. The plate is then introduced into the furnace (or kiln).

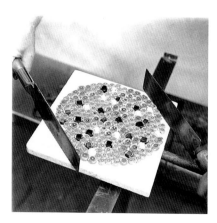

48 When the sections have softened, they are compressed inwards to fill up the tiny spaces between them. A solid disc results.

49 The disc is pressed flat to make the upper surface smooth. With additional reheating, this and the previous step are repeated several times to fuse and smooth the sections.

50 Attaching the network cane to form the rim. The cane is held in the furnace until about 6–8 inches (15–20 cm) of its length become soft.

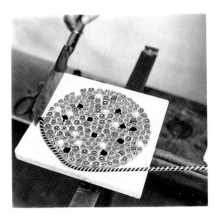

51 The hot end is quickly attached to and wrapped around part of the edge of the disc. Both are then returned to the furnace for reheating.

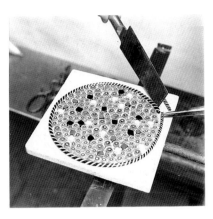

52 After the remainder of the disc has been wrapped with the cane, any excess is trimmed off and the two ends are united by manipulation.

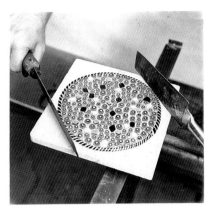

53 Following reheating, further compressing of the outer edge smooths the join between the disc and the rim cane.

54 Slumping. While still hot, the disc is 'draped' over a ceramic form made in the shape of the final object, in this case a hemispherical bowl.

55 The disc and form are reintroduced into the furnace (or kiln) and, as the glass softens, gravity causes the disc to move downwards over the form.

56 As the glass flows downwards, the mosaic sections develop an oblique slant. In addition, the glass at the highest point of the object becomes thinner, while that at the lowest point becomes thicker.

57 Any folds which may have occurred around the lower part of the bowl during the slumping can be pressed flat with tools.

58 While still hot, the object is given a few sharp taps and prised free of the form. After cooling, the inside and sometimes the outside of the piece may be ground and polished to remove any marks.

Mould-pressing, or casting in an open mould

FIGS 59–64

From earliest time to the present. First practised by Mesopotamian glassworkers; thereafter in the classical world. Although little used during the medieval period, the technique was revived in Renaissance Venice and continued therafter.

Equipment A glass-melting furnace or a kiln, a crucible, an open mould of a material which can withstand contact with hot glass (clay, stone or plaster), a slumping form, tongs (for manipulating the crucible) and shears.

Materials Cullet, canes or molten glass.

Notes In the nineteenth century the mechanisation of mould-pressing, particularly in the United States, permitted the mass-production of attractive and relatively inexpensive objects on a previously unknown scale.

59 Early Roman mould-pressed and slumped (pillar-moulded) bowl, mid-1st century BC. Made in one of the western provinces, probably Gaul, since it was found at Vaison, Vaucluse, France. H. 19.5 cm. See Pl. 67.

60 **Pouring glass for the blank**. Molten glass is poured from a crucible onto a metal or ceramic surface until it spreads to form a thick disc. The band-like stream of glass from the crucible is then cut with shears.

61 A mould with an incised radiating rib pattern is pressed into the disc of glass. The soft glass is forced upwards into the recesses, so forming the ribs, and outwards, so becoming thinner and wider in diameter.

62 The mould is removed from the glass disc while it is still soft, so that no reheating is required for the initial stages of the slumping process which follows.

63 The disc is transferred, with the ribs uppermost, to a slumping form (see Figs 54–7). The tops of the ribs become partially flattened by manipulation, creating a need for a plain band under the rim.

64 The bowl is removed from the form and cooled. The narrow zone below the rim is then ground smooth so that all the ribs end at an equal distance from the rim. The interior may also be finished by grinding.

Free-blowing

FIGS 65–87

75/50 BC to the present; first practised extensively in the Roman world, and later in all glassmaking centres.

Other techniques shown Using the sofietta.

Equipment A glass-melting furnace, a marver, jacks, pincers, blow-pipe, and a pontil. NB Glassblowing may also be conducted by the flame-working technique, using a glass-working lamp. However, the scale of objects made in this way is necessarily very limited, particularly before the twentieth century.

Materials Molten glass (in the case of flame-working, tubes of glass).

Notes While glassblowing fundamentally consists of inflating soft glass to form a bubble, the making of useful objects by blowing is a process which involves a number of steps. In most typical free-blown vessels, these can be reduced to five basic stages: 1. Shaping the gather of glass and blowing the bubble; 2. Separating the bubble from the blow-pipe; 3. Attaching a pontil (or clamp) at the bottom end of the bubble; 4. Reheating and shaping the opening; 5. Separating the vessel from the pontil (or clamp).

Of the six basic glassmaking processes described in this chapter, glassblowing requires the greatest mastery of the material and the greatest dexterity and speed. Although this is true of virtually any period and style, it is at its most apparent in the spectacular Venetian glass of about 1500–1725.

65 The 'Aldrevandin' beaker. The enamelled decoration (here photographed against a paper lining for clarity) is applied on both the interior and exterior of the beaker. Venetian, early 14th century. H. 13 cm. See Pl. 192.

66 **Gathering**. The end of the blow-pipe is introduced into the furnace to determine the level of glass in the crucible.

67 After submerging the blow-pipe about 1 in (2.5 cm) into the glass, it is rotated slowly to pick up an even coating. The faster the rotation, the more glass is collected around the blow-pipe.

68 When the required amount of glass has been gathered, the blow-pipe is brought to a horizontal angle, then removed from the furnace.

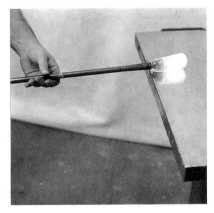

69 **Marvering**. The glass is rolled back and forth across the marver to make it cylindrical and perfectly concentric with the blow-pipe.

70 **Blowing the bubble**. While the still soft glass is kept carefully centred by the rotation of the blow-pipe, air is blown into the opposite end to form a bubble.

71 The blowing continues until a bubble of sufficient size for the finished object is formed.

72 Using the jacks, a constriction is made in the bubble, near the blow-pipe. The diameter is reduced to no more than one-quarter that of the bubble.

73 The lower portion of the bubble is reheated in the furnace while holding it down at an angle of 20–30°. As the glass softens, the bubble elongates and becomes conical.

74 The bubble is further inflated until the desired diameter and degree of tapering is achieved.

75 The rounded end of the bubble is pressed flat with the handle of the jacks to form the bottom of the vessel.

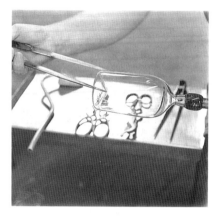

76 Making the kick. Using the pointed tip of a blade of the jacks, the centre of the flat bottom is pushed inwards to become conical in shape.

77 Adding the base-ring. A bit of glass hot from the furnace is attached to the edge of the base, then pulled away slightly to form a trail.

78 As the vessel is turned, the trail of glass eventually overlaps its starting point; the pontil is then rapidly pushed away from the vessel, breaking the thread.

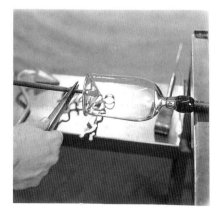

79 Transferring the vessel to the pontil. A pontil, its tip thinly coated with soft glass, is attached to the vessel at the apex of the kick.

80 The constriction between the vessel and the blow-pipe is grasped firmly with pincers. Minute cracks are thus formed as the relatively cool tips of the pincers touch the hot glass.

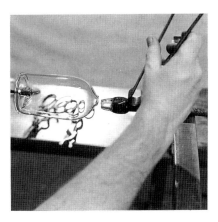

81 A sudden sharp tap on the blow-pipe with the pincers fractures the vessel's neck where the constriction is greatest and where the cracks have formed.

82 **Shaping the opening**. The vessel, attached to the pontil, is held with its open end inside the glory-hole until the glass reheats and softens.

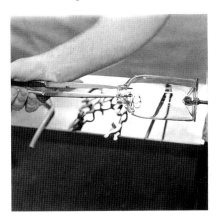

83 While the pontil is slowly turned, the jacks are used to dilate the opening to a diameter of about 1 in (2.5 cm).

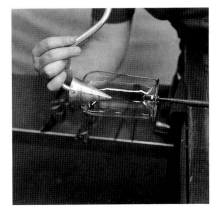

84 Following reheating, the sofietta is lightly pressed against the opening, while air is blown through it to inflate the vessel further, extending it outwards to form a shoulder.

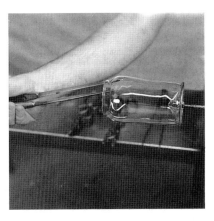

85 After a final reheating of the open end of the vessel, the jacks are used to dilate the rim to its final diameter.

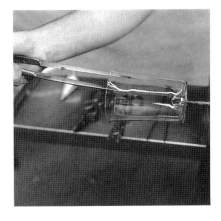

86 By lifting the jacks and opening their blades while the glass is still soft, the profile of the sides is extended smoothly to the upper edge of the vessel. Continuous rotation of the pontil ensures symmetry.

87 A sharp blow to the pontil breaks it away from the vessel, leaving the characteristic 'pontil mark'. After cooling in the lehr, enamels may be painted onto both surfaces of the glass and fired.

Blobbing and clamping
FIGS 88–92

Before the invention of blowing, a richly polychrome effect was achieved by using canes of coloured glass, either in strips or slices (see Figs 40–58). The glassblower discovered, however, that with a transparent glass (clear or coloured) on the end of the blow-pipe, he could pick up chips of opaque glass scattered on the marver and swiftly obtain an equally polychrome effect with far greater ease.

88 Roman *amphoriskos* in transparent blue glass with blobs of opaque white, yellow and red. Probably made in Syria, first half of the 1st century AD. H. 11.7 cm. Corning, New York, The Corning Museum of Glass.

89 **Blobbing**. Soft glass on a blow-pipe or pontil is rolled on a marver on which chips of coloured glass are scattered. These become embedded in the surface and rapidly fuse with it.

90 After reheating, the body of the object is blown and then stretched to form the neck, resulting in the enlargement and elongation of the blobs.

91 **Clamping**. The vessel is first broken off the blow-pipe (see Figs 80–81) onto a bed of sand or onto charred wood.

92 Held with the pincers, the vessel is slid into the two wire arms of the clamp. As the arms are forced open, spring tension grasps the vessel firmly while handles and other additions are manipulated.

Cracking off
FIGS 93–97

Soon after the invention of blowing, in the late 1st century BC, the glassblower discovered a speedy and satisfactory method of creating a vessel rim in the thinly blown glass while still hot and close to the furnace.

93 Blown glass bowl with enamelled decoration, from Greece but probably made in the eastern Mediterranean, AD 50–75. H. 7 cm; D. of rim 8.2 cm. See Pl. 87.

94 After the blank has been fully blown and shaped, the constriction near the blow-pipe is grasped firmly with the pincers.

95 A sharp tap on the blow-pipe separates it from the vessel (see Figs 80–81), which is then placed in the lehr to cool.

96 A gob of hot glass is applied at the point where the edge is to be, then pulled to a thread and wrapped around the body. The glass immediately under the thread cracks because of the stresses created.

97 The unusable upper portion of the blank is removed, leaving the vessel with a sharp upper edge. This may be ground smooth with abrasive materials.

Casing and flashing
FIGS 98–108

Both in antiquity and since the nineteenth century, the glassmaker has been eager to imitate hardstone cameos, and soon after the invention of glassblowing succeeded in fusing a glass of one colour with a layer of a different colour, so that when carved it could rival the effects of banded stones, like onyx. With a glass vessel there are two ways to achieve this layered effect: either by fusing onto the *inner* surface of a vessel (the casing or 'cup-overlay' method: see Glossary) or by fusing onto the *outer* surface (the flashing or 'dip-overlay' method: see Glossary).

98 Cameo glass amphora, known as the Portland Vase. The lower part was broken in antiquity, but is most convincingly reconstructed as tapering to a point. Probably made in Italy, early 1st century AD. See Pl. 75.

99 Flashing ('dip-overlay method'). An elongated bubble of glass is marvered and shaped to a cylindrical form.

100 The cylinder is partially dipped into a crucible containing glass of a contrasting colour.

101 The newly gathered glass is marvered in order to distribute it evenly around the original cylinder.

102 Blowing and shaping the body. The still soft glass of the double-layered cylinder is blown to a spherical shape. The sphere, held downwards, is then heated to produce a spheroidal shape (see Fig. 73).

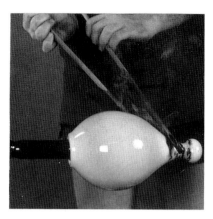

103 Using a pair of wooden sticks, the lower part of the spheroid is constricted to form a ball at the end.

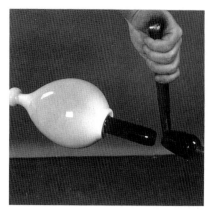

104 A pontil thinly coated at the end with opaque white glass is attached to the ball. Water is dripped onto the constriction in the glass near the blow-pipe, and with a sharp tap the blow-pipe is broken off.

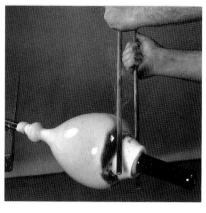

105 Shaping the shoulder and opening. After reheating, the shoulder is constricted and flattened to its final shape using the wooden sticks.

106 The opening is dilated, and the lip is flared.

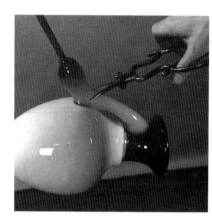

107 Making the handles. Additional glass on a pontil, having been marvered to a cylindrical shape (see Fig. 69) and still hot, is attached to the vessel's neck and shoulder. The glass is cut free of the pontil.

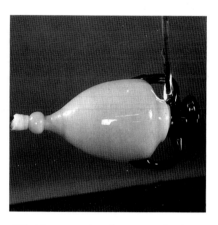

108 After repeating the process for the second handle, both are given their final shape using a wooden stick. The blank is broken off the pontil and placed in the lehr.

Millefiori cane-making and dip-mould blowing
FIGS 109–119

The glassmakers of the Italian Renaissance, particularly in late fifteenth-century Venice, sought to recreate the effect of the so-called mosaic glass of the ancient world by slicing coloured, patterned canes and embedding them within the glass at the end of a blow-pipe. Subsequent developments led to the application of the technique to furniture, as in the Louis XIV table, made before 1681 (Pls 7–8).

109 Miniature *millefiori* bottle of dark blue glass embedded with gold leaf and slices of canes; a white trail added at the rim. Venetian, 17th century. H. 10 cm. See Pl. 209.

110 Making *millefiori* canes. A gather of glass is pressed into a dip mould. Successive coatings of contrasting colours are each pressed into progressively larger dip moulds, each one having a slightly different pattern.

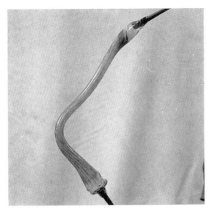

111 After the final coating has been marvered smooth, a second pontil is attached at the other end and the glass stretched to make a cane, sometimes over 30 ft (9 m) long. This is cut into slices or small sections.

112 Gold-leaf gilding. A thick cylindrical bubble of soft glass on the end of the blow-pipe or pontil is rolled over gold leaf on the marver. The gold immediately melts and sticks to the surface of the glass.

113 Picking up the *millefiori*. The slices, placed at random on a ceramic plate, are introduced into the furnace. When they have begun to melt, the gold-covered glass is rolled over them, picking them up.

114 Dip-mould blowing. After reheating and marvering, the bubble of glass covered in gold and *millefiori* is lowered into the dip mould.

115 Air is blown into the blow-pipe at the highest possible pressure, forcing the glass into the deepest recesses of the mould.

116 The glass is pulled vertically out of the mould: the tapered profile (wider at the top) allows for easy release.

117 Blowing and shaping the object. The glass is then blown – but at a considerably lower pressure than before – to the full size of the vessel's widest part.

118 The neck is formed by constricting the bubble near the blow-pipe, then pulling the glass outwards. The bottom is flattened, and the vessel is transferred to the pontil.

119 Attaching the edge trail. On the end of a second pontil, soft opaque white glass is attached to a point on the neck rim. As the vessel is turned, the white glass is drawn around the rim in a thin trail.

Assembling compound objects on the blow-pipe
FIGS 120–136

The glassblower discovered that by skilful manipulation he could create objects of a complex design, especially if a particular sequence of manufacture was observed. The speed and accuracy with which additions have to be made at each stage are fundamental to the success of this process.

120 A drinking glass of thin *cristallo*, with applied 'chain' ornament and scrolls. Venetian, 16th century. H. 17.1 cm. British Museum.

121 Making the bowl. A thin bubble is blown at the end of a blow-pipe.

122 While still soft, the bubble is flattened by pressing the bottom in towards the blow-pipe. Next, a constriction is made in the glass nearest the blow-pipe (see Fig. 72).

123 After reheating, the thick point at the centre of the flattened end of the bubble is pulled away from the blow-pipe. The long taper of glass is then trimmed to the required length.

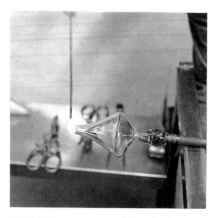

124 Making a merese. A bit of soft glass is added to the tip of the bowl. The glass remaining on the pontil is separated from the bowl by giving it a rapid pull.

125 The glass is flattened using the handle of the jacks.

126 With one blade of the jacks on each side of the flattened glass, a thin disc is formed by squeezing the blades together as the blow-pipe is rotated.

127 Making the stem. On a second blow-pipe, a small bubble of glass is blown and allowed to elongate into the shape of a teardrop. With the first blow-pipe almost vertical, the bubble is attached to the merese.

128 Using shears, the bubble is cut from its blow-pipe. The lower part of the stem is trimmed to the required length and then another merese is added, in the same way as before.

129 Making the foot. Another bubble, similar to that for the stem but less elongated, is added to the second merese, then cut from its blow-pipe.

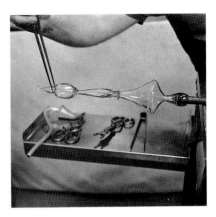

130 Using the jacks, a constriction is made near the tip of the bubble that is to form the foot.

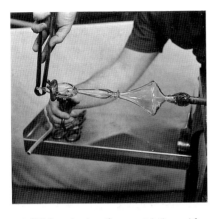

131 While gripping the constriction with shears, the excess glass extending beyond the constriction is given a sharp tap with the pincer handle.

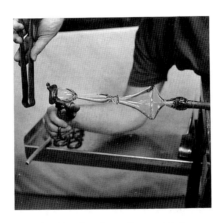

132 The glass breaks at the constriction, leaving a hole at the end of the bubble that will form the foot.

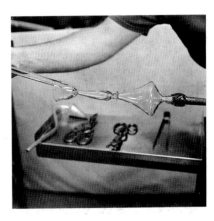

133 Following the reheating of this bubble, the hole is dilated and the bubble flattened to form a disc.

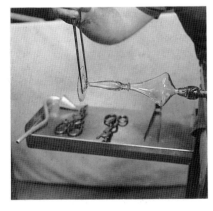

134 The jacks are used to give the foot a tapered, flaring profile as it is pulled outwards. The vessel is then transferred from the blow-pipe to the pontil, which is attached to its foot (see Figs 79–81).

135 Shaping the bowl. Pointing downwards at the glory-hole, the bowl softens and centrifugal force from rapid rotation of the pontil causes the shoulder and the opening to enlarge.

136 As heating and rotation continue, the edge turns outwards. Adjustments to the pontil's downward angle and the speed of rotation produce the required shape.

Assembling compound objects on the pontil
FIGS 137–150

The glassblower could obtain effects of great virtuosity by making an object in several sections and finally uniting them to form a single entity, without any apparent sign of the joins and without detracting from the perfect proportions and harmony of the whole.

137 'Serpent' goblet with a stem of ribbed cane enclosing a blue thread; the eyes, cresting and wings of applied blue glass. Venetian, 17th century. H. 25.3 cm. British Museum.

138 Making the serpent. After having been pressed into a dip mould (see Figs 115–17), a gather of glass is twisted and pulled into a long tapering cane, then swiftly wrapped around a tapering metal rod.

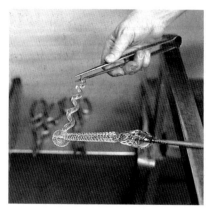

139 The metal rod is removed and the resulting coil is wrapped onto the remaining straight portion of the cane.

140 Following reheating, the end of the cane is held with pincers while the pontil is rotated. The coil is thus completely wrapped onto the cane, which now forms the straight central stem.

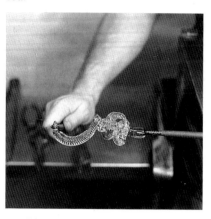

141 The serpent's body is then transferred to a second pontil, this time attached to its base. After reheating, the neck is bent to the required shape and trimmed to the required length.

142 The jaws are made by adding a bit of hot glass to the tip of the neck, then cutting it from its pontil.

143 By pressing the side of the pincer blade into the soft glass, it is divided into two halves. Next, each half is pressed flat with pincers.

144 The two flattened pieces of glass are pulled at their ends with pincers, then bent to form the upper and lower jaws.

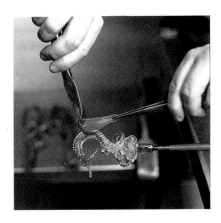

145 The wings and comb are made by applying a bit of glass of a contrasting colour at the required point, flattening it with pincers, then pulling both ends outwards simultaneously with two pairs of pincers.

146 While the wing is still hot from the application of glass, shears are used to cut a feather pattern into it. Next the serpent is transferred to a new pontil, now attached to the top of its neck.

147 Assembling the wine-glass. A bit of glass still hot from the furnace is applied to the base of the serpent.

148 The serpent is pressed onto the foot assembly which was made earlier and kept hot in the lehr. The soft glass immediately fuses to the foot. This assembly is transferred to a new pontil, which is attached to the foot.

Insertion form moulding
FIGS 151–152

The glassblower working at the furnace and wishing to vary – without using a mould – the circular rim which inevitably resulted from blowing, devised a swift method of creating hexagonal and octagonal shapes by inserting a form into the upper part of the vessel.

149 After a bit of glass has been added to the top of the serpent's neck, the bowl assembly is picked up and fused.

151 'Winged' goblet with a twisted rod stem encasing white, blue and red threads. Venetian, or possibly Netherlandish *façon de Venise*, 17th century. H. 19 cm. British Museum.

150 The entire goblet is reheated to ensure that all parts reach the same temperature. Using the pincers, the parts are aligned accurately with the pontil. Finally the wine-glass is annealed in the lehr.

152 A finished conical bowl (see Figs 66–73, 79–86) is thoroughly reheated and an octagonal tapered form inserted. The bowl is then placed into a lehr prior to the attachment of a stem and foot assembly.

Full mould blowing

FIGS 153–156

The use of a closed mould to make one specific part of a vessel, such as the knop of a stem, could provide a highly decorative effect while simultaneously offering a suitably strong surface for constant handling. The glassmakers of the Renaissance frequently incorporated mould-blown elements into their free-blown vessels.

153 Tazza of *cristallo*, with a stem incorporating a mould-blown knop of alternating lions' heads and cartouches. Probably Netherlandish *façon de Venise*, 16th century. H. 15.9 cm. British Museum.

154 An elongated bubble of soft glass attached to the end of a blow-pipe is placed between the two open halves of a mould, and the mould is then tightly closed.

155 Air is blown into the blow-pipe with enough pressure to force the glass into the mould's deepest recesses. Blowing continues until the glass has cooled sufficiently to retain its shape when the mould is opened.

156 The glass, now impressed with the mould's shape and pattern, is removed. The moulded element can be incorporated into a compound object or annealed in the lehr.

Air-twist

FIGS 157–161

The creation in England by the end of the seventeenth century of a pure, light-reflective lead glass encouraged glassmakers to experiment with trapping air within the glass to create attractive visual effects. The serviceable, sturdy stems of wine-glasses, for example, were made to appear less heavy as the air-twists within them created patterns of light and movement.

The following sequence shows a stem being made, using a pontil; a separately made bowl and foot can then be added. Alternatively, the entire sequence can be carried out on a blow-pipe which has at its end enough glass to make both the stem and the bowl, the foot being made by adding another piece of glass.

157 Drinking glass with air-twist stem and, above, a hollow bulb on the outside of which are applied three 'raspberry' prunts. The bowl is wheel-engraved. H. 8.5 in. See Pl. 241.

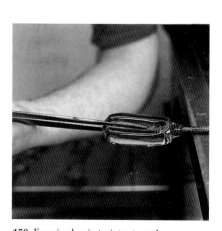

158 For single air-twists, two deep furrows are formed in a gather of glass, by squeezing it with the blades of the jacks. For multiple air-twists, specially made tools are used to make impressions as required.

159 Trapping the air. The gather is again dipped in molten glass. Because of its viscosity, this second layer of glass fails to flow into the furrows made in the first gather, and so the air is trapped.

160 Making the twist. While the tip of the glass is held still, the pontil is rotated, causing the pair of elongated air-bubbles trapped inside to twist and form a double helix.

161 Pulling the stem. As rotation continues, the tip of the glass is pulled outwards away from the pontil, forming a straight stem. A separately made bowl and foot can be added.

Mezza-forma (half-moulding); making a folded rim; gold-leaf 'gilding' with enamels

FIGS 162–178

The glassblower wishing to use mould-blown high-relief ornament on a section of the vessel's surface found a method that could be part of the continuous process of blowing and did not require either a closed mould or a separate stage for joining it onto the other part of the vessel.

162 Low-footed tazza with twelve gilded ribs in high relief and an enamelled doe in the centre. Venetian, about 1500. H. 6.8 cm, D. 27 cm. See Pl. 201.

163 Half-moulding. Glass is gathered on the tip of a very thick bubble at the end of a blow-pipe.

164 The bubble is plunged firmly downwards into a dip mould, thus forcing the soft glass to travel upwards, filling the mould's grooves.

165 The glass is removed, then reheated and redipped into the dip mould. As a result, the glass becomes resoftened, but the ribs retain their definition.

166 While the tip of the glass is held still, the blow-pipe is rotated, causing the ribs to spiral.

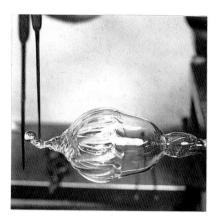

167 Inflating and shaping the body. The glass nearest the blow-pipe – unaffected by the half-moulding process – blows out smoothly; the rest is covered with spiral ribs.

168 While air is gently blown into the blow-pipe, the bottom of the bubble is pushed inwards with the jacks. The bubble becomes short and flattened as a result.

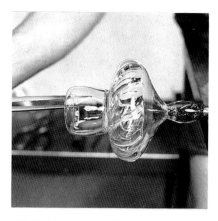

169 Making a folded foot rim (inner-fold). A second bubble is added to form the foot (see Figs 129–32). Before this is fully opened, the end is flattened and the edge of the opening is turned inwards.

170 The jack blades are then lifted and opened to press the folded glass against the inside surface of the bubble, thus forming a double thickness.

171 After reheating, the foot is spread to its final shape and diameter using the jacks. The vessel is transferred to the pontil, reheated and the opening enlarged to a diameter of about 1 in (2.54 cm): see Figs 79–83.

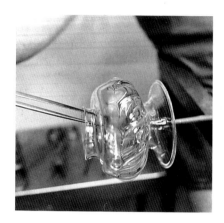

172 Making the dish's folded rim (outer-fold). Following reheating, the glass around the opening is flared sharply outwards, then upwards, before being turned over and pressed against the shoulder of the vessel.

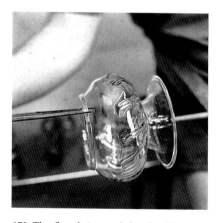

173 The flared ring and the shoulder are grasped and squeezed between the blades of the jacks, thereby fusing the two surfaces together.

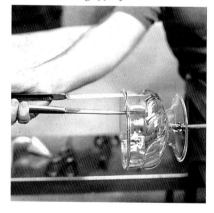

174 Completing the blank. After reheating, the sides of the vessel are given a vertical shape. After cooling in the lehr, gold leaf is applied using gum arabic and water as an adhesive, and enamels added.

175 Firing the gold and enamels. When the enamels have dried, the vessel is placed in a cool lehr and gradually reheated to just below softening point. It is then attached to a pontil, thinly coated with soft glass.

176 The vessel is reintroduced into the furnace, the edge being heated first to begin softening the rim.

177 The entire vessel is put in the furnace and left until all the enamels glow and appear fused. As the heating continues, the glass becomes soft and flexible.

178 The vessel is withdrawn from the furnace and rotated rapidly. Centrifugal force causes the softened sides and rim to expand and curve outwards, the speed of rotation determining the final shape, curve and diameter.

'Nipt diamond waies'

FIGS 179–183

The glassblower creating a mesh design in relief on the exterior of a blown glass vessel could achieve it either by blowing into a mould or by creating parallel ribs of glass and then pinching them together in an alternating fashion. The English glassmaker George Ravenscroft (1618–81) described the latter method (in his price list of 1677) as 'nipt diamond waies', and his phrase is now universally used.

179 Beaker with a high kick and applied pincered foot-ring; gilded on the pinched ribs and rim. Venetian, second half of the 15th century. H. 11.2 cm. See Pl. 199.

180 Making the ribs. These are made in a dip mould, as shown in Figs 163–5. Alternatively, the ribs may be made from applied canes of glass (see Figs 185–7).

181 Making the diamond pattern. Using pincers, alternating pairs of ribs are squeezed together horizontally, forming a diamond pattern along the entire length of the bubble.

182 During the pincering of the ribs, the bubble is continuously inflated.

183 Blowing continues until the bubble has been inflated to the outer tips of the ribs. The object is then completed by standard glassblowing procedures (see Figs 75–87).

Vetro a fili (broadly spaced canes); *vetro a retorti*

FIGS 184–188

The Venetian glassblower began in the second quarter of the sixteenth century to apply thin white (*lattimo*) canes. These could either be picked up on the gather and kept in high relief or they could be embedded in the thickness of the glass by repeatedly rolling on the marver: both forms are known as *vetro a fili*. The thin white canes could also be twisted into a spiral pattern (*vetro a retorti*) and the same techniques applied.

184 Drinking glass with foot and stem of typical *vetro a fili*; the bowl with *vetro a fili* in relief and, above, two horizontal bands of *vetro a retorti*. Venetian, mid-16th century. H. 15.2 cm. See Pl. 216.

185 Lengths of glass canes, *a fili* and *a retorti*, are laid in grooves in a ceramic plate and heated until soft. They are then picked up on the outside of a heated glass bubble on the end of a blow-pipe.

186 The canes laid at right angles to the blow-pipe encircle the bubble horizontally, while those laid parallel to the blow-pipe become attached vertically at regular intervals.

187 After reheating, the ends of the canes horizontally encircling the bubble are joined together, leaving only a narrow seam.

188 Making the bowl. After reheating, the bubble is further inflated, then the additional elements required to finish the object are added – a knop, mereses, and a foot (see Figs 124–36).

Vetro a fili (closely spaced canes); closed cylinder blowing

FIGS 189–199

By the middle of the sixteenth century the Venetian glassblower, seeking to create an overall effect of closely packed white stripes with no areas of clear glass, devised a method of fusing the *lattimo* canes so that the clear glass between them was reduced to a minimum.

189 Goblet and cover of *vetro a fili*, with clear glass mereses (above and below the knop) and a clear finial. Venetian, late 16th century. H. 35 cm. British Museum.

190 Fusing the canes. Canes of *vetro a fili* are laid side by side on the flat surface of a ceramic plate with no gaps between them.

191 The canes are heated in the furnace until they begin to soften and fuse together.

192 The canes are compressed from the sides to ensure complete fusing of the individual canes, so that a single rectangle of glass is formed.

193 While the canes are still soft, a collar of hot glass at the end of a blow-pipe is attached to one corner of the rectangle, then rolled along the edge, thus picking up the canes.

194 After one revolution of the blow-pipe, the rectangle of canes fully encircles the glass collar. Following reheating, the join is adjusted to produce as imperceptible a seam as possible.

195 After reheating, the ends of the canes are constricted to form a closed cylinder.

196 Twisting the canes. After further reheating, the end of the closed cylinder is held still while the blow-pipe is rotated, producing a spiral pattern. Gentle blowing keeps the cylinder from folding or collapsing.

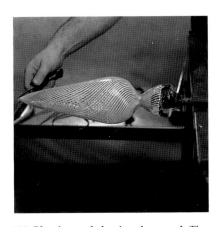

197 Blowing and shaping the vessel. The glass is further inflated, then, after a constriction has been made near the blow-pipe, the end of the glass is elongated and further inflated to form a cone (see Figs 72–3).

198 As a result of the pull, the canes in the lower half of the vessel become noticeably less twisted. After reheating, the jacks are used to constrict the glass at regular intervals.

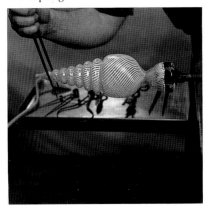

199 The constrictions are continued to the tip of the vessel. Finally, the additional elements required to finish the object are added: a knop, merese and foot (see Figs 124–34), and a separate cover is made.

Vetro a reticello; fused sandwich gold
FIGS 200–204

The virtuosity of the Renaissance glassblower reached a new level with the invention of *vetro a reticello*, a material entirely composed of single white threads or canes, creating a very small mesh. Occasionally, gold leaf was even trapped between the criss-crossing white threads.

200 Beaker of *vetro a reticello* combined with a 'sandwich' of gold leaf. Venetian or, more probably, *façon de Venise* from the Southern Netherlands, third quarter of the 16th century. H. 15.7 cm. See Pl. 218.

201 A tube of glass with *vetro a fili* canes (see Figs 190–96) spiralling in an anti-clockwise direction is rolled in gold leaf and positioned over a tall glass cup composed of canes spiralling in the opposite direction.

202 Carefully avoiding any contact with the sides of the glass cup (which has been kept in a lehr near its softening point), the tube is lowered inside it to its full extent.

203 The tube is rapidly inflated, causing the two layers of glass to fuse. However, the surfaces of both tube and cup remain ribbed because of the contour of the canes from which they were made.

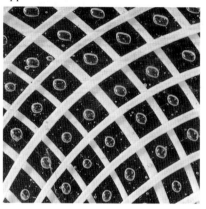

204 As a result, tiny air bubbles are trapped in the small cavities between the high points of the intersecting ridges. The vessel is then completed by the usual processes of glassblowing (see Figs 74–86).

Claw prunts
FIGS 205–209

The glassblower's virtuosity, often using glass with many impurities, led in late Roman times to three-dimensional decorative features being added to the vessel's exterior surface and also directly connected with the interior, so that the liquid could flow into the 'claws'.

205 Claw beaker of green glass, with blue trails on the upper row of claws and at the neck and base. Probably Frankish, late 5th to early 6th century AD. H. 26.2 cm. See Pl. 130.

206 Having blown a vessel to the required shape (see Figs 66–73), a gob of hot glass is applied to the vessel's side, then separated from its pontil. The new hot glass rapidly resoftens the vessel wall at that point.

207 Air is blown into the blow-pipe until the newly added glass and the vessel wall immediately beneath it simultaneously inflate and unite to form one bubble of glass of hemispherical shape.

'Finger-cup' prunts; milling
FIGS 210–214

The glassblower's liking for novelty took many forms as he experimented and, perhaps playfully, demonstrated his skill and versatility. Despite the dangers, the glassmaker's blow-pipe could be sucked instead of blown, and unique effects thus achieved.

208 The bubble, while still soft, is grasped with pincers and pulled outwards to become conical and elongated. The tip is then bent over and attached to a lower part of the vessel, leaving a gap between it and the wall.

210 Barrel-shaped drinking vessel of green glass with six finger-grips protruding inwards: the seven circuits of applied glass each have milled decoration. German, late 17th century. H. 20 cm. British Museum.

209 A trail of glass is added to the spine of the claw (see Figs 77–8) and milled (Fig. 211). When all the claws have been made, the vessel is attached to a pontil and its opening shaped (see Figs 79–86).

211 Milling an applied trail or thread. A trail of glass is applied to the surface of a blown vessel (see Figs 66–75) and a roulette rolled over the still soft glass, leaving an impressed pattern.

212 Making a 'finger-cup' prunt. A gob of glass is added wherever it is intended to make one of these prunts (see Fig. 206).

213 The hot glass is pressed firmly with the handle of the jacks against the side of the vessel, thus causing it to flatten and spread.

214 Air is sucked from the blow-pipe, causing the still hot glass and the vessel wall immediately beneath it to inflate simultaneously and to be drawn inwards, so that the prunt protrudes into the vessel.

GLOSSARY

This glossary, compiled with the help of the six contributors, lists the glassmaking (hot-working) terms found in this book and sets out the way in which they have been used. Because so many glassmaking terms (for instance, casing and flashing) have in the past been given different shades of meaning – not only in English, but also in other languages – these definitions should, where necessary, be read in conjunction with the pictorial sequences in the section 'Techniques of Glassmaking and Decoration' (subsequently referred to as *Techniques*).

NB Cross-references to full definitions are shown in SMALL CAPITALS.

Air-twist Longitudinal channels of air trapped in a mass of glass which has been elongated and twisted in the process of forming a CANE. See *Techniques*, Figs 158–61.

Annealing The process of gradually cooling a completed object at the end of the hot-working process. It takes place in a LEHR and allows the thicker and thinner parts of the object to cool at a uniform rate, thereby preventing the development of stresses within the glass.

Annealing chamber or oven See LEHR.

Batch The mixture of raw materials – sand, soda, lime, lead, etc. – which are heated in a crucible within a glass furnace to form the glass from which objects are made.

Bead-forming In antiquity, the making of glass beads on metal rods (and possibly by other methods). See CORE-FORMING and FLAME-WORKING.

Blobbing The process by which chips of coloured glass are embedded in the thickness of blown glass, thereby forming an irregular scatter of blobs of contrasting colours over the entire surface of an object. See *Techniques*, Figs 89–90.

Blowing The process of forming an object by inflating a gob of soft glass gathered on the end of a hollow tube (BLOW-PIPE) or by inflating a closed cylinder of soft glass (composed of CANES, for example). See *Techniques*, Figs 66–87 (free blowing), 114–17 (dip-mould blowing), 154–6 (full mould blowing), and 194–6 (closed cylinder blowing).

Blow-pipe A hollow tube for blowing glass. The blow-pipe is usually made of metal; however, in FLAME-WORKING it is made of glass.

Bubbles See AIR-TWIST, SEEDS and TEARDROPS.

Cane-making The process of stretching glass into thin rods or strips. Glass of any colour can be used, and several colours can be incorporated in a single cane, often to create a specific pattern. See *Techniques*, Figs 23–5 (polychrome band), 26–8 (GOLD BAND), 39–45 (MOSAIC) and 110–11 (MILLEFIORI).

Canes Thin rods or strips of glass. See CANE-MAKING.

Casing A term that has come to describe the technique by which glass of one colour is fused onto the *inner* surface of glass of a different colour, using a preformed 'cup' of one colour and introducing into it a glass of a different colour. By repetition, a multicoloured layered glass can be produced. This technique is sometimes referred to as the 'cup-overlay method'.

NB This technique was used in the nineteenth century for making cameo-glass blanks, Bohemian multicoloured layered blanks and paperweights with a coloured background or exterior. Unlike the related technique of FLASHING, with which it is sometimes confused, casing does not seem to have been practised in antiquity; until a comprehensive examination of all examples surviving from antiquity has been carried out, this must remain a tentative generalisation.

Casting A process by which moulds – either open or closed – are filled with glass which, because of its viscous nature, has to be forced into the recesses – and even into the finest intaglio designs – of the mould. When using an open mould, the hot glass may be poured into the mould or, alternatively, the mould may be pressed onto the soft glass on the MARVER; see MOULD-PRESSING (*Techniques*, Figs 60–64). There are certain categories of 'cast' glass vessels in antiquity in which subsequent reworking of the surface has obscured the precise method of manufacture.

Chair The name given to the glassblower's bench, at which he sits and with one hand rolls the BLOW-PIPE or PONTIL back and forth on the flat extended arms of the chair while working the soft glass with a tool held in his other hand. The chair as we know it today probably dates from the seventeenth century. In the late sixteenth century the Italian practice was to strap boards to the glassblower's thighs; this method may have derived from Roman practice (see Pl. 1).

'Chair' is also the name given to the team of craftsmen making glass at the furnace.

Cire-perdue See LOST-WAX PROCESS.

Clamp A tool often used in place of a PONTIL, to hold a blown glass vessel at its closed end while the open end is being shaped. Its use speeds up production and avoids the occurrence of a PONTIL MARK. See *Techniques*, Figs 91–2.

Closed cylinder blowing See BLOWING.

Combing A decorative technique whereby bands of coloured glass on the surface of an object are dragged while still soft at right angles, usually with a pointed instrument, to form a repetitive pattern. See *Techniques*, Figs 8 (vertical combing) and 31–2 (horizontal combing).

Core-forming A process for making vessels by building glass around a removable core. The core, generally composed of an organic substance (probably animal dung) and a binding agent (probably clay), is fixed to one end of a metal rod and modelled to the shape required for the interior of the glass vessel. See *Techniques*, Figs 2–15.

The same technique – using a similar material as a separating agent – can be used to produce small glass beads at the end of a metal rod. See *Techniques*, Figs 17–21.

NB In some recent publications, this technique for making beads has been called 'rod-forming', even though a separating agent was still used; the intention was to distinguish it from the use of a much thicker core in the making of vessels. It should be stressed that in antiquity there may have been other methods of making beads.

Cracking off A technique by which the rim of a blown glass vessel is created: by using the point of a diamond (or similar sharp stone) and a trail of soft glass, the vessel is separated from the 'OVERBLOW'. This method is most frequently used in the making of thin-walled vessels, often those which have been blown into moulds. The edge can, if required, be ground smooth. See *Techniques*, Figs 96–7.

Crackle glass See ICE-GLASS.

Crizzling A state of increasing deterioration in the chemical make-up of glass, probably due mainly to the presence of an excess of alkaline elements in the glass reacting to moisture in the atmosphere, resulting in the formation of droplets or 'tears' of alkaline moisture on the surface. Glass suffering from this phenomenon is sometimes referred to as 'weeping', 'sweating', 'sick' or 'diseased'. It should not, however, be confused with WEATHERING (iridescence) or DEVITRIFICATION.

Cullet Glass assembled for the glassmaker's use, whether specially made (i.e. 'raw' glass) or scrap glass (i.e. recycled fragments) intended to be melted for use in a hot process.

'Cup-overlay method' See CASING.

Devitrification A state of deterioration in which crystals have formed within the glass, probably due mainly to a technical fault in the manufacturing process. It should not be confused with CRIZZLING.

Dip-mould blowing See BLOWING.

'Dip-overlay method' See FLASHING.

'Diseased' See CRIZZLING.

Enamelling A decorative technique whereby finely powdered coloured glass suspended in a liquid medium is applied to the surface and fired until the two are fused together. See *Techniques*, Figs 174–8.

Fili More correctly, *vetro a fili*, see FILIGRANA.

Filigrana An abbreviation of *vetro a filigrana*, the old term used to encompass all varieties of blown glass made with white, and sometimes coloured, CANES. The three principal types are (a) *vetro a fili*, in which all the canes form a series of parallel lines; (b) *vetro a retorti* (or, occasionally, *retortoli*), in which each of the canes has been twisted into a spiral pattern; (c) *vetro a reticello* (literally, glass with small network), in which all the canes – whether composed *a fili* or *a retorti* – crisscross each other to form a fine mesh, in which tiny air bubbles may be trapped. See *Techniques*, Figs 185–204.

Flame-working A technique whereby heat is applied to glass in a strictly localised manner. The source of the heat is usually from a specially designed lamp – hence the term 'lamp-work'. See *Techniques*, Figs 17–21.

Flashing A term that has come to describe the technique whereby glass of one colour is fused onto the *outer* surface of glass of a different colour, by taking a gather of the inner colour – sometimes partly inflated – and dipping it into a crucible containing molten glass of the outer colour. By repeating the procedure, a multicoloured layered glass can be produced. This technique is sometimes referred to as the 'dip-overlay method'. See *Techniques*, Figs 99–101. NB This technique was used both in antiquity and in later periods, for example to make Roman cameo glass, which, contrary to recent published opinion, was not made by CASING. Bohemian glass of the nineteenth century is often described as 'flashed' when it has a very thin layer of coloured glass, even though this thin layer was most often achieved using the technique of casing.

Folded rim A double thickness of glass forming a narrow border around the edge of a blown glass vessel – most commonly found on the foot of an object – to give greater strength and minimise the risk of chipping. For a description of the process of manufacture, which takes place during the opening of the vessel, see *Techniques*, Figs 169–71 (inner-fold) and 172–3 (outer-fold).

Form A heat-resistant object used to create a final shape. Used in the SLUMPING process (see *Techniques*, Figs 53–8) and in insertion forming (*Techniques*, Fig. 152).

Founding Making glass by melting and fusing the materials in a FURNACE.

Free blowing See BLOWING.

Frit A calcine mixture of sand and fluxes ready to be melted to form glass. See FOUNDING.

Full mould blowing See BLOWING.

Furnace A construction, however small, in which glass can be made or, alternatively, melted to the required temperature. Glass in a furnace is readily accessible to the glassmaker through the GLORY-HOLE.

Fusing The process of melting two or more pieces of glass together. See *Techniques*, Figs 46–8.

Gathering The collecting of hot glass (or, as it is more commonly called, soft glass) from the FURNACE on the end of the BLOW-PIPE and the PONTIL. See *Techniques*, Figs 66–8.

Gilding See GOLD-LEAF GILDING and GOLD PAINTING.

Glory-hole Traditionally, an opening in the side of a glass FURNACE at which the glassmaker gathers the soft glass and reheats it during the manufacturing process. More recently, this term has been applied to any furnace that is exclusively used for the reheating of a glass object during manufacture.

Gold band A term used to describe a flat CANE made by 'SANDWICHING' gold leaf between two layers of fused glass.

Gold-leaf gilding A technique whereby gold leaf is used to decorate the surface of an object. See *Techniques*, Figs 26–8 (picked up on hot glass and fused) and 175–7 (applied cold and then fused).

Gold painting A technique whereby gold in a solution is brushed or painted onto the surface of a glass object to produce a gilded or gold painted appearance. It is then fixed to the surface by firing.

Ice-glass A decorative technique (also known as 'crackle glass') whereby the surface of the glass is deliberately made rough and opaque, like cracked ice. The effect is created by plunging a PARAISON of soft glass into cold water early in the blowing process so that the surface is fissured. After gentle reheating (to avoid smoothing the surface), the final blowing enlarges the web of cracks to create a frosted appearance. A slightly similar effect can be achieved by rolling a soft paraison over a mass of splintered glass on the MARVER.

Iridescence See WEATHERING.

Jacks A glassmaker's tool, sometimes known as *pucellas*, for the shaping of glass during the blowing process. See *Techniques*, Figs 72, 83 and 85–6.

Kick A concavity in the base of an object where it has been pushed in by the PONTIL. At the apex of the kick, a PONTIL-MARK can often be seen.

Kiln A construction for heating glass at temperatures slightly below those in the glass FURNACE and significantly higher than those normally found in a LEHR, thereby enabling FUSING and SLUMPING to be carried out. A kiln can also serve as a lehr when the temperature has been reduced to the level required for the ANNEALING process.

Lamp-working See FLAME-WORKING.

Latticino (or latticinio) An Italian term which was formerly used to describe *vetro a filigrana* but which, because of past confusion about its meaning, has now been abandoned. See FILIGRANA.

Lehr A construction in which ANNEALING can be carried out. When built as an auxiliary part of the FURNACE, this chamber draws its heat from the furnace, but if it is built as a separate unit it requires an independent heat source. The lehr can also be used for firing ENAMELS and LUSTRE PAINTING on glass objects at low temperatures. Furthermore, cold finished objects awaiting further decoration or additions at the furnace are first returned to the lehr for gentle reheating.

Liquid gilding See GOLD PAINTING.

Lost-wax process A method of casting whereby a wax or wax-coated model is embedded in clay and then baked, so that the wax melts and is 'lost', leaving a mould into which the soft glass can be poured. The mould has to be broken in order to retrieve the object.

Lustre painting A technique of glass decoration which uses metal oxides, especially silver and copper, to create a coloured stain. When the painted object is fired in the FURNACE, the compounds of silver and copper change colour because they become reduced – all oxygen being consumed by the flames. The amber or reddish-brown film which remains fused onto the glass has a slightly lustrous sheen. See also STAINING.

Marver A metal or stone surface on which heated soft glass is rolled or pressed to shape it and often to pick up surface embellishments, such as gold leaf or small pieces of coloured glass. See *Techniques*, Figs 24 (making soft glass flat), 69 (making soft glass round), 26 and 112 (picking up gold leaf), and 89 (BLOBBING).

Merese A small disc of glass typically seen between the bowl and stem and stem and foot of a goblet. It is usually ornamental, but also has a practical function in giving greater strength to the object. Mereses can appear singly or stacked one above another, often in groups of two or three. See *Techniques*, Figs 124–6.

Metal A term traditionally used to refer to the substance of the glass, both during the manufacture of an object and thereafter.

Mezza-forma (or mezza-stampatura) Literally 'half-moulding', this term is used to describe the technique for producing ribs on the lower portion of a blown glass vessel. See also 'NIPT DIAMOND WAIES'.

Millefiori A term used to describe the technique whereby glass objects are blown and embedded with thinly sliced sections of glass canes of multicoloured chevron, floral or other patterns in alternating concentric bands (see CANE-MAKING). See *Techniques*, Figs 110–11.

For another method of making glass objects embedded with thin sections of coloured canes, see MOSAIC.

Moil See OVERBLOW, for which this is another name.

Mosaic A technique whereby glass objects are formed by FUSING thin slices or lengths of previously manufactured canes (see CANE-MAKING). See *Techniques*, Figs 39–48.

Mosaic should be distinguished from the later technique of MILLEFIORI.

Mould-pressing A process whereby the glassmaker presses a mould onto the soft glass on a MARVER or exerts force, other than by blowing, to push soft glass into the recesses of the mould. Because the glass rapidly begins to harden as it touches the surface of the mould, it must be made to travel swiftly into the depths of any intricate designs cut in the sides as well as into the furthest corners of the mould. See *Techniques*, Figs 60–64.

Mould See BLOWING, CASTING, OVERBLOW.

Muffle kiln A construction, sometimes placed within the FURNACE itself, for heating the materials without exposure to the direct action of the fire.

'Nipt diamond waies' The PINCERING of adjacent ribs on a vessel to form a diamond pattern, the ribs having usually been created by the MEZZA-FORMA technique. See *Techniques*, Figs 179–83.

Overblow A term often associated with the mould-blowing process, describing that small portion of the PARAISON, after its insertion into the mould, which forms between the BLOW-PIPE and the mould. After the ANNEALING process, the overblow is removed, usually by CRACKING OFF. See *Techniques*, Figs 94–7 and 154–6.

Overlaying An imprecise term describing the process of creating two or more fused layers of different coloured glass, by one of the following three methods: CASING ('cup-overlay method'), FLASHING ('dip-overlay method') or CASTING (for the production of flat objects such as the cameo plaques of ancient Rome).

Paraison A term given various meanings by different authorities at different times. In this book, it is used to refer to the blown glass on the end of a BLOW-PIPE.

Pincering The technique of shaping soft glass by manipulating it with pincers. It is used for making entirely functional – or perhaps structural – elements of an object, and also for purely decorative ones. See *Techniques*, Figs 9–10, 12–13 (functional) and 21, 143–5 (decorative).

'Plating' A nineteenth-century term, used especially in America, to describe the technique of CASING; hence 'plated' glass was a popular description. (The term should not be confused with 'plate glass', which was first used in the nineteenth century to describe fine quality flat glass for windows etc.)

Pontil A metal rod used during hot manufacturing processes which enables the glass-worker to hold and manipulate an object with ease while working on it. A BLOW-PIPE that has been used to inflate a blown glass object can also serve as its pontil during the finishing processes. The pontil can also be used for GATHERING glass from the FURNACE in order to make additions to an object in the course of manufacture. See *Techniques*, Figs 79, 148–9 (pontil) and 11, 36, 77–8 (gathering).

Pontil mark A scar of roughened glass on an object to which a PONTIL was attached. In blown glass vessels it is usually centred on the base and appears as a relatively small round area. Other forms include a ring-shaped mark, indicating the probable use of the BLOW-PIPE as a pontil.

The absence of any pontil mark may mean that it has been (a) ground away, or (b) that the vessel was opened by CRACKING OFF, thereby obviating the need for a pontil, or (c) that a CLAMP was used to hold the object during its final shaping. For examples of processes which leave pontil marks, see *Techniques*, Figs 79, 149–50 and 175–8. For examples of processes which do not leave pontil marks, see *Techniques*, Figs 92 (clamping) and 94–7 (cracking off).

Pontil rod See PONTIL.

Press-moulding See MOULD-PRESSING.

Pressed glass Objects produced by a mechanised process, either hand-operated or fully automated, for pressing glass into moulds. See MOULD-PRESSING.

Prunts Decorative additions of glass, usually on the sides of vessels, in the form of small circular blobs which are variously left plain, manipulated with pincers, stamped with relief ornament or inflated by the glassblower. See *Techniques*, Figs 206–14.

Pucellas See JACKS, for which this is another name.

Punty (puntee) See PONTIL, for which this is another name.

Reticello More correctly, *vetro a reticello*; see FILIGRANA.

Retorti More correctly, *vetro a retorti*; see FILIGRANA.

'Rod-forming' See CORE-FORMING.

Sandwich A technique whereby decoration is introduced between two layers of glass. It can be achieved without any heat, for example as in the late third-century BC bowls from Canosa (Pls 54–5) or the eighteenth-century Bohemian *Zwischengoldglas* (Pl. 237), or by FUSING the two glass surfaces and trapping the decoration between them, as in Late Roman (Pl. 123) and Renaissance examples (Pls 207–8). See also GOLD-LEAF GILDING. For a description of fused sandwich gold, see *Techniques*, Figs 26–8.

Seeds An imperfection in glass consisting of small bubbles, usually a result of impurities in the BATCH. Seeds can also be caused by insufficient heat or time in the FURNACE during the melting and refining process.

'Sick' See CRIZZLING.

Slumping The process of heating glass until gravity forces it to conform to the shape of the FORM on which it rests. See *Techniques*, Figs 53–8.

Sofietta The Italian name for a tool used by the glass-blower as a puffer, to inflate still further a vessel after it has been separated from the BLOW-PIPE and while it is still attached to the PONTIL. See *Techniques*, Fig. 84.

Staining The decorative colouring of glass by the technique of LUSTRE PAINTING.
NB The subject of stained window glass is excluded from this survey, and there is therefore no discussion of the techniques involved.

'Sweating' See CRIZZLING.

'Teardrop' The name commonly used to describe teardrop-shaped bubbles of air deliberately trapped in the glass for purposes of decoration when forming the stem of a goblet or wine-glass, for example. See also AIR-TWIST.

Tooling The shaping of soft glass by squeezing or pressing it with JACKS or other tools while it is being rotated on the BLOW-PIPE or PONTIL.

Trailing A process whereby a strand of glass is pulled directly onto the surface of an object from a relatively large mass of soft glass. It is used to produce spiral, circular or meandering patterns. The trailed glass can subsequently be PINCERED etc. into other shapes. See *Techniques*, Figs 6–7 (spiral trailing) and 77–8 (circular trailing).

Vetro a fili, vetro a reticello, vetro a retorti See FILIGRANA.

Weathering The harmful effects of age, moisture and chemical action which lead to the decomposition of glass, on or under its surface. In its most usual form, weathering causes the glass to develop thin layers of rainbow-like colours (iridescence). Often found in conjunction with surface pitting, iridescence obscures not only the original transparency and decorative details, but also destroys the original colour of the glass. However, in the nineteenth century its colourful effects were considered attractive and were deliberately copied by European and American glassmakers.

'Weeping' See CRIZZLING.

Window glass The subject of window glass is excluded from this survey, and there is therefore no discussion of the techniques involved.

FURTHER READING

The following select list of books published since 1940, mainly in English, has been arranged to correspond with the order of the text.

For those who wish to pursue the subject in detail or have a more specialised interest in the British Museum's collection of glass, attention is drawn to the following sources:

1. GEORGE S. DUNCAN, *A Bibliography of Glass from the earliest records to 1940* (published for the Society of Glass Technology, Sheffield), London 1960.

2. Each volume of the annual *Journal of Glass Studies* (The Corning Museum of Glass, Corning, New York, commencing Vol. I, 1959—) contains a 'Check List of Recently Published Articles and Books on Glass', which is very helpfully arranged under five main headings: General, Technological, Historical, Stained Glass, and Beads. The 'Historical' publications, being the largest section, are divided chronologically and, after the medieval period, are subdivided geographically.

3. Each issue of the annual *New Glass Review* (The Corning Museum of Glass, Corning, New York, commencing Vol. I, 1979—) contains a similar 'Check List for Contemporary Glass', which in addition includes architectural flat glass and technology.

4. The British Museum collections:

A. NESBITT, *Catalogue of the Collection of Glass formed by Felix Slade, Esq., and bequeathed to the British Museum in 1868*, London 1869 and 1871.

O. M. DALTON, *Catalogue of Early Christian Antiquities and Objects from the Christian East*, British Museum, London 1901.

Masterpieces of Glass, exh. cat. compiled by D. B. Harden, K. S. Painter, R. H. Pinder-Wilson and Hugh Tait, British Museum, London 1968.

J. D. COONEY, *Catalogue of Egyptian Antiquities in the British Museum*, IV, *Glass*, London 1976.

HUGH TAIT, *The Golden Age of Venetian Glass*, British Museum, London 1979.

D. B. HARDEN, *Catalogue of Greek and Roman Glass in the British Museum*, I, London 1981.

D. BARAG, *Catalogue of Western Asiatic Glass in the British Museum*, I, London 1985.

J. RUDOE, *Decorative Arts 1850–1950: A Catalogue of the British Museum Collection*, London 1991 (2nd edn 1994).

HUGH TAIT, *Catalogue of the Waddesdon Bequest*, IV, *Enamels, Glass, Nielli and Maiolica* (forthcoming).

TECHNOLOGY

D. B. HARDEN, 'Glass and Glazes', in C. Singer *et al.* (eds), *History of Technology*, Oxford 1956.

F. KULASIEWICZ, *Glassblowing: The Technique of Free-blown Glass*, New York 1974.

J. PRICE, 'Glass', in D. Strong and D. Brown (eds), *Roman Crafts*, London 1976.

W. A. WEYL, *Coloured Glasses*, Society of Glass Technology, Sheffield 1976 (paperback reprint).

K. CUMMINGS, *The Technique of Glass Forming*, London 1980.

I. FREESTONE, 'Looking into Glass', in S. Bowman (ed.), *Science and the Past*, London 1991.

HISTORICAL STUDIES

B. NOLTE, *Die Glasgefässe im alten Ägypten*, Berlin 1968.

D. B. HARDEN, 'Ancient Glass', I, II and III, *Archaeological Journal*, 1969, 1970 and 1971.

J. PRICE, 'Glass', in M. Henig (ed.), *Handbook of Roman Art*, Oxford 1983.

D. B. HARDEN *et al.*, *Glass of the Caesars*, Milan 1987.

V. EVISON, contributions in *The Making of England: Anglo-Saxon Art and Culture AD 600–900*, exh. cat., ed. L. Webster and J. Backhouse, British Museum, London 1991.

K. REYNOLDS BROWN *et al.*, *The Treasury of San Marco*, Venice and Milan 1984.

S. FUKAI, *Persian Glass*, trans. E. B. Crawford, New York 1977.

J. GLUCK and C. J. PENON, 'Glass', in J. and S. H. Gluck (eds), *A Survey of Persian Handicraft*, Tehran, New York, London and Ashiya 1977.

F. BAYRAMOĞLU, *Turkish Glass Art and Beykoz-ware*, Istanbul 1970.

R. SOAME JENYNS, *Chinese Art*, II, *The Minor Arts*, London 1965, rev. ed. New York 1982.

AN JIAYAO, *Early Chinese Glassware*, Oriental Ceramic Society Translations no. 12, London 1987.

C. BROWN and D. RABINER, *Clear as Crystal, Red as Flame: Later Chinese Glass*, China House Gallery, New York 1990.

A. POLAK, *Glass: its Makers and its Public*, London and New York 1975.

E. BAUMGARTNER and I. KRUEGER, *Phoenix aus Sand und Asche: Glas des Mittelalters*, Munich 1968.

A Travers le Verre: du Moyen Age à la Renaissance, exh. cat., ed. Danièle Foy and Geneviève Sennequier, Musées et Monuments Départementaux des Antiquités, Rouen 1989.

G. H. KENYON, *The Glass Industry of the Weald*, Leicester 1967.

E. S. Godfrey, *The Development of English Glassmaking, 1560–1640*, Oxford and Chicago 1957.

G. Mariacher, *Italian Blown Glass from Ancient Rome to Venice*, London 1961.

K. Hettes, *Old Venetian Glass*, trans. O. Vojtisek, London 1960.

G. Boesen, *Venetian Glass in Rosenborg Castle*, Copenhagen 1960.

A. W. Frothingam, *Spanish Glass*, London 1963 and New York 1964.

J. Barrelet, *La Verrerie en France de l'Epoque Gallo-Romaine à nos Jours*, Paris 1953.

A. von Saldern, *German Enamelled Glass*, Corning Museum of Glass, New York, 1965.

R. Chambon, *L'Histoire de la Verrerie en Belgique*, Brussels 1955.

E. Meyer-Heisig, *Der Nürnberger Glasschnitt des 17. Jahrhunderts*, Nuremberg 1963.

F. G. A. M. Smit, *Frans Greenwood 1680–1763, Dutch Poet and Glass Engraver*, Peterborough 1988.

O. Drahotova, *European Glass*, New York 1983.

B. Klesse and H. Mayr, *Veredelte Gläser aus Renaissance und Barock: die Sammlung Ernesto Wolf*, Vienna 1987.

R. von Strasser and W. Spiegel, *Dekoriertes Glas: Renaissance bis Biedermeier: Katalog Raisonné der Sammlung Rudolph von Strasser*, Munich 1989 (with full bibliography, especially concentrating on Austrian, Bohemian, Dutch and German enamelled and engraved glasses).

L. M. Bickerton, *An Illustrated Guide to Eighteenth-Century English Drinking Glasses*, with bibliography by D. R. Elleray, London and New York 1972.

W. A. Thorpe, *English Glass*, 3rd edn, London 1961.

P. Warren, *Irish Glass: the Age of Exuberance*, London 1970.

R. J. Charleston, *English Glass and the Glass used in England, c.400–1940*, London 1984.

C. Witt, C. Weeden and A. Palmer Schwind, *Bristol Glass*, Bristol 1984.

A. C. Revi, *Nineteenth Century Glass, its Genesis and Development*, rev. edn, New York 1967.

H. Wakefield, *Nineteenth Century British Glass*, London 1982.

Y. Amic, *L'Opaline Française au XIX Siècle*, Paris 1952.

P. Jokelson, *Sulphides, the Art of Cameo Incrustation*, New York 1968.

P. Davis, *The Development of the American Glass Industry*, Cambridge, Massachusetts, 1949.

A. C. Revi, *American Cut and Engraved Glass*, New York 1965.

J. S. Spillman and E. S. Farrar, *The Cut and Engraved Glass of Corning 1868–1940*, Corning Museum of Glass, New York, 1977.

L. Innes, *Pittsburgh Glass 1797–1891*, Boston 1976.

L. W. Watkins, *Cambridge Glass 1818–1888*, New York, n.d.

K. M. Wilson, *New England Glass and Glassmaking*, New York 1972.

J. S. Spillman, *Pressed Glass 1825–1925*, Corning Museum of Glass, New York, 1983.

J. Measell, *Greentown Glass: the Indiana Tumbler & Goblet Company*, Grand Rapids Public Museum, Minnesota, 1979.

J. S. Spillman and S. K. Frantz, *Masterpieces of American Glass*, New York, 1990.

S. M. Goldstein and L. S. and J. K. Rakow, *Cameo Glass. Masterpieces from 2000 Years of Glassmaking*, Corning Museum of Glass, New York, 1982.

P. Hollister Jr, *The Encyclopedia of Glass Paperweights*, New York, 1969.

J. S. Spillman, *Glass from World's Fairs*, Corning Museum of Glass, New York, 1986.

D. B. Burke et al., *In Pursuit of Beauty: Americans and the Aesthetic Movement*, New York, 1986.

R. Koch, *Louis C. Tiffany's Art Glass*, New York, 1977.

H. F. McKean, *The 'Lost' Treasures of Louis Comfort Tiffany*, Garden City, New York, 1980.

A. Duncan and G. de Bartha, *Glass by Gallé*, New York, 1984.

W. Warmus, *Emile Gallé Dreams into Glass*, Corning Museum of Glass, New York, 1984.

P. V. Gardner, *Frederick Carder: Portrait of a Glassmaker*, Corning Museum of Glass, New York, 1971.

P. V. Gardner and P. Vickers, *Glass*, The Smithsonian Institution, Washington DC, 1979.

A. Polak, *Modern Glass*, London, 1962.

R. Flavell and C. Smale, *Studio Glassmaking*, New York, 1974.

PUBLICATIONS ON OTHER COLLECTIONS IN BRITAIN AND NORTH AMERICA

W. B. Honey, *Glass: a Handbook . . . to the Collections in the Victoria and Albert Museum*, London 1946.

H. Tait, *The Pilkington Glass Museum*, reprinted from *The Connoisseur*, December 1964, January 1965.

Art in Glass: a Guide to the Glass Collections, Toledo Museum of Art, Toledo, Ohio, 1969.

M. Greenshields, *Glass in the Cecil Higgins Art Gallery, Bedford*, Bedford 1969.

Glass in London, Museum of London, 1970.

J. W. Hayes, *Roman and Pre-Roman Glass in the Royal Ontario Museum*, Toronto 1975.

S. H. Auth, *Ancient Glass at the Newark Museum*, Newark, New Jersey, 1976.

I. N. Hume, *Glass in Colonial Williamsburg's Archaeological Collections*, Williamsburg, Virginia, 1976.

I. Wolfenden (ed.), *English Rock-Crystal Glass*, exh. cat., Dudley Museum and Art Gallery, 1976.

C. P. Kaellgren, *A Gather of Glass*, The Royal Ontario Museum, Toronto, 1977.

M. Archer, R. J. Charleston and M. Marcheix, *The James A. de Rothschild Collection at Waddesdon Manor: Glass and Enamels*, The National Trust, 1977.

English Drinking Glasses in the Ashmolean Museum, Oxford 1977.

Glass at the Fitzwilliam Museum, Cambridge 1978.

S. M. Goldstein, *Pre-Roman and Early Roman Glass in the Corning Museum of Glass*, Corning, New York, 1979.

Historic Glass from Collections in North-West England, Merseyside County Museum, Liverpool, 1979.

Glass in the British Isles, Bulletin de l'Association Internationale pour l'Histoire du Verre, no. 8, Liège 1980.

S. B. Matheson, *Ancient Glass in the Yale University Art Gallery*, Yale 1980.

J. R. Charleston, *Masterpieces of Glass from the Corning Museum of Glass*, Corning, New York, 1980.

C. Truman, *An Introduction to English Glassware to 1900*, Victoria and Albert Museum, London, 1984.

M. Jenkins, *Islamic Glass: a Brief History*, The Metropolitan Museum of Art Bulletin, XLIV, no.2, Fall 1986.

C. Brown and D. Rabiner, *The Robert Clague Collection: Chinese Glass of the Qing Dynasty*, Phoenix Art Museum, 1987.

D. F. Grose, *Early Ancient Glass in the Toledo Museum of Art*, New York 1989.

J. Barnes, *Catalogue of the Turner Museum of Glass*, University of Sheffield, 1993.

D. P. Lanmon with D. B. Whitehouse, *The Robert Lehman Collection, XI, Glass*, New York and Princeton, 1993.

ILLUSTRATION CREDITS AND MUSEUM ACCESSION NUMBERS

Except where stated, references are to British Museum registration numbers. The Museum Departments are abbreviated as follows:

EA Egyptian Antiquities
GR Greek and Roman Antiquities
MLA Medieval and Later Antiquities
OA Oriental Antiquities
PRB Prehistoric and Romano-British Antiquities
WAA Western Asiatic Antiquities

Half-title page OA 1938.5–24.301
Title page Corning Museum of Glass, New York, 74.3.24
Contents page OA G. 1983.330, 95.3–22.1, 77.1–16.43

1 Photo © Scala, Milan
2 WAA 120960
3 Photo courtesy Stuart Crystal
4 British Library, Sl. MS 857
5 MLA S.829
6 MLA 1991.1–8.1
7–8 Private collection, photos Sotheby's
9 GR 1906.5–22.3
10 GR 1958.2–11.1
10a OA 89.5–7.11
11 MLA W.B. 59
12 Metropolitan Museum of Art, New York
13–14 Corning Museum of Glass, photos courtesy Christopher Sheppard
15 WAA 901952
16 WAA 120659
17 WAA 134901
18 WAA 130076
19 GR Glass Cat. 56
20 GR Glass Cat. 14
21 EA 22819
22 EA 47620
23 EA 55193
24 EA 64333
25 EA 4741
26 EA 64342, 47983
27 EA 4742, 4743
28 EA 29210
29 EA 64338
30 EA 64335, 64334
31 EA 4749
32 *Centre:* EA 27727; *clockwise, from top left:* EA 68391, 68388, 64125, 64124, 64163, 68394, 65660, 68398
33 EA 24391
34 EA 65774
35 EA 16374
36 *Top:* EA 64186, 64297; *centre:* EA 2895, 64162, 65535; *bottom:* EA 29258, 29264, 63347, 68531, 16443
37 *Top:* EA 64215, 37527, 64216, 17597; *bottom:* EA 16375, 54264, 64121, 54925
38 *Top:* EA 65544, 6261, 16682, 64284; *bottom:* EA 64280, 6242, 65655
39 WAA 118120
40 WAA 91521
41 WAA 134900
42 GR 1869.6–24.16
43 GR Glass Cat. 377
44 GR Glass Cat. 80
45 GR Glass Cat. 231, 159, 127, 258
46 EA 16536, 64220, 16531, 64222, 62580, 63728
47 GR Glass Cat. 423
48 GR Glass Cat. 311, 295, 297
49 GR Glass Cat. 357, 338, 352
50 EA 63772
51 GR 1870.6–6.7
52 GR 1896.6–30.2
53 GR 1871.5–18.3
54 GR 1871.5–18.7, 1871.5–18.9, 1871.5–18.2
55 GR 1871.5–18.2
56 GR 1873.8–20.420, 1836.2–24.488
57 GR 1849.11–21.1
58 Metropolitan Museum of Art, New York, 91.1.1303
59 EA 16597, 64211, 16588, 16598, 29396
60 EA 15720, 64276, 20871, 64272
61 *Top:* EA 64224; *centre:* EA 64248, 64266, 64263; *bottom:* (wings) EA 64231, (head) 642226

62 EA 37496
63 EA 71019
64 GR 1868.1–10.509
65 GR 1896.12–15.2
66 GR 1868.5–1.75, WAA 1895.6–2.1, GR 1851.3–31.9
67 PRB 1923.6–5.1, GR 1851.8–13.460
68 GR 1879.7–15.1, 1896.6–30.3, 1856.12–26.1132
69 GR 1869.6–24.20, 1868.5–1.153
70 GR 1873.8–20.127
71 PRB 1967.2–2.1 to 24
72 GR 1879.5–22.47, 1883.6–21.39, 1814.7–4.1190, 1870.2–24.1
73 EA 64642 a–f
74 EA 29374
75 GR Gem Cat. 4036 (1945.9–27.1 and 1948.10–18.1)
76 Photo Vincenzo Carcavallo, Naples
77 GR Gem Cat. 4036 (1945.9–27.2)
78 EA 16630
79 GR 1867.5–8.586
80 GR 1866.5–4.43
81 PRB 1932.3–14.1
82 GR 1868.5–1.924, 1869.6–24.30
83–4 GR 1856.12–26.1122
85 GR 1878.12–30.97
86 PRB 1868.5–1.264, 1883.12–13.319
87 GR 1905.11–7.2
88 GR 1887.6–13.8
89 GR 1893.10–16.1
90 GR 1876.11–14.4
91 PRB 1870.2–24.3
92 GR 1869.6–24.5
93 GR 1878.12–30.60, 1878.12–30.58
94 GR 1872.7–26.1
95 GR 1870.9–1.2
96 GR 1878.10–20.1, 1892.6–13.50
97 GR 1856.12–26.1203
98 GR 1772.3–17.1
99 PRB 1840.10–15.2
100 PRB 1299–170, GR 1881.4–6.1, PRB 1922.5–12.1
101 PRB 1922.5–12.1
102 GR 1876.11–14.3
103 GR 1901.4–13.3174
104 GR 1984.7–16.1
105 GR 1868.1–5.52, 1868.1–5.49
106 GR 1881.6–4.2
107 GR 1888.11–12.1
108 National Museum, Copenhagen; photo Lennart Larsen
109 Corning Museum of Glass, New York, 78.1.1; photo © Mario Carrieri
110 GR 1868.5–1.321
111 GR 1868.5–1.919
112 GR 1922.10–25.1
113 GR 1900.10–15.1
114 GR 1891.10–17.6
115 Ashmolean Museum, Oxford, 1957.186
116–17 MLA 1958.12–2.1
118 George Scott, Edinburgh
119 GR 1868.5–1.261, 1877.8–12.3
120 Römisch-Germanisches Museum, Cologne, N 150; photo © Mario Carrieri
121 MLA 1881.6–24.1
122 GR 1877.5–7.2
123 MLA 1863.7–27.3, 1863.7–27.9
124 MLA 1891.6–24.1
125 GR 1915.5–22.105
126 MLA 1971.10–2.1, 1911.5–13.1
127 WAA 134638
128 Museo Archeologico, Cividale; photo Elio Ciol
129 Römisch-Germanisches Museum, Cologne, N 6082; photo © Mario Carrieri

130 MLA 1947.10–9.1, Mucking 843
131 MLA 1973.5–2.212
132 MLA 1921.11–1.381
133 MLA 1894.12–16.8
134 Cambridge University Museum of
Archaeology and Anthropology, Ac.1977.831
135 MLA 1901.4–13.3989
136 Topkapi Sarayi Müsezi Müdürlüğü, Istanbul;
MS H.1344
137 WAA 132985
138 WAA 134373
139 WAA 134909
140 WAA 91498A
141 OA 1959.2–18.1, 1959.2–18.3
142 OA 1956.7–30.2, 1969.3–17.3
143 OA 1964.12–17.1, 1913.11–4.1
144 OA 1913.10–9.1, 90.3–14.2
145 OA 1964.12–10.1
146 OA 1966.4–18.1
147 Treasury of San Marco, Venice; photo ©
Mario Carrieri
148 OA 1966.12–11.1
149 OA 1945.10–17.263, +520
150 OA +7409
151 OA 1976.11–2.1
152 OA 1927.5–16.1
153 OA 1913.5–23.115
154 OA 1964.12–17.2
155 OA 1978.10–11.2
156 OA 1978.6–23.1
157 OA 1902.5–17.8
158–9 OA 1959.4–14.1
160 OA 1945.10–17.260
161 OA 1913.5–22.100
162 OA 1913.5–2.39
163 OA 1906.7–19.1
164 OA 79.5–22.68
165–6 OA 69.1–20.3
167 OA 75.7–17.1
168 OA S.333
169 OA 69.6–24.1
170 OA 81.9–9.3
171 OA 1924.1–25.1
172 OA S.334
173 OA 87.10–15.4
174 OA 77.1–16.45, 42, 43, 47
175 OA S.343
176 OA S.341
177 OA 1961.10–16.1
178 OA 1935.1–15.3
179 OA 1938.5–24.285, 1938.5–24.599,
1940.12–14.110
180 OA 1940.12–4.108
181 OA SL.1696
182 OA 73.12–15.1, 88.5–15.4
183 OA 1945.10–17.341
184 OA +505
185 OA 1948.10–20.14
186 MLA S.461, W.B. 58
187 Treasury of San Marco, Venice; photo ©
Mario Carrieri
188 MLA 1977.7–1.1
189 MLA 1971.10–2.3
189a OA 1910.4–16.3

190 Clockwise, from top left: MLA S.323, 52.4–23.4,
S.947, 74.5–19.9, 83.6–21.5, OA (old
acquisition) 835, 70.11–26.16
191 Musée d'Art et d'Histoire de la Ville de Saint-
Denis, 16.1680.5; photo by Emmanuelle
Jacquot; drawing by Michaël Wyss; courtesy
Unité d'Archéologie de Saint-Denis
192 MLA 76.11–4.3, 1943.4–2.3
193 Musée des Beaux-Arts et d'Archéologie,
Besançon, fouille J. O. Guilhot; photo F.
Dugué, Musées Départementaux de la Seine
Maritime
194 Municipal Museum, Prague; photo Antonín
Krčmář
195 Vatican Library, Rome, MS Palat. Lat. 291,
f.211
196 MLA 75.3–5.2, 73.5–2.214, 1958.5–3.1, 69.1–
20.6
197 MLA S.875, 69.1–20.7
198 British Library, Add. MS 24189, f.16r
199 MLA 78.12–30.279, 1904.7–6.19
200 MLA S.391, 82.4–24.7
201 MLA S.377
202 MLA 1979.4–1.1
203 MLA W.B. 55
204 MLA 69.6–24.62, 69.6–24.71
205 MLA 54.3–2.4
206 MLA S.824
207–8 MLA S.390
209 MLA S.799, S.803, S.796, S.801, 69.6–24.40
210 MLA 78.12–30.266, 70.9–1.6, S.815
211 MLA W.B. 56
212 MLA 55.12–1,197
213 MLA 1924.3–11.1, S.592, S.661
214 MLA S.660, S.688, S.609
215 MLA 1987.7–2.2, AF.3134, AF.3133
216 MLA 55.12–1.156
217 MLA BL. 2867, 55.12–1.156
218 MLA BL.3332, 73.10–29.1
219 MLA 55.12–1.129, 78.12–30.268
220 MLA 71.6–16.6, 95.6–3.17
221 MLA 1956.10–4.1, 80.6–17.6
222 MLA S.607
223 MLA S.587, S.486, S.495
224 MLA 72.12–1.12, S.894
225 MLA S.874, 73.12–4.1
226 MLA S.849, S.836, S.851
227 MLA S.859
228 MLA 1958.4–3.1
229 MLA S.826, 80.6–17.38
230–31 MLA 63.5–8.1
232 Private collection, on permanent loan to the
British Museum
233 MLA 1982.5–5.1
234 MLA 69.1–20.17
235 MLA 1925.2–16.1, OA (old acquisition) 110
236 MLA AF.3147, S.870, 1907.7–26.1
237 MLA S.866, 70.12–1.10
238 MLA S.860
239 MLA 86.11–13.1
240 MLA S.886
241 MLA 1934.1–17.56, 64.5–12.1, 1934.1–17.45,
1924.10–22.6, 1957.12–1.57

242 MLA 69.6–24.89, S.903
243 Courtesy Paul Hollister
244 Corning Museum of Glass, New York,
74.3.129
245 Corning Museum of Glass, New York, 66.3.20
246 Corning Museum of Glass, New York, 65.3.68
247 Chrysler Museum, Norfolk, Virginia, GAS
59.787/71.7769A, 59.788/71.7769B
248 Corning Museum of Glass, New York, 54.2.16
249 Corning Museum of Glass, New York,
84.4.165
250 Corning Museum of Glass, New York,
51.4.536
251 Corning Museum of Glass, New York,
89.4.30, 89.4.32, 89.4.34
252 Chrysler Museum, Norfolk, Virginia, 81.13
(GAS 81.4), 71.4458 (GAS 59.610), 71.4471 (GAS
59.471A)
253 Corning Museum of Glass, New York, 62.4.4
254–5 Photo Sotheby's
256 Corning Museum of Glass, New York,
79.3.330, 79.3.466
257 Birmingham Museums and Art Gallery
258 Photo Leo Kaplan Antiques Ltd
259 Chrysler Museum, Norfolk, Virginia, GAM
68.12/71.4994, 65.12/71.5004, 64.14/71.4996
260 Photo Christie's, New York
261–2 Musée des Arts Décoratifs, Paris; photo
Corning Museum of Glass, New York
263 MLA 1980.11–8.1
264 Corning Museum of Glass, New York, 74.3.27
265 Corning Museum of Glass, New York, 65.3.48
266 Rockwell Museum, New York, 76.353

Techniques of Glassmaking and Decoration
Fig. 1 GR 78.12–30.3
Fig. 16 Toledo Museum of Art, Toledo, Ohio,
76.57, Gift of Edward Drummond Libbey
Fig. 22 GR 95.6–2.1
Fig. 36 GR 73.8–20.420
Fig. 59 GR 51.8–13.460
Fig. 65 MLA 76.11–4.3
Fig. 88 Corning Museum of Glass, New York,
59.1.88
Fig. 93 GR 1905.11–7.2
Fig. 98 Drawing by Pamela Becker, reproduced
from Corning Museum of Glass, Journal of
Glass Studies, vol. 32 (1990), p. 111
Fig. 109 MLA S.801
Fig. 120 MLA S.426
Fig. 137 MLA S.491
Fig. 151 MLA S.583
Fig. 153 MLA S.476
Fig. 157 MLA 64.5–12.1
Fig. 162 MLA S.377
Fig. 179 MLA 78.12–30.279
Fig. 184 MLA S.640
Fig. 189 MLA 80.6–17.27
Fig. 200 MLA 73.10–29.1
Fig. 205 MLA 1947.10–9.1
Fig. 210 MLA 70.2–24.8
All other photographs by Steven Barall

HUGH TAIT, formerly Deputy Keeper of the Department of Medieval and Later Antiquities in the British Museum, is currently engaged on the five-volume *Catalogue of the Waddesdon Bequest in the British Museum*: vol. I, *The Jewels*, was published in 1986, vol. II, *The Silver Plate*, in 1988 and vol. III, *The 'Curiosities'*, in 1991; vols IV, *The Enamels, Glass, Nielli and Maiolica*, and V, *The Sculpture, Miniature Carvings and Metalwork*, are in preparation. His other publications include *The Golden Age of Venetian Glass* (1979), 'European glass (post 1200)' in the British Museum's catalogue *Masterpieces of Glass* (1968), and, as editor, *The Art of the Jeweller, A Catalogue of the Hull Grundy Gift to the British Museum* (1984) and *Seven Thousand Years of Jewellery* (1986). He is an Honorary Fellow of the Corning Museum of Glass and a former President of the International Association for the History of Glass.

CAROL ANDREWS is an Assistant Keeper in the Department of Egyptian Antiquities at the British Museum, and author of *Egyptian Mummies* (1984), *Ancient Egyptian Jewellery* (1990), *Amulets of Ancient Egypt* (1994), *Catalogue of Egyptian Jewellery in the British Museum* (1981) and *Catalogue of the Demotic Papyri in the British Museum*, vol. IV (1990).

WILLIAM GUDENRATH, former President of the New York Experimental Glass Workshop, is a Fellow of the Corning Museum of Glass and has contributed articles to the *Journal of Glass Studies*.

PAUL HOLLISTER is both an artist who has exhibited widely and a glass specialist with a particular interest in paperweights. Apart from numerous articles, his publications include *The Encyclopedia of Glass Paperweights* (1969). He has also lectured extensively throughout Europe and the United States.

RALPH PINDER-WILSON was formerly a Deputy Keeper in charge of the Islamic collection at the British Museum and was a contributor to the catalogue *Masterpieces of Glass* (1968). His other publications include *Studies in Islamic Art* (1985) and articles in the *Journal of Glass Studies*. He is a former Director of the British Institute of Afghan Studies in Kabul and Director of the Royal Asiatic Society.

VERONICA TATTON-BROWN is an Assistant Keeper in the Department of Greek and Roman Antiquities at the British Museum. She is author of *Ancient Cyprus* (1987) and editor of *Cyprus and the East Mediterranean in the Iron Age* (1989).

Numbers in italics refer to illustration captions; Fig. numbers refer to the technical sequences on pp. 214–41.

Abbasids 112, 114
abrasion 90, 100; *112*
acid-etching 192, 203, 205, 210; *265*
Adana, Turkey 162
Afghanistan 70, 76–8; *140*
Africa, North 50, 70, 81, 88, 98, 100, 102, 114, 206; *46*
Agricola, Georgius, *De Re Metallico* 166
Agrippina the Younger 66
Ahmedabad, India 176
air-twist *241*; Figs 157–61
Akhenaten 28, 33, 36; *37*
al-'Aziz 119
al-Mu'izz 114
alabastra 39–40, 41–2, 43, 44, 50, 55; *15, 42, 44*; Figs 1, 22
Alalakh, Syria 18
Albert, Prince 200, 201
Albintimilium (Ventimiglia), Italy *87*
Aldrevandin Beaker 151–2; *192*; Fig. *65*
Aldrevandin Group of vessels 151–3
Aldrevandino family 151
Aleppo, Syria 131; *126, 165–6*
Alexander the Great 44, 47, 50, 132, *192*
Alexandria 50–51, 65, 97, 149
lighthouse 78
Alexius I, Emperor 145
Alfonso, King of Naples 157
Alicante, Spain 149
Aliseda, Spain 40
Alloa, Scotland 11
Altare, Italy 16, 163, 176; *229*
Amarna period 36; *37*
Amathus, Cyprus *48*
'Amberina' 200, 204
Ambras, palace of 174
Amenophis II 31, 35; *32, 35*
Amenophis III 26, 31, 35
America 191, 193–9, 204–5, 211; *249–53*
see also Corning, N.Y.; New York
American Research Centre in Egypt, Fustat 114
Amlash, Iran *138*
Amman, Jordan Archaeological Museum 101
amphoriskoi 40, 42, 44, 69; Fig. 88
Amsterdam, Rijksmuseum 158–9
amulets 35–8; *38*
Anatolia 50, 126, 135; *162–3*
Anglo-Irish glass 188, 198, 201
Anglo-Saxon glass 103, 154; *124, 130, 133–4*; Fig. 205
see also Britain
Ankan, Emperor *138*
Ankara, Museum 61
Anne of Brittany 159
annealing chamber *see* lehr
Ansedonia (Cosa), Italy 76
Antakya, Turkey *see* Antioch, Syria
Antalya, Turkey, Archaeological Museum 100
Antikythera 55
Antioch (Antakya), Syria 24, 122, 156
Prince of 149
Antwerp, Belgium 163, 165–6; *207, 218–20*
Aphrodite of Knidos 61
applied blobs 82, 83–5, 90, 94, 97, 100, 108; *84, 120, 121, 122, 127*

see also prunts
Aquileia, Italy 66, 80; *69*
Aramantus (Aramanthus) 78
Argonne, France 153
Argy-Rousseau, Gabriel 205; *260*
Aristeas 70
Aristophanes, *Acharnians* 47
Arles, France 102
Armenia 130
Arslan Tash, Syria 39
Art Deco 205, 209; *260, 266*
Art Glass 204, 205
Art Nouveau 194, 206, 209
Artas 70
aryballoi 42
Asia, Western 38–47
Asia Minor 47, 50, 64, 88, 145; *96*
Assyria 39, 46; *15, 39–41*
Astarte 18
Asulanus, Franciscus 166
atef crown 46, 50
Athens 80
Augsburg, Germany 18; *227, 236*
Augustus, Emperor 55, 60
Aurangzib, Emperor 177
'Aurene', Blue and Gold *263*
Austria 66; *221, 237*
see also Innsbruck; Linz; Vienna
avventurina glass 165
Ayyubids 129, 132

Baccarat glassworks 192, 195, 201, 202
Bacchus, George, & Sons 193, 202
Baden, Germany 223
bag beakers 108
Baiae, Italy 90
Bakewell, Benjamin 198
Bakewell, John P. 197
Bakewell, Page & Bakewell 197, 201
Bar-sur-Seine, France 210
Barcelona, Spain 160, *204*
barilla 149
Barking, Essex 109
Barnwell, Cambridgeshire 86
Barovier, Angelo 157
Barovier, Maria (Marietta) 157, 163
Bartolomeo da Zara 151, 152
base-ring, making of a Figs 77–8
Basil II, Emperor 145
Basle 151
Batavia 138
Baur, Tobias 236
Bayford, Kent 86
beads 108, 109, 131, 140, 153, 163; *46–7, 209*
forming Figs 6–21
Beatrix of Aragon, Queen of Hungary 159
Beauwelz, Belgium 212
Begram, Afghanistan 70, 76–8; *140*
Beijing 141; *181*
Belfast 10, 186
Belgium 83, 97, 103, 105, 106, 108, 126, 188–90, 198, 201; *124*
bell beakers 106
bell flasks 116, 122, *152*
Bella, Stefano della 166
Bergamo, Italy 156
Berkmeyer 197
Berlin, Islamic Museum 122
see also Potsdam

Besançon, France 153
    Musée des Beaux-Arts et
        d'Archéologie 193
Beykoz, Turkey 137
Bianco, Bacchio del 166
Biedermeier period 191
Biemann, Dominik 192; 246
Bigaglia, Pietro 201
Bing, Siegfried (Samuel) 206, 207
Bingerbrück, Germany 131, 196
Biringuccio, Vannoccio, Pirotechnia
    170
Birmingham 202
    Museums and Art Gallery 203; 257
Blades, Mr 188
blobbing 38, 66; 38, 81, 82; Figs 88–90
blobs see applied blobs
blowing, invention and technique of
    12, 48, 55, 61, 62–5, 140, 141,
    153, 168; Figs 65–87
    closed-cylinder Figs 189–99
    dip-mould Figs 114–18
    see also mould-blowing
Bo Shan, China 143
Bodrum Museum, Turkey 154
Bohemia (Czech Republic) 136, 137,
    153, 155, 159, 177–93 passim, 193,
    202; 194, 198, 246, 248
Böhm, August 192
Bologna, Italy
    Museo Civico 40
    San Salvatore monastery 160
Bonn 69
    Landesmuseum 86
Bontemps, Georges 197
Bonus Eventus plaque 18; 10
Borgo, Corsica 72
Bortolo d'Alvise 165
Boston 193
    Museum of Fine Arts 61
Boston and Sandwich Glass
    Company 197, 202; 247, 259
bow drill 119
Box Lane burial ground, Hemel
    Hempstead 99
Brandenburg, Elector of 182
Brescia, Italy 156
    Museo Cristiano 97
Breslau (Wrocław), Poland 159
Breteuil-sur-Noye, France, Musée de
    109–10
Briati, Giuseppe 182
Brierley Hill, W. Midlands 193
brilliant cutting 194; 250
Brindisi, Italy 95
Bristol 203
Britain 66, 72, 79, 87, 91, 98–100
    see also Anglo-Saxon glass; England
British Museum see under London
Broadfield House Glass Museum,
    Kingswinford see Dudley
brooch-runners 41
Broomfield, Kent 133
Brussels 177
Buquoy, Count Georg 181, 191
Burghley, Lord, tankard of 215
'Burmese' 204; 259
Burns, Robert 201
Bussolin, Domenico 201
Butteri, Giovanni Maria 1
Byzantine glass 98, 101, 124, 128,
    130–31, 145–8, 151; 147, 158–9,
    187–9

cage cups see diatreta
Cairo 114, 122, 125, 131, 132
    Islamic Museum 135
calcedonio (chalcedony) 210
Callot, Jacques 166
cameo glass 10, 11, 60, 64, 119, 128,
    143, 203, 204; 75, 77–8, 83, 148,
    258; Figs 98–108

Camirus, Rhodes 44–5
Campania, Italy 56, 66; 82, 83
canes 48, 49, 66, 110, 163, 168, 174;
    52, 56, 58, 65, 209, 254–5; Figs
    22–58, 88–92, 109–19, 184–99,
    200–204
Canosa, Italy 48; 53–4
Carbone, Ludovico 157
Carder, Frederick 194, 200, 209–10;
    263, 266
Cardiff, National Museum of Wales
    72, 76
Carlevaris, Luca 177
Carlsthal glassworks 201
carnival glass 200
Carolingians 108–9
Carpaccio, Vittore 159
Carthage, Tunisia 46–7; Figs 6–21
cased glass 192–3, 195, 203, 206; 248
casing Figs 99–108
Castiglione, Count Baldassare 159
casting 33–6, 52, 57; 68–70, 74
    cire perdue (lost-wax) method 35,
        40, 57, 61, 76, 209; 15, 35, 70
Castle Eden, Co. Durham 130
Catcliffe, S. Yorkshire 11
Caucasus 152
cesendello 136
chalices 109
Chardin, Sir John 137
Charlemagne 108–9
    Cup of 135
Charles Martel 108
Charles V, Emperor 212
Charpentier, M. 188
Chartres Cathedral 135
Chicago
    World's Fair (1893) 194, 199, 207
Chinese glass 135, 140–43; 171,
    178–85
chinoiserie 135, 141, 191
Choisy-le-Roi glassworks 192
Christian II of Saxony 232
Christianity 97, 106, 109, 124, 150
Chur, Switzerland 151
Cicero 50
cire perdue method see under casting
Cividale, Italy 150; 128
clamping Figs 91–2
Claudius, Emperor 66
claw beakers 103, 104–5, 108, 109,
    154; 129–30; Figs 205–9
claw prunts Figs 205–9
Clichy-la-Garenne, glassworks 13,
    202; 5, 254–5
closed cylinder blowing Figs 189–99
coats-of-arms, German 18–19; 11, 12,
    226, 233
Colchester, Essex 79
cold cutting 34
cold painting 85, 131
Coleman, Samuel 206
Colinet glassworks, Netherlands 174
    Catalogue Colinet 212
Cologne 66–9, 79–97 passim, 104,
    105, 106, 110; 86, 106, 109, 112,
    120–21, 129, 197a
    Rheinische Glashütten 256
    Römisch-Germanisches Museum
        69, 84, 88, 94, 97; 120, 129
coloured glass 21, 56, 80, 84, 88–90,
    94, 100–110 passim, 119, 126, 163,
    165, 166, 172, 191, 192, 200, 204;
    Figs 88–92
Combe, Taylor 18
combing 129, 130, 177; 160, 162; Figs
    8, 31–3
Comestor, Pierre, Bible historiée 153
cone beakers 105, 106; 124, 127,
    131
cones, glass 10, 11; 3
Constantine, Emperor 80

Constantinople (Istanbul) 90, 98,
    145, 147, 161
    Sack of 148
    see also Istanbul
Copeland, W. T. 193
Copenhagen
    David Collection 124
    National Museum 74, 97; 108
    Rosenborg Castle 165, 177
'Coralene' 205
Cordel, Germany 109, 110–11
core-forming 22–5, 31, 40–6, 54–5;
    20, 28–31, 43–8, 66; Figs 1–21
Corinth, Greece 64, 150, 151
Cork, Ireland 186
Corning, New York 250
    Corning Museum of Glass 19, 69,
        87, 94, 188, 193, 194, 209; 13, 14,
        70, 109, 118, 212, 244–6, 249, 256,
        264–5; Fig 88
    Corning Glass Works 251
        Steuben Division 266
Cornwall, Richard, Earl of 192
Corsica 72
Cosa, Italy 76
Coty 209
cracking off 90; 130; Figs 93–7
Crete 39, 47, 54; 52, 68
cristallo 157, 159, 166, 168, 170, 179;
    212–13, 215; Figs 120, 153
crizzling 143, 184; 181
Cros, Henri 205
'Crown Milano' 205
Crusades 135, 145; 187
'crystal' (Bohemian) 179–82;
    (19th-century) 188–94
    see also 'lead-crystal'
Crystal Palace, London 191; 243
crystallo-céramie 201
Culross, Scotland 196
Cumae, Italy 51
Cuthbert, abbot of Jarrow 110
cutting 78, 86–8, 103, 115–19, 179,
    188–94; 111
    see also brilliant cutting; cameo
    glass; facet-cutting; relief cutting;
    wheel-cutting/engraving
Cyprus 40, 43, 46, 62, 69, 73, 85, 130;
    20–21, 48, 90, 102, 107
Cyrenaica 50
Cyzicus, Turkey 96, 119
Czechoslovakia 201
    see also Bohemia

Dalmatia 78, 80
Damascus 131, 132, 133, 136, 156;
    167–70
    National Museum 87
Dammouse, Henri 205
Daoguang 143
d'Artigues, Aimé Gabriel 188
Darius the Great 62
David, Gerard 159
Décorchement, François-Emile 205;
    260
Delfos, Abraham 186
Demetrius, St 151
Dendera, Egypt 52; 61
Denmark 59, 74, 85, 97, 106, 165
Desarnaud, Mme 190
Despret, Georges 205
Desprez, Barthélemy 201
d'Huyvetter, Jean 230–31
diamond-point engraving 11–12,
    174, 179, 184; 222, 225, 234, 242
diatreta (cage cups) 11, 76, 80, 91–4,
    108, 209; 116–17
Dionysos 65, 92
dip-overlay method see flashing
Donino da Zara 151
Dorflinger, Christian, & Sons 194
Douai, France, Museum 135

double-cone glass 155
Doyle & Co. 199
Dresden, Germany 181; 232, 236,
    239
    Grünes Gewölbe 165
    Schiesshaus 226
dropper-flasks 84; 106
Dry Drayton, Cambridgeshire 134
Dublin 10, 186
Dudley, E. Midlands
    Broadfield House Glass Museum,
        Kingswinford 92, 195
Dura Europos, Syria 87
Durand, Asher B. 206
Düsseldorf, Germany,
    Kunstmuseum 197a
Dvin, Armenia 130

ear ornaments 36
Eastlake, Charles, Hints on Household
    Taste 202
Eder, Paulus 233
Edinburgh 203
    National Museum of Scotland 94
Edis, Robert W. Decoration and
    Furniture of Town Houses 202
Egermann, Friedrich 191; 245
Egypt 24, 25, 26–38, 46, 49–52, 60,
    70, 82–90 passim, 97–136 passim,
    152, 156, 161, 188; 21–38, 46,
    59–63, 74, 78, 110, 112, 114, 127,
    143, 147–50, 154–5, 157, 160, 162,
    164
el-Amarna, Egypt 24, 28, 33, 34; 23,
    29, 32, 34
Elgin Marbles 194; 257
Elgin Vase 194, 203; 257
Elizabeth I, Queen 215
Elizabeth Petrovna, Empress of
    Russia 240
enamelling 66, 85–6, 103, 112, 119,
    124, 125, 130–35, 138, 141, 143,
    146, 148, 151–2, 157–61, 166, 177,
    182, 191, 206; 107–9, 123, 128,
    147, 164–6, 171, 175–6, 199–204,
    206–8, 226, 230–31; Figs 87,
    175–8
England 102, 103, 105–11 passim,
    135, 149, 182–6, 188, 192, 193,
    198, 202–4; 234, 242, 248, 257–8
    see also Anglo-Saxon glass; Britain;
    London
engraving 90–91, 191–4, 203, 206
    see also diamond-point engraving;
    wheel-cutting/engraving
Enkomi, Cyprus 20
Ennion 70, 72, 73; 90
Esanville, Chevaliers d' 151; 191
Escalier de Cristal 188
Este, Isabella d' 163
Estonia 152
etching see acid-etching
Etruria 40, 50; 43
Eugenes 102
European glass, 11th–20th centuries
    136–7, 145–212; 186–246, 248,
    254–8, 260–62, 264–5
eye-paint containers 31, 33–4; 30, 33

facet-cutting 57, 76, 78, 86, 90, 101,
    115–16, 126, 128; 140, 143–4, 155,
    158–9, 245
façon de Venise 163, 165, 172, 177, 179;
    204, 207, 211–12, 217–20, 223,
    225; Figs 151, 153, 200
Faiyum, Egypt 8; 26, 71
faking 17–19; 9–14
Farfa, Italy 153
Faversham, Kent 108; 100–101, 133
'Favrile' 206; 263
Felix 82; 100–101

Ferdinand, Archduke of Tyrol 12, 174
Ferdinand I, Emperor 174
Ferdinand V, King of Aragon 160
Ferro, Bernardino 159
Fikellura cemetery, Camirus 45
filigrana see vetro a filigrana
'finger cups' prunts Figs 210–14
flame-working 7, 229; Figs 6–21
Flanders 207
flashing (dip-overlay method) 193; 75; Figs 99–108
Flaxman, John 10
Florence 157, 165–6; 1
flower glasses see verres à fleurs
flute glasses 153; 194, 224
fluting 198
Fontenelle, Julia de, Manuel Complet du Fabricant de Verre et de Cristal 190
foot, making of a Figs 129–34
Ford, John 201
forest glass 153, 155; 196, 198
Fort Shalmaneser, Nimrud 41
Fortetsa, Crete 39
France 72, 78, 82, 87, 91, 94, 102–9 passim, 150–54 passim, 163, 176, 191, 198, 200–202, 205; 67, 102, 122, 124, 135, 191, 193, 206–7, 229, 230–31
see also Frankish glass; Gaul
Franchini, Giovanni 201
Frankfurt 151, 181; 196
Frankish glass 119, 124, 129, 130, 135
Franklin, Benjamin 201
Franks 94, 98, 102, 103–6, 154
Františkovy Lásně (Franzenbad), Czech Republic 192
Frederick II, Emperor 128
Frederick Augustus, Elector of Saxony 239
Frederik IV, King of Denmark 165, 177
French National Exhibition (1819) see under Paris
Fritsche, William 195
fritting 8
Frotinus bottles 82
furnaces 8, 10–11, 103, 110, 155, 179, 211; 1, 136, 195, 198
Fustat, Egypt 114, 122, 125, 131, 152

Gallé, Emile 206; 256, 261–2
Gardner, Paul V. 209
Gate, Simon 195
Gates, John 251
Gateshead, Tyne and Wear 200
Gaul 66, 72, 78, 81, 83, 91, 97; 67, 91, 102, 122
see also France
Genoa, Italy 156
Georgia 42
Germany 18, 66–9, 85, 87, 91, 103, 106, 110, 128, 150, 153, 154, 177, 179, 182, 184, 193; 11, 12, 104–6, 124, 131, 223, 226, 227, 234, 236
see also Rhineland; Saxony
gilding see gold painting; gold-leaf gilding; sandwich gold glass
Gillinder & Sons 199
Gladstone, William Ewart 201
glasspot, covered 10
Glastonbury, Somerset 110
Goblet of the Eight Priests 135
gold painting 112, 125, 130–48 passim, 157–61, 166, 177, 182, 192; 123, 164–71, 175, 177, 189, 202–3
see also gold-leaf gilding
gold-band glass 55–6; 66, 68
see also sandwich gold glass

gold-glass 97; 123, 155
gold-leaf gilding 97, 110, 148, 161, 168; 175–8, 219, 226; Fig 112
see also gold painting
gold-ruby glass 181–2; 236
Gordion, Turkey 40, 49
Göttingen, Germany 128
Granada Cathedral 160
grape-flasks 73, 83; 93
Great Exhibition, London (1851) 191, 192; 243
Greece 24–5, 44, 46, 48, 50, 64, 92, 111, 145, 150; 19, 65, 87; Fig 93
Green, J. G. 193
Greene, John 12; 4
Greenwood, Frans 242
Gregorio da Napoli 151
Grice, Edwin 203
Guild of Glassmakers 16
Gutenbrunn, Austria 182; 237

Hablingbo, Sweden 132
Hague, The 184–6
Haida, Bohemia 193
Hald, Edward 195
half-moulding see mezza-forma
Hama, Syria 129, 132
Hamwih (Southampton) 109
Han period 140
Hancock, Daniel 203
Harborough, Earl of 221
Hasan, Sultan 168, 170
Hasanlu, Iran 39
Havemeyer, H. O. 207
Hawkes, T. G. 209
Hawkes, T. G. & Co. 250
head-flasks 73, 83; 102
Hedwig, Queen of Denmark 232
Hedwig glasses 126–8, 146; 158–9
Heemskerk, Willem Jacobz. van 225
Hellenistic glass 18, 47–55, 97, 110, 122; 10a, 52–66
Henry, Duke of Silesia and Poland 126
Henry VII, King of England 159; 202
Henry VIII, King of England 159, 172
Heraclius, Emperor 144
Herculaneum, Italy 64, 73, 74
Hermes 96
Hess, Johann 181
Hobbs, Brockunier & Co. 199, 204
Hodgetts, Richardson & Co. 203, 204
Hoffmann, Josef 14; title page
Hoffnungsthal glassworks 201
Hofheim cups 65
Hohenstaufen 128
Holland see Netherlands
Hope, Adrian 17
Hope Goblet 17
Hörlin family 18
horns
   drinking 102, 106, 109; 94, 131
   ink 109
Horus, Sons of 71
hot- and cold-working techniques 11–12, 213
Humpen, Reichsadler 226
Hungary 156, 159
'Hyalith' 191
hydriskai 42, 44

Ialysos, Rhodes 19
ice-glass 170; 219
Idalion, Cyprus 102
'Imad al-Din Zangi, Atabeg 130; 163
India 112, 138–40, 188; 174–7
Indiana Tumbler and Goblet Company 200; 253
inlays 38–9, 46, 52, 60, 85, 140; 37, 39, 62–3, 71

Innes, Georges 206
Innsbruck, Austria 174; 221
insertion form moulding Figs 151–2
Iran 39, 40, 111, 146, 153
   see also Persia
Iraq 20, 39, 41, 114, 146; 140
   Museum 23
Ireland 152, 186, 188
Isabella of Castile 160
Isfahan, Iran 137; 174
Islamic glass 112–38, 128, 140, 146, 148, 152; 136–77
Israel 39
Istanbul (Constantinople) 90, 136–7; 173, 187
   Topkapi Sarayi Library 137
   Topkapi Sarayi Museum 136
   see also Constantinople
Italy 40, 43, 48, 49, 50, 62, 65–6, 70, 78–111 passim, 128, 150, 152, 202; 43, 48, 51, 53, 56, 68–9, 79, 80, 82, 83–5, 88, 95, 128; Fig. 98
   see also Rome; Venice
ivory-carving 128

jacks Figs 125, 168, 171–3
James II, King of England 235
Janousek (Helmbach) works 181
Japan 115
Jarrow, Tyne and Wear 110
Jarves, Deming, Reminiscences of Glass-Making 197
Jason 70
jasper ware 203
Jenkinson, James 203
Jerusalem 62, 100, 126, 135; 126
   Israel Museum 62
Johann Georg, Duke of Sachsen-Weissenfels 236
Johann Georg II, Elector of Saxony 226
John II, Emperor 145

Kabul, Afghanistan, Museum 78
Kangxi, Emperor 143; 181
Karanis, Egypt 86
Karnak, Egypt 46
Kaş, Turkey 24, 25
Kempston, Bedfordshire 124
Kempten, Abbot of 165
Kent 105, 106, 108, 109
   Maidstone Museum 108
Kerch, Ukraine 69, 70; 189a
Keulengläser 153–4; 194
Khurasan 141, 147
kick, making of a Fig. 76
Kisling, Moise 251
Knidos, Turkey 61
Kny, Frederick E. 194
Koblenz, Germany 104
Kohl, Johann Georg, Austria, Vienna, Prague, etc. 191
kohl tubes 41–2; 30
Konya, Turkey 135
Kothgasser, Anton 191
kraters 49
Krautstrünke 154; 197a
Kretschmann, Adolf 195
Kufic 122, 124, 147; 147, 157
Kunckel, Johann, Ars Vetraria Experimentalis 181–2

Labino, Dominick 211
lacework see network
Lafayette, Marquis de 201
lagynoi 40
Lalique, René 207–9; 264
Lando, Elena de 157
Lanna Collection, Prague 19
latticino decoration 136

lattimo 159, 166, 168, 177; 203, 209, 228; Figs 184–99
'Lava' 204
Le Brun, Charles 192
lead glass 182–6, 199, 209; 234, 235, 241, 242
'lead-crystal' (English) see lead glass
Lebanon 38
Lehmann, Caspar 179–81; 232
lehr (annealing chamber) 10, 110, 155, 200; 1, 136, 195, 198
Leiden, Netherlands 184; 225
   National Museum of Antiquities 97
Leighton, Henry B. 193
Leighton, William 199
Leith Flint Glass Works 203
Lemington, Tyne and Wear 11
Leuna, Germany 110
Libbey, Edward D. 204
Libbey Glass Company 194, 199
Libisch, Josef 251
Libya 81
Ligozzi, Jacopo 166
Linz, Austria, Oberösterreichisches Landesmuseum 66
Lisht, Egypt 33; 29
'Lithyalin' 191; 245
Littleton, Harvey 211
Liège, Belgium 177; 223
   Musée Curtius 222
Lloyd & Summerfield 193
Locarno, Switzerland 66
Locke, Joseph 203, 204
Lombards 98, 103, 106; 128
London 149, 151, 174, 191, 203; 215, 220
   British Museum 12–14, 17, 18, 26, 66, 72, 73, 74, 92, 116, 122, 129, 130, 132, 141, 147, 151, 163, 177
   Crystal Palace 191; 243
   St Paul's Cathedral 202
   Savoy glasshouse 236
   Victoria and Albert Museum 132, 135, 193
lost-wax method see under casting
Louis IX, King of France 151; 191
Louis XII, King of France 159
Louis XIV, King of France 229
   glass table of 14–16; 7–8
Louis C. Tiffany and Associated Artists 206
Low Countries see Netherlands
Luck of Edenhall goblet 135
Ludwig of the Palatinate 155; 195
lustre painting 100, 112, 124, 130; 157
Lycurgus Cup 11, 92; 116–17
Lyons, France 80
Lysle, Anthony de 220

Maaret al-Nu'man 189
McDonald, Philip 250
Macedonia 43, 44, 48, 111
Macquenoise, Belgium 83
Madrid, Museo Arqueológico Nacional 40, 92
Maës, J. 13; 5
Maghrib 114
Magna Graecia 50
Maigelein 196
Mainz, Germany 110, 152
Maison d l'Art Nouveau 206, 207
Malik al-Nasir 132
Malkata, Egypt 33, 34, 35; 29, 32, 34
mallet flasks 116; 172
Mamluks 126, 129, 132; 154, 168, 171
Manchester Exhibition (1849) 193
Manship, Paul 251
Mansson, Peter 161
Mantua, Italy 163
Manuel I, Emperor 145

Marinot, Maurice 210, 211; *265*
marqueterie de verre 206
Martial 76, 80
Martino da Canale, *Chronicle* 49
marvering 94, 102, 129, 168, 206; *18,
    33–5, 69, 136, 160; Figs 30, 89, 99,
    107, 184–8*
Massachusetts Charitable Mechanic
    Association 193
Matthias Corvinus, King 159
Mauretania 80
Maximilian Emanuel, Elector of
    Bavaria 227
Medici, Cosimo I de', Grand Duke
    165
Medici, Francesco de', Grand Duke *1*
Medici family 166
    glasshouse of *1*
Medinet Gurob, Egypt 31; *29*
Meges 70
Memphis, Egypt 31; *25, 27*
Mendes, Egypt 46; *50*
Menshiya, Egypt 33; *29*
Merchant's Magazine 198–9
Mercury 96
Mercury flasks 81, 83
mereses 179, 225, 252; *Figs 124–8*
Mérida, Spain, Museo Nacional de
    Arte Romano 80
Merovingians 103, 104; *124, 135*
Merret, Christopher 182
Mesopotamia 8, 21–6, 40, 43, 50,
    110–15 *passim*, 125, 126, 135; *2,
    16, 17, 43, 137, 140, 145, 152, 156*
mezza-forma (half-moulding) *Figs
    163–6*
Milan 156, 157
    Duke of 157
Mildner, Johann Joseph 237
millefiori 163, 201, 202, 209; *7, 8, 209,
    254–5; Figs 22–35, 109–19*
Milton Vase 10
minai pottery 131
Ming period 141
Minutoli, Heinrich von 201
Miotti family 165; *228*
mirrors 177
Mohn, Gottlob and Samuel 191
Mongols 126, 131, 135, 137
Monkwearmouth, Tyne and Wear
    110
Monte Cassino, Abbey of 155; *195*
Montpellier, Bibliothèque de la
    Faculté de Médecine 153
Moore, Edward C. 206
Morea, Greece 151
Morelli, Allesio 12; *4*
Morgan, Mary 204
Morocco 80
mosaic glass 23, 48–50, 51–2, 54–5,
    56, 101, 110, 122; *17, 32, 38,
    52–3, 56–61, 67–8, 156; Figs
    22–35, 40–46, 109–19*
Moscow, Pushkin Museum 49
mosque lamps 131, 132, 136, 148;
    154, 167–70
Mostagedda, Egypt 46
mould-blowing 70–74, 80, 81, 83,
    100, 110, 116, 119–22, 153, 154,
    170, 198; *Figs 89–96, 100–103,
    126, 149, 153–6, 196, 207, 210,
    212, 221*
mould-pressing *120, 122; Figs 59–64*
    see also pressed glass
Mount Washington Glass Company
    204, 205; *259*
Mozetto, Nicolo 157
Mucking, Essex 104, 105; *130*
Mughals 112, 136, 138; *177*
Muhammad b. Qala'un, Sultan *169*
Müller, Michael 181
Munich *227*

Murad III, Sultan 137; *136*
Murano, Italy 14, 18, 135–77 *passim*,
    182, 201, 202; *6, 228*
    Museo Vetrario 200
Mycenae, Greece 24–5
Myra, Turkey 100

Najim al-Din 132
Namur, Belgium 105, 106
Nancy, France 206
Nanking, China 140
Naples, Museum *75; Fig. 98*
Napoleon I 198
narghileh 138
natron 21, 111
Navagero, Andrew (Andreas
    Naugerius) 160, 166
Navarre, Henri 210
Naylor & Co. 193
Nectanebo II 51
Nefertiti, Queen 28, 36
nef 212
Neikon 70
Neri, Antonio, *L'Arte Vetraria* 165,
    181, 182
Netherlands 12, 13, 76–8, 94, 153,
    163, 174, 184–6; *176, 196, 197,
    212, 217–19, 223, 234; Figs 151,
    153, 200*
network, lacework 49, 50, 55, 110; *52,
    56, 68; Figs 37–9*
Nevers, France 16, 177; *229*
New England Glass Company
    (NEGC) 193, 195, 197, 202, 204,
    205
New York 193, 203
    Brooklyn Museum 34; *35*
    Experimental Glass Workshop 213
    Metropolitan Museum of Art 19,
        73, 97, 207; *12, 58*
Newcastle upon Tyne 242
Newton, Sir Isaac 10
Nijmegen, Netherlands 76–8
    Museum 76
Nimrud, Iraq 39, 40; *15, 39–41*
Nineveh, Iraq 140
'nipt diamond waies' 163; *199, 210,
    234, 235; Figs 179–83*
Nishapur, Iran 114
Norfolk, Virginia, The Chrysler
    Museum 252, 259, *247*
Normandie 209
Normandy 79
Normans 128, 150
Northumbria 110
Northwood, John I 10, 195, 203, 209;
    257
Northwood, John II 203–4
Nottingham 10
Novogrudok, Byelorussia 128
Nové Hrady, Czech Republic 181
Nuremberg, Germany 18, 179; *225,
    233*
    Germanisches Nationalmuseum
        233

Obizzo, Giovanni Maria 159; *202–3*
Ohio 198
oinochoai 40, 41; *43, 45*
Olbia, Ukraine 17, 49; *9*
Olympia, Greece 47
opal glass 165; *211, 230–31*
'Opaline' 192
Oppitz, Paul 193
Orchard, John 193
Orléans, France 16
Orrefors 194
Osler, F. & C. 191; *243*
Ottoman Turks *see* Turks, Ottoman
Oude, Nabob of 188
Oxyrhynchus, Egypt *112*

Padua, Italy 156
    Basilica of San Antonio *221*
Pairpoint Manufacturing Company
    205
Palermo, Sicily 152
Palestine 40, 43, 46, 52, 62, 65, 70,
    84, 88, 90, 100, 101; *48, 64, 126,
    Fig 22*
Palestrina, Italy 39
palm cups 103–4, 106–8, 109; *135*
palmettes 116; *60, 145–6, 152, 158–9*
Panticapaeum (Kerch), Ukraine 69,
    70
paperweights 201, 202; *254–5*
Paphos, Cyprus 147
Pargeter, Philip 203
Paris 151, 201, 205, 206
    Exhibition (1819) 190
    Exhibition (1878) 194, 207; *256*
    Exhibition (1900) 207
    Exhibition (1925) 194, 210
    James Barrelet Collection 72
    Louvre 192
    Musée des Arts Décoratifs *261–2*
Passe, Crispin de *232*
Passgläser 191
'Patent Queen's Ivory' 200
Pavlovsk Palace Museum 188
'Peachblow' 204
Pegasus Vase 203
Pellatt, Apsley 192, 201
    Curiosities of Glass Making 197
Pellatt & Co. 193
Pellipario, Nicolo 157
Perrot, Bernard (Bernardo Perroto)
    16, 176
Persia 18, 40, 49, 112–19 *passim*,
    126–40 *passim*, 188, 192; *137–8,
    141, 145–6, 148–9, 151, 152, 154,
    160, 162, 174, 176*
    Shah of 188
    see also Iran
Petronius, *Satyricon* 65
Petrus (enameller) 151, 152
Pfohl, Karl 192
phalerae 60–61; *72*
phiale-mesomphalos 40
Phidias 47
Philadelphia 194, 199
Philip II, King of Macedonia 49
Philip II, King of Spain 170
Philippos 70
Phillips, Dobson & Pearce 193
Phoenicia 38–9, 40, 42, 43, 47, 70, 73;
    39–42, 89, 90, 93
Phrygia 40
Pietro di Giorgio 157
pilgrim flasks 132; *165–6*
pillar-moulding 56; *67; Figs 59–64*
Pinzolo/Trentino, Italy, church of
    Santo Stefano 150
Pisa, Italy 165
Pistoia, Italy 128
Pittsburgh, Pennsylvania 198
Pius IV, Pope 174; *222*
Pliny the Elder 74, 78, 79, 94, 111
    Natural History 20, 56, 57, 59
Po Valley 66
Pohl, Franz 246
Poland 128
'Pomona' 205
Pompeii, Italy 64, 65, 73, 74; *69, 75;
    Fig. 98*
Pomposa, Abbey of 150
pontil 38; *38; Figs 79–82, 86–7,
    107–8, 140–42*
Portland Vase 10, 11, 64, 209; *75, 77;
    Fig. 98*
Portugal 79, 157, 160, 188
potash glass 179–82
Potsdam, Germany 182; *236, 240*
Powell, Harry J. 203

Pozzuoli (Puteoli), Italy 90; *42, 82*
Prague 19, 151, 153, 179–81, 191;
    232
    beaker 179
    Lanna Collection 19
    Municipal Museum *194*
    'Pressed Amberina' 204
pressed glass 54, 186, 197–200; *252–3*
Priego, Marquis of (Count of Feria)
    160
Priene, Turkey 64
Prouvé, Victor 206
Providence Flint Glass Works 198
prunts 94, 131, 153, 154; *120, 139,
    194, 197, 225, 241*
    claw *Figs 205–9; see also* claw
        beakers
    'finger-cup' *Figs 210–14*
    see also applied blobs
Ptolemaic period 52; *59–63, 74*
Ptolemy V 52; *63*
Puteoli *see* Pozzuoli
pyxides 72
pâte de verre 205, 209; *260*

Qa'it Bay, Sultan 135
Qing dynasty 141
'Queen's Burmese Ware' 204
Qur'an 124, 132, 133; *167–70*
Quyunjik, Iraq *140*

Rabanus Maurus, *De Universo* 155;
    195
Radnage, Buckinghamshire 67
Ramesses II 31; *29, 37*
Ramesses III 37
Ranftbecher 191
Raqqa, Syria 131
Ravenscroft, George 182–4; *235; Figs
    179–83*
recipes 8, 111, 165, 181, 184; *2, 236*
Red House Cone, Wordsley 10, 11; *3*
Reims, France 87; *122, 135*
relief cutting (relief carving) 112, 116,
    119, 128, 143; *141, 146, 158–9*
Restormel Castle, Cornwall 152; *192*
Rhineland 65, 66, 79–111 *passim*, 122,
    153–5 *passim*; *86, 97, 104–6, 110,
    116–17, 120–21, 129, 196, 197*
Rhodes 40, 43, 44, 49, 161; *19,
    43–6; Figs 1, 16*
ribbing 56–7, 110, 130, 153, 198; *67,
    139, 150, 174, 201, 238; Figs
    179–83*
Rice Harris & Son 193, 202
'rich-cut' patterns 194
Richardson, W. H., B. and J. 193
Richborough, Kent *81*
Riedel, Josef 259
rims, folded *Figs 169–73*
Robert Lehman Collection 19; *12*
Robinson, Enoch 197
rock-crystal engraving 115, 193
'rod-forming' *Figs 16–21*
Roger of Helmarshausen 147
Roman Empire, glass of 50, 55–61,
    62–98, 102–6, 112, 122, 140, 145,
    148, 161; *9, 71, 78, 79, 86, 90, 93,
    98*
Rome 64, 80, 98, 161; *70, 75, 77, 123*
    catacombs 97
    Museo Sabatini 18; *10*
    Vatican Library *195*
'Rose Amber' 204
Rosenborg Castle 165, 177
rotary presses 200
Rouen, France 153
'Royal Flemish' 205
Rubi (Ruvo di Puglia), Italy *48*
ruby glass *see* gold-ruby glass
Rudolph II, Emperor 174, 179
Russia 130, 188; *47, 240, 244*